The Granth of Guru Gobind Singh

Essays, Lectures, and Translations

KAMALROOP SINGH
GURINDER SINGH MANN

OXFORD
UNIVERSITY PRESS

OXFORD
UNIVERSITY PRESS

Oxford University Press is a department of the University of Oxford.
It furthers the University's objective of excellence in research, scholarship, and education by publishing worldwide. Oxford is a registered trademark of Oxford University Press in the UK and in certain other countries

Published in India by
Oxford University Press
22 Workspace, 2nd Floor, 1/22 Asaf Ali Road, New Delhi 110002

First Edition published in 2015
23rd impression 2025

ISBN-13:978-0-19-945897-4
ISBN-10:0-19-945897-9

Typeset in Scala Pro 10.5/13
by Tranistics Data Technologies, New Delhi 110 044
Printed in India by Rakmo Press, New Delhi 110 020

To the Guru Khalsa Panth
and many others who keep the flag flying

'I gave you the *Kesh* so you would glisten like the Sword'

—Guru Gobind Singh

Contents

Figures

Acknowledgements

We are indebted to the current *jathedars* of the Guru Khalsa Panth and Buddha Dal, most importantly the late Akali Nihang Baba Surjit Singh and the late Akali Nihang Baba Santa Singh, who shared with us valuable manuscripts and traditions. We are very much in debt to Jathedar Sant Baba Kulwant Singh and Bhai Ram Singh of Takht Hazur Sahib. We are very grateful to the learned Jathedar Baba Iqbal Singh, the present head of Takht Harimandir Sahib, Patna Sahib. We are indebted to Jathedar Joginder Singh Vedanti who gave permission to photograph the *Dasam Granth* manuscripts in Bhai Santokh Singh Library, Amritsar. We are thankful to the Damdami Taksal, the late Sant Baba Thakur Singh, the learned Giani Hardeep Singh (Hazuri Taksal), Giani Surjit Singh, Giani Amolak Singh, and the honourable Sant Baba Gurharkirpal Singh 'Rājayogī', for their help. We are very thankful to Baba Mohan Singh, Baba Surjit Singh 'Sewāpanthī', and the late Baba Sucha Singh of Jawadi Taksal. We are also indebted to the Nirmalā Sampradāyā, in particular Sant Mittar Parkash Singh.

Our academic credit is just as much, as we are heavily indebted to Dr David Cheetham (University of Birmingham), the Marc Fitch Fund, Dr Imre Bangha, Dr Harpal Singh Pannu (Punjabi University, Patiala), Dr Jeevan Singh Deol (University of Cambridge) for valuable references, Anurag Singh for his support, Dr Nigel Allen (Wellcome Trust), the late Dr Chanan Singh 'Chan', Professor Pashaura Singh (University of California, Riverside), Dr Louis Fenech (University of Northern Iowa), and Professor Gurinder Singh Mann (University of California, Santa Barbara). We are also grateful to the various staff members at Guru Nanak Dev University (Amritsar), Punjabi University (Patiala), Khalsa College (Amritsar), Punjabi Sahit Academy (Ludhiana), Panjab

University (Chandigarh), Marina Chellini (British Library), School of Oriental and Asian Studies (London), Royal Asiatic Library (London), and the Wellcome Trust Library (London).

There are many individuals around the world who have provided us with valuable sources: Vijaydeep Singh (India), Lakhwinder Singh (USA), Dr Ripudaman Singh (Denmark), Jatinder Pal Singh (India), Gurchanjit Singh Lamba (USA), Sukhdeep Singh (Canada), Attul Jetha (China), Arvinder Singh (Canada), Mary Pat Fisher (Gobind Sadan, New Delhi), Kirpal Singh (Gobind Sadan, New Delhi), Joginder Singh Ahluwalia (USA), and the late Amarpreet Singh Badesha (Canada). In the UK this includes Davinder Singh Panesar, Surjit Singh Bains, Francisco Luis, Hardeep Singh Kainth, Amardeep Singh, Bhupinder Singh 'Bob', Sukhwinder Singh 'Sodhi', Harminder Singh Bharj, Hamandeep Singh Gill, Nihang Sher Singh, Jasmeet Singh Nihang and family, and Manpreet Singh 'Ram Janga'. As this publication has taken some years to be published, we are sure to have missed somebody out, so we also thank the many other individuals not mentioned who have helped us in our research.

We would also like to thank our families for being supportive and giving us time and space in order for us to complete our research. In particular, we both thank our fathers, Sardar Baldev Singh and Sardar Balbir Singh Mann, who have been very supportive. We would like to thank all our friends for their emails and discussions on social media, and the many helpful suggestions they have given about the subject. Finally, we are equally indebted to the reviewers of the manuscript and their feedback.

Abbreviations

AG	*Ādi Srī Gurū Granth Sāhib*
DG	*Srī Dasam Granth Sāhib*
SGPC	Shiromani Gurdwara Parbandhak Committee
vs	Vikram Samvat

Introduction

The Sikh religion, founded in the fifteenth century under Guru Nanak, has flourished into a large international community, if not a sovereign nation without borders. Numerically, in comparison to faiths like Islam, Christianity, and Hinduism, it is a much smaller religion. The contribution of this young faith has mostly been felt in the Indian subcontinent; however, Sikhs have served all over the world in World War I and World War II. From looking at the transformation of a Sikh to the Khalsa, the impact of Guru Gobind Singh is clear, and is comparable to the metamorphosis of a caterpillar to a butterfly. By consecrating the scripture and the fraternity the *Shabad Gurū* in the form of the *Ādi Srī Gurū Granth Sāhib* (*AG*) and the Khalsa, the transformation of *Sant* to *Sant Sipāhī* solidified the traditions of the previous Gurus. The history of the Sikhs took a novel direction due to the projects at Anandpur Sahib and Paonta Sahib, as both of these centres became focal points for innovative literary projects, and are famous for being the sacred locations where symposiums for the poets were held. Some of the poets were from the court of Emperor Aurangzeb, including the poet laureate of the Sikhs, Bhai Nand Lal, while others were inherited from the previous *darbar* (court) of Guru Tegh Bahadur. Prior to the literature composed in the court of the Tenth Guru, Sikh scripture already had an extensive canon, and consisted of the *Pothī Sāhib*, and secondary theological and hagiographic works, for example, the *Prāṅ Sangalī*, Bhai Balla's *Janamsākhī*, the *Vārs* and *Kabitts* of Bhai Gurdas, and so forth. In order to finalize the *Graṅth* and Panth, the canon had to be formalized, and this took place in the new literary renaissance in the darbar. The poets undertook the translations of Indian and Islamic literature including the Mahābhārat, Qur'an, Purāṇas, and *Hitopedesh* to supplement the Sikhs' understanding of wider scripture. The compositions of the *Srī Dasam Granth Sāhib* (*DG*) were composed mainly at Anandpur, and some at Paonta Sahib, with the finalization of the first complete edition at Bhabaur Sahib. This location is cited in Sikh history as the one where the completion of the *Srī Charitropakhyān* took place. The verses from the final composition, known as *Chaupaī Sāhib*, are said to have been recited here by the Guru and, as a result, a large fair takes place every year to commemorate this event. The compositions within the *DG* were written by Guru Gobind Singh and compiled between 1680 and 1705. Shortly afterwards the *Granth* was recompiled by his devotees including Bhai Mani Singh and Baba Dip Singh. New research presented herein highlights the roles of scribes such as Bhai Haridas and Bhai Shia Singh in writing compilations of the *DG*.

After the martyrdom of Guru Gobind Singh's father, Guru Tegh Bahadur, a new requirement of all Sikhs to follow the new military doctrine was introduced. The position put forward by the authors in this publication is that this warrior or *chhatri* ideal was actually formulated in the *DG* and also led to the injunction for a distinctive appearance for the Sikhs. The unique form and ideology of the Khalsa was also to combat the *masand* system, so that this new sovereign corporeal body was solely based on the doctrines of the *AG*, and the *dharam yudh* (righteous war) ideology that is the central leitmotiv of the *DG*. The double-edged sword (*bhagautī*) would now initiate a Sikh, with the prayers recited from the *AG* and the *DG*. Due to explicit prescriptions for the Khalsa, the importance of the Khalsa over the Brahmins, and a statement about the abolition of caste, it can be argued that the *DG* is the Khalsa scripture.[1] The Guru's own struggle against the Mughals and their allies is recorded in the powerfully worded letter known as the *Zafarnāmah*, which was delivered to Emperor Aurangzeb. It was most likely to have been subsequently compiled into the *DG* at the Guru's encampment, in the area of Dina in AD 1705. Within the compositions of the *DG* there are a number of colophons that help us formulate a clear understanding of its textual history.

This new research highlights the intrinsic relationship of the *Scripture of Guru Gobind Singh* to the *marayādā* (tradition), which includes the *shastras* (weapons), the *takhts* (thrones of polity), and the warriors known as the Akali Nihangs. This work also takes into consideration the historical context that the scripture was written in, and its link with battlefield sciences of the period. This was in line with the concept of *mīrī–pīrī* that was institutionalized by Guru Hargobind. His army was led by Baba Buddha, a veteran Sikh who survived many gurus. He is credited for devising the martial training for Sikhs and, consequently, the Akali Nihangs are named as 'Buddha' Dal after him. In the late seventeenth century, throughout the eighteenth century, and till the middle of the nineteenth century, the Nihang Sikhs were heavily adorned with weapons, served as the vanguard of the Khalsa, and made a great number of sacrifices.[2] It was also during the reign of Guru Hargobind that the first of several battles with the Mughal authorities occurred. This martial tradition was then further solidified by the creation of the Khalsa.

The *DG* and the *Sarabaloh Granth* contain the following features: (*a*) weapons are equated with Akal Purakh (the One beyond time, or God); (*b*) the role and method of weapons in warfare are described as a part of the narrations; and (*c*) the compositions are to be recited before and during battle. The new chattrī ideal formalized by the Guru now required the saint who venerated the *AG* to also refer to the warrior scripture, the *DG*.

If we take some of earliest Sikh history to be accurate, then the *prakāsh* (ceremonial opening and reading) of the *DG* took place in the Guru's lifetime, and this is another important area of discussion that forms a part of this book. Consequently, we shall see that the story of the compilation by Bhai Mani Singh is a contrived story. As there was no controversy in eighteenth-century texts, various accounts were engineered to form a new ambiguous discourse. The early relationship of the *DG* with Sri Akal Takht is examined in light of Sikh history, as the enthronement of the *DG* no longer takes place there, but the marayādā continues at Takhts Patna and Hazur Sahib. During the early twentieth century, a number of leaders attempted to ensure that the *DG* was not only discredited and edited, but also physically destroyed. Teja Singh 'Bhasauria' became most vocal in his opposition to the *DG*, one objection being that the *DG* should not be placed together with the *AG*. This was put into effect by groups who later lobbied and joined the Shiromani Gurdwara Parbandhak Committee (SGPC), and removed the custodians, the Akali Nihangs, from their traditional duty at the takht, along with committing the sacrilegious act of tossing the *DG* out of the window. The prakāsh of *DG* takes place in many gurdwaras across India including those run by the Akali Nihang, Namdhari, Nirmale, Sewapanthi, Udasi, Nanaksar, and the schools of the Damdami Taksal. This tradition is now becoming popular outside of India with the *akhaṅḍ pāṭhs* (uninterrupted readings) of the *DG* taking place in the UK and other parts of the Sikh diaspora.

To date, there are scarce academic works about the *DG*, but a few rare exceptions are D.P. Ashta,[3] Trilochan Singh,[4] Randhir Singh,[5] P. Sehgal,[6] R.S. Jaggi,[7] and C.H. Loehlin.[8] Recently, Gurinder Mann of Santa Barbara covered some early sources of history about the life of Guru Gobind Singh, which included *DG* manuscripts.[9] In the following year our book *Sri Dasam Granth Sahib: Questions and Answers* was released.[10] This book was an introductory guide to familiarize readers about the *DG*. In the same year, R. Rinehart presented her research, *Debating the Dasam Granth*, on how the contents and authorship of the *DG* had been debated in recent times.[11] In this book, we present the first translations of the 'apocryphal' compositions of the *DG*. This contribution to the field provides a useful supplement to the popular translations of the *DG* presently available, mainly by Dharam Singh and Jodh Singh,[12] S.S. Kohli,[13] and P.S. Sandhu.[14] This book adds to the previous academic research on the *DG*, and would be useful to both academics and individuals interested in the subject.

Many of the previous studies have employed little evidence from the manuscripts and are generally uncritical. The main criticism is that with the same material being constantly quoted, the secondary sources have been exhausted. The discussion of primary sources only includes a small number of manuscripts and the letter purported to be by Bhai Mani Singh sent to the wife of the Guru, Mata Sundari. Generally, scholars have only looked at the authorship issue, and have therefore neglected its role in the eighteenth-century Khalsa. There are some areas which we have not included like the discussion of the language—Braj Bhāshā, and the importance of this language throughout the history of Gurmukhī literature. Another area, which is beyond the scope of this book, is the various types of verses employed throughout the scripture. A detailed study of this was made by Dharam Pal Ashta who has examined them at length in his thesis, *The Poetry of the Dasam Granth*.[15] There are studies on the court poet literature from the darbar of Guru Gobind Singh; for example, B.B. Chaudhry's *Gur Govind kī Darbārī Kavī* and Piara Singh Padam's *Gurū Gobind Singh jī de Darbārī Rattan*.[16] In Sikh studies the work of the *kavīs* (poets) has only received passing comment, other than the recent and extensive research by Louis E. Fenech, in *The Darbar of the Sikh Gurus—The Court of God in the World of Men*.[17] In addition, there has been a recent renewal of interest in the Sikh martial art, *Shastravidiā*, and there have been some new publications including the *Shastranāmā* by Manjit Singh[18] and 'Gatka' in *The Oxford Handbook of Sikh Studies* by Kamalroop Singh, one of the authors of this book.[19]

As noted by Rinehart,[20] in recent times, the *DG* has been the focus of much interest and volatile debate. This debate has its roots in the aforementioned Sikh reform. On 14 May 2000 Sri Akal Takht issued a *hukamnāmā* (written order), and then made a further reiteration on 7 August, asking the Sikh diaspora not to engage in public discussion about the *DG*. The directive was made by Jathedar Joginder Singh Vedanti. This edict was later reversed in 2006 asking scholars to give befitting replies to those individuals who doubted the *DG*; this was further reiterated in 2013. When faced with the predicament of Vedanti Sahib's previous directive one of the authors of this book, Gurinder Singh Mann, was completing his MA in South Asian Religions at De Montfort University, Leicester. This edict made him question whether he should continue with his research, but he decided to persevere, and his MA was completed in 2001. His study titled 'The Role of the Dasam Granth in Khalsa' looked at the various compositions of the *DG* and how they were employed in Sikh practices, for example, the *khaṇḍe kī pāhul* and their use in the daily liturgical ritual of the *nitnem*. He discussed the Sikh *ardās* or supplication and showed that the opening parts of this composition were taken from the *DG* composition *Chaṇḍī dī Vār*. This study is one of the few academic studies on the *DG* in the West after C.H. Loehlin's thesis of 1955, which was published as *The Granth of Guru Gobind Singh and the Khalsa Brotherhood* in 1971.

Kamalroop Singh embarked on his part-time postgraduate research on the textual history and manuscripts of the *Granth of Guru Gobind Singh* at the University of Birmingham in 2005. He completed his PhD with his thesis titled *Dasam Granth Re-Examined* in 2012. In this work he was the first to construct the textual history of the *DG*, which was achieved by examining new primary sources such as manuscripts and hagiographies, from which he concluded that the *DG* was in fact compiled during the Tenth Guru's lifetime. Therefore, this evidence challenged the accepted narrative by the Singh Sabha that the *DG* was compiled by Bhai Mani Singh after the ascension of Guru Gobind Singh. Another feature of his thesis is the analysis of the compositions of the *DG* that reveals that the rubrics in the compositions in conjunction with manuscripts attributed to Bhai Mani Singh demonstrate that Bhai Mani Singh was actually recompiling the scripture. In his thesis he also briefly explored the standardization of the *DG* in 1897 and the 'apocrypha', and this publication contains the translations of the 'apocryphal' compositions that were originally intended for his PhD, but due to word count limitations they were not included in his final thesis. In 2007 we met and discussed some of the issues about the study of the *DG* and their individual research. They both decided that due to the large amounts of information involved only a collaborative project would allow different aspects of the history of the *DG* to come to light.

Gurinder Singh Mann spent a substantial amount of time locating new material evidence in the form of relics, and their histories, which feature in this joint research. It is important to mention some of the related issues here, as the use of such evidence has led to a delay in our publication. Before the auctioning of the *chārāinā* armour (attributed to Guru Gobind Singh) that made headlines in 2008, we collated much of the research and created an extensive portfolio of information related to various relics, and were intending to release this prior to the auction. As we did not want to contribute to the ongoing controversy that was brewing up in India and the UK, we delayed our publication. We decided it was best to wait and proceed cautiously, due to the strong reaction of the Sikh community to the sale. The onus of our publication is to present the evidence about the *DG*, and not the authenticity of the chārāinā armour. Had we published at the time, we are quite certain that this issue would have overshadowed all the other research herein.

The most controversial and volatile discussion is that of the authorship, which is the most polemical and opinionated argument one could ever experience. Our book is not centred on the issue of authorship, but our discussions are based mainly on primary sources. More importantly, the history of how the *Granth of Guru Gobind Singh* was created is discussed, where we consider the transmission of manuscripts which demonstrate how and where the *DG* was created and how its liturgical scripture has proliferated through smaller *guṭkās* and *pothīs*. It took a number of years to track down manuscript copies of the *DG* in India and the UK, and we have supplemented the manuscript evidence with information about them from secondary source material. The unique portion of this work is the introduction of new manuscripts as well as supplementation from oral traditions of the Akali Nihang Singhs. Kamalroop Singh has conducted an extensive survey of manuscripts worldwide, undertaken fieldwork with this traditional institution, and has learnt some of their oral traditions and rituals. Complementing this research, the relationship of the relics of Guru Gobind Singh and the role played by the scriptures at the takhts has been researched by Gurinder Singh Mann.

This book was written in the UK and supplemented with fieldwork in India. We have also relied on British institutions like the Wellcome Trust, the British Library, and other university libraries where there are relevant manuscripts. We have uncovered new material and introduced it in this book. Both of us have been approached on numerous occasions to provide our academic opinion on this subject, and we have intended this publication to fulfil the requests of many hundreds of emails and phone requests over the years. The academic community has also contacted us in this regard, and we have had a number of dialogues on the subject. Naturally we are heavily indebted to our colleagues who have furthered our understanding through the dialogue we have enjoyed with them. As the *DG* is the secondary scripture of the Sikh canon, this book is a useful guide for scholars, and it fills the large gap on the subject in the growing field of Sikh studies.

We have intended this book to create discussion about the *DG* and avoid the rhetoric that currently surrounds the subject. We hope that it opens up fresh areas of interest and further research. This book discusses a range of ideas, although on reflection it is clear that there is an intrinsic relation between the chapters. We have endeavoured to bring to light the traditional praxis of the *DG*, instead of focusing solely on the text of the scripture. This joint work contains a multidimensional discussion of the *DG*, ranging from the compilation, the apocrypha, and the practices to the purpose of the *DG*. Much of the research presented herein was a set of several essays written and lectures delivered by us over the years. As a result, we both have covered various themes on the *DG*. The reviewers of the draft suggested that a more holistic approach should be taken. Consequently, after careful editing, several of the essays and lectures have now been revised in order to highlight their interconnectedness. This book is a combined effort of many years of research by us, and during this time, we have located other sources that are beyond the scope of this book to discuss, which will be presented in future papers and lectures. We also aim to create a repository of unpublished evidence and material on the Internet that will supplement and enrich this research. We hope this book serves as a guide to both scholars and laymen, many of whom have been patiently awaiting this publication.

Notes on Orthography

For ease of reading, we have omitted diacritics in common terms such as 'jathedār', 'bābā', 'giānī', 'takht', 'Akālī', 'Nihaṅg', 'Buddhā Dal', 'Akāl Purakh', and so on, which are originally used with diacritics. Where we feel it is necessary for the reader and where they show the form of the original Gurmukhi, we have included them. In order to prevent any ambiguity, there is a need to explain some of the commonly used terminology in our book. We have used different names for the same institution including Akali, Nihang, Akali Nihang, Buddha

Dal, which all mean the traditional Sikh warriors whose official name is Shiromanī Khālsā Paṅth Akālī Buddhā Dal Panjvā Takht Chaladā Vahīr. *Khās patre* and *daskhat* refer to the Tenth Guru's signature folios. Pothī and guṭkā are in reference to smaller liturgical recensions. 'Takht' and 'throne' refer to the sovereign seats of Sikh polity. For the translations, we have employed a separate system that is more familiar to South Asian scholars of language, and have provided a separate transliteration table in Chapter 2 so that the original orthography can be determined.

Notes

1. In the *Sarabaloh Graṅth*, a scripture also attributed to Guru Gobind Singh, there is another famous description of the virtues of the Khalsa that begins with the verse '*Khalsā mero rūp hai khās*'.

2. See our forthcoming publication: G.S. Mann and Kamalroop Singh, *The History of the Akali Nihang Singh Khalsa from 1800–1920* AD (Brill, 2015).

3. D.P. Ashta, *Poetry of the Dasam Granth* (Delhi: Arun Prakashan, 1959).

4. Trilochan Singh, 'History and Compilation of Dasam Granth', *Sikh Review* 3, no. 4 (1955): 51–60.

5. Randhir Singh, *Shabad Mūrat: Dasave Pātishāh ke Graṅth dā Itihās* (Amritsar: SGPC, 1962).

6. P. Sehgal, *Gur Govind Singh unkā Kaviyā* (Lucknow: Hindi Sahit Mandir, 1965).

7. R.S. Jaggi, *Dasam Graṅth dā Kartritav* (New Delhi: Panjābi Sāhitt Sabhā, 1966).

8. C.H. Loehlin, *The Granth of Guru Gobind Singh and Khalsa Brotherhood* (Lucknow: Lucknow Publishing House, 1971); Sehgal, *Gur Govind Singh unkā Kaviyā*.

9. Gurinder Singh Mann, *Journal of Punjab Studies* 15, nos 1 & 2 (2008).

10. Gurinder Singh Mann and Kamalroop Singh, *Sri Dasam Granth Sahib: Questions and Answers* (London: Archimedes Press, 2011).

11. R. Rinehart, *Debating the Dasam Granth* (New York: Oxford University Press, 2011).

12. Jodh Singh and Dharam Singh, *Sri Dasam Granth Sahib*, Text and Translation, 2 vols (Patiala: Heritage Publications, 1999).

13. S.S. Kohli, trans., *Sri Dasam Granth Sahib*, 3 vols (Birmingham: Sikh National Heritage Trust Publishing, 2003).

14. P.S. Sandhu, *Selections from Sri Dasam Granth Sahib*, 2 vols (Amritsar: Singh Brothers, 2004).

15. Ashta, *The Poetry of the Dasam Granth.*

16. Piara Singh Padam. *Srī Gurū Gobiṅd Siṅgh jī de Darbārī Rattan* (Patiala: New Patiala Printers, 1976); B.B. Chaudhry, *Gur Govind ki Darbarī Kavī* (Delhi: Svasitak Satiya Sadan, 1979).

17. Louis E. Fenech, *Darbar of the Sikh Gurus: The Court of God in the World of Men* (New Delhi: Oxford University Press, 2008).

18. Manjit Singh, *Shastranāmā* (Amritsar: Chattar Singh Jivan Singh, 2005).

19. Kamalroop Singh, 'Gatka', in *The Oxford Handbook of Sikh Studies*, eds, Pashaura Singh and Louis E. Fenech (New York: Oxford University Press, 2014).

20. Rinehart, *Debating the Dasam Granth.*

1

Compilation of the *Dasam Granth*

In this chapter we shall discuss the earliest manuscripts of the *Srī Dasam Granth Sāhib* (*DG*) and its textual transmission. This is based on the PhD research of Kamalroop Singh who examined the textual history and compilation of the *DG*. He uncovered a number of modern myths surrounding the text, which earlier historical sources and manuscripts contradict. This chapter is a synopsis of his findings together with important contributions from Gurinder Singh Mann, which include new research on relics and manuscripts.

The analysis of early manuscripts by scholars[1] has been used to formulate arguments about the authorship, rather than tackling the core issue which is the textual history of the volume. In this chapter we shall consider a number of historical sources and examine how their selective use has led to myths being created. It seems that two different stories have been amalgamated into a new romanticized myth about the compilation of the *Granth of Guru Gobind Singh*. The standard text and manuscripts of the *DG* provide us with colophons that consist of the dates and locations where various chapters of the *Granth* were composed. The compositions we shall consider are from the standard edition of the *DG*, authorized by the Sodhak Committee or 'Committee of Corrections' in AD 1898, which has 1,428 pages, two pages less than the standard *Ādi Srī Gurū Granth Sāhib* (*AG*).[2] There are items of material heritage, including several relics attributed to the Tenth Guru, which have received little attention, and it is possible that they could shed light on the *DG*. The majority of the research on the Tenth Guru's writings has been polemic, and as a result, this has hindered any serious investigation about the scripture.

Some writers have asserted that there is no history attached to the *Granth* and its compilation, and that the volume is heterogeneous and inconsistent.[3] Recently, however, some scholars have concluded that the *DG* was written in the court of the Guru.[4] They argue that the current manuscript evidence does not reveal the authorship of the scripture.[5] Some go further and suggest that the whole work should be attributed to the court poets.[6] In this chapter, the introduction of new evidence brings the viewpoints of the aforementioned scholars into question.

Historical sources are clear that the secondary *granth* to the *AG* is the *Dasam Pādashāh kā Granth*.[7] It is important to note that there is no manuscript bearing the title *Dasam Granth*, as it was a colloquial name given to it much later.[8] A scripture may begin with a title, but, throughout its development, it may take on new ones.[9] This is also dependent on the interaction the audience has with a scripture. The primary scripture, the *AG*, started off as a small manuscript (*pothī*) and was then given the title of *Pothī Sāhib* by Guru Arjan Dev. The *Pothī Sāhib* was subsequently given the name of *Ādi Granth* when additional compositions were added to it. To reflect its final status, the title of 'Guru' was given to the scripture by Guru Gobind Singh, which is seen by the reverence given to the scripture by Sikhs of today.[10] In primary and secondary sources we see the titles *Pothī Sāhib*, *Gurū Granth Sāhib*, *Granth jī*, *Ādi Granth*, and *Ādi Gurū Granth Sāhib* being employed for the *AG*.[11] Similarly, we see the titles *Bāṇī Srī Mukhvāk Pātishāhī 10*, *Bachitra Nāṭak Granth*, *Dasaveṅ Pātashāh jū kā Granth*, and *Dasam Gurū Granth* for the *DG*.[12] Some recensions of both scriptures record the title *Granth jī*, which may have led to the term *Ādi* (the first or primal) being employed to differentiate the *AG* from the *DG*. However, it is clear that the Guruship passed onto the *AG*, the story of which is recorded in key eighteenth-century texts, for example, by Kuir Singh in AD 1751.

The Compositions of the *Dasam Granth*

We shall begin our discussion by examining the compositions in the standard edition of the *DG*. The language of the *Granth* is essentially Braj Bhāshā with two compositions written in Persian, and one composed in Panjabi; and like the *AG* it is recorded in the Gurmukhi script. The compositions within the *Granth* can be categorized as devotional, historical, mythological, and didactic. The common leitmotiv throughout most of the compositions is holy war or *dharam yudh*.

The first composition of the *DG* is *Jāp Sāhib* or 'Recitation' which consists of 199 verses and after Guru Nanak's *Jāp jī Sāhib* is the second prayer of the *nitnem*, the daily liturgy of the Sikhs. The prayer starts with the title *Srī Mukhvāk Pātashāhī Dasvīṅ* or 'The Oration of the Tenth Sovereign'.[13] The traditional view is that this validates that the composition was written by Guru Gobind Singh. The first composition the Guru composed was the *Jāp Sāhib*, and in the tradition and historical sources it is said to have also been recited at the first *khaṇḍe kī pāhul* ceremony in AD 1699.[14] Its content has been compared to the Sanskrit *Viṣhṇusahasranām* or 'Vishnu's Thousand Names' by Macauliffe.[15] In reality, there are 950 different names that are used to describe the Creator. The *Jāp Sāhib* shares similarities with the *Jāp jī* of Guru Nanak, as the writer expresses his devotion to Akal Purakh, and this name for the Divine is consistently employed throughout the *DG*.[16]

The second composition, *Akāl Ustati*, or 'Praises to the Timeless', is another example of devotional poetry. It starts with 'Utār Khāse Daskhat kā Pātasāhī Dasvīṅ' or 'Copy of the Verses Written by the Tenth Sovereign'.[17] It is composed of 271.5 verses and appears unfinished, which has led to the romanticized notion amongst scholars that the Guru said the praise of Akal was infinite and so must be left open.[18] It is written in Braj Bhāshā with interspersing words of Arabic and Persian. The Guru describes Akal Purakh as 'Sarabaloh' or 'All-Steel', 'Sarabkāl' or 'All-Death', and 'Mahāloh' or 'Great-Steel'. The use of the word 'steel' thus symbolizes God as the Sword, which is a dominant theme throughout the *DG*.[19] The writer also dispels the notion of a 'chosen people', as he expresses that all of mankind is the same, even though they may reside in different lands and have different appearances. He articulates that people worship the same Divinity, even though they have diverse rituals and different places of worship. The Guru categorically states, '[M]ānas kī jāti sabai ekai pahichānabo', or 'Recognise all mankind as one.'[20] Stanzas numbered 21 to 30 are known as the 'svaiye' and form a part of the nitnem and khaṅḍe kī pāhul ceremony. The tradition records that this composition was composed prior to the Vaisakhi ceremony of AD 1699.[21]

The *Bachitra Nāṭak* or 'Wondrous Drama' is composed of various chapters or *adhiāi*. The composition starts with the heading 'Srī Mukhvāk Pātashāhī Dasvīṅ'. After the eulogy of Akal Purakh the introductory chapter is known as 'Apanī Kathā', and it is written in the first person and considered biographical.[22] This chapter is written in 401 verses and describes Guru Gobind Singh's early life and vividly describes the battles he fought. It also emphasizes that the spirit of Guru Nanak ran through each consecutive Guru. The Tenth Guru stresses the importance of the martyrdom of Guru Tegh Bahadur within his 'Own Narration'. Much of the history we know about the Tenth Guru is based on this composition.[23] The *Bachitra Nāṭak* also includes the *Chaṇḍī Charitra*, *Chaubīs Avatār*, *Brahmā Avatār*, and *Rudra Avatār*, as the concluding rubrics of the compositions state that they are a part of *Bachitra Nāṭak Granth*. The Guru rejects the idea of Divine incarnation and states that all prophets are the creation of Akal Purakh, which is equivalent to the theology of the *AG*.

The *DG* also contains three different narrations of the battles of Chandi, the Indian goddess of war, and two of the Chandi compositions record *Pātashāhī 10* as a heading. The *Chaṇḍī Charitra Ukati Bilās* or 'Recitation of the Deeds of Chaṇḍī' records that it is derived from the story of *Mārkaṇḍeya Purāṇa*.[24] The second exposition is simply known as *Chaṇḍī Charitra* and in the standard edition does not have any rubrics recording the source of the composition, but it forms a part of the *Bachitra Nāṭak*. Both the compositions have been written in Braj but the third version, known as *Chaṇḍī dī Vār* or 'The Ballad of Chandi', is the only composition written in chaste Panjabi.[25] It begins with an invocation to the ten gurus and the first verse is employed as a part of the Sikh *ardās*. The compositions of the goddess describe her battles with various demons and she takes on different forms including Chandi, Durga, Bhavani, and Kali. The tales symbolize the epic battle between good and evil where the demons represent different types of evil. There are several differences between the Guru's accounts of Chandi and the original account.[26] The term *Ukati Bilās* refers to a style of poetry where there is an elaborate use of similes. It contains the Sikh national anthem, 'deh sivā baru mohi ihai', and the reference to the poetic 'sentiment of dread' or *Rudra Ras* by the author clearly shows its purpose as a martial scripture. This is in reference to the gory scenes of death and bloodshed within its verses.[27] It seems that the reason for three different compositions was to allow for the expression of the story in different styles of poetry.

The *Giān Prabodh* or 'Awakening of Knowledge' contains the salutations to Akal Purakh, which is similar in style to the *Akāl Ustati*. It starts with the heading *Pātishāhī Dasvīṅ* and was written in 336 verses. It contains descriptions of ritualistic sacrifices of kings from the Mahābhārat.[28] The poet narrates a dialogue between the soul and Akal Purakh and proceeds to elaborate on the four stages of *dharam* or righteousness. The stages are: *Bhog*-dharam (principles of family life), *Rāj*-dharam (political morality), *Dān*-dharam (principles of charity), and *Mokhsa*-dharam (the codes of salvation). The composition appears to be unfinished as only the principle of *Dān*-dharam has been elaborated on.[29]

The *Bachitra Nāṭak* continues by recounting the *avatārs*: *Chaubīs Avatār, Brahma Avatār,* and *Rām Avatār*. The three works begin with the title of the Tenth Guru (*Pātashāhī 10*) and describe the different incarnations of Vishnu, Brahma, and Rudra respectively.[30] The *Chaubīs Avatār* describes the 'Twenty-Four Incarnations' of Vishnu, and its longest episode is the *Krishnā Avatār*, while the others are brief in comparison. Within it there are a number of colophons and the final one states that 'this work has been completed in the year 1745 of the *Vikramī* era in the *Sudi* aspect of the moon in the month of *Sāvan* (July 1688), in the town of Paonta at the auspicious hour, on banks of the flowing Yamuna'.[31] The prologue to the 'Twenty-Four Incarnations' begins with the poet's view on incarnation, which is that Akal Purakh is the sole Creator of the Vishnu incarnations.[32] He gives his opinion on their importance:

> I shall not invoke Ganesh first of all.[33] I shall never contemplate on Krishna or Vishnu. I have heard about them but know them not. My devotion is concentrated on the feet of the Lord.[34]

The poet continues by stating, 'First of all I remember God. Then I compose poetry of different moods.'[35] In *Rām Avatār* the warrior feats of this *deva* are narrated, and its concluding verses are recited as part of the *Rahirās Sāhib*, which is the evening prayer of the Sikhs. At the end of this panegyric, the Guru refutes the supremacy of the Islamic and Hindu scriptures and asks for the benediction of the Divine Sword. He employs the pen name 'Gobind Das', which was his childhood name.[36] Its colophon reads, 'This Granth has been completed and improved in the year 1755 of the *Vikramī* era in *Vadī* first in the month of *hāṛh* (July 1698); if there has remained any error in it then kindly correct it.'

The *Shastra Nām Mālā Purāṇ* or 'Rosary of Weapons from Puranic Literature' describes the various weapons that were utilized at the time of the Guru, and its title indicates its ancient context. It begins with the title of the Tenth Sovereign and it is composed of 1,318 verses. The text includes riddles and practical information, that was an aid for the Khalsa warriors who were trained in *Shastravidiā*, and continues the theme of dharam yudh. The composition equates various weapons with Akal Purakh, and hence the poet considers that God has ordained that a primal power is present in the weapons. Some of the weapons described in this composition can be seen ceremonially placed at many gurdwaras in front of the Sikh scriptures.[37]

The didactic piece known as *Srī Charitropakhyān* also bears the hallmark of martial tones.[38] It also begins with the title of the Tenth Sovereign and is one of the largest compositions, and is composed of 7,555 verses.[39] The debate about the *DG* has focused on this composition and some have questioned whether the Guru could have authored the *Charitrās*.[40] Like the previous compositions narrated, it also contains mythological stories and these have also been labelled as 'Hindu'. The *Srī Charitropakhyān* has been described as 'wiles of women' which is incorrect, as there are stories related to both men and women. The word 'pakhyān' translates as 'short tale' and 'charitrā' translates as 'account or adventure'. There are tales derived from various sources including religious and secular texts from the Hindu, Buddhist, Islamic, and Christian traditions.[41] The *Chaupaī Sāhib* is the concluding charitrā of this composition which is traditionally recited twice daily, in the nitnem and *Rahirās Sāhib*, and as part of the khaṅḍe kī pāhul ceremony. At the end of the *Srī Charitropakhyān*, the author clearly expresses that the *DG* has been completed (*pūran karā Graṅth tatakālā*).[42] The *Srī Charitropakhyān* colophon records, 'The Granth was completed in the year of 1753 *Vikramī* on the 18th day of month of *Bhadoṅ* (August 1696) on the banks of river Satluj.' This place is noted to be Gurdwara Bhabaur Sahib, Nangal; and the tradition records that the *Chaupaī Sāhib* was written here. As the author of *Srī Charitropakhyān* clearly refers to the completion of the *Graṅth*, this would suggest the finalization of the *DG*, which was before the addition of the *Zafarnāmah*, and other smaller compositions.

The *Zafarnāmah*, or the 'Epistle of Victory', was a letter written in AD 1705 addressed to the Mughal Emperor Aurangzeb. It is written in Persian and describes the military stand-off with Aurangzeb, and was composed after the Guru's withdrawal from the besieged Anandpur Sahib. The author accuses Aurangzeb of breaking his oath, and the treachery of his army whilst at the siege of Chamkaur in December 1704. The Guru lost two of his sons, Sahibzada Ajit Singh and Sahibzada Jujhar Singh, in the battle with Wazir Khan's battalion.[43] The *Zafarnāmah* is a first-hand account of the Guru's relationship with the Mughal Empire and therefore a very important source of Sikh history. After this composition follows the Persian *Hikāitāṅ* or 'tales', which are numbered starting at two, and has a total of 868 verses. The name derives from the internal rendering of the words *Hikāyat shunidan* or 'we have heard the story of', which starts at the beginning of each tale.[44] The *Hikāitāṅ* are to some extent a repetition of a few stories in the *Srī Charitropakhyān*; for example, tales 4 and 5 are the same as the *Charitrās* 52 and 267 respectively.[45] The *Hikāitāṅ* follow the *Zafarnāmah*, which would suggest that the stories are addressed to Aurangzeb, to give him a didactic message.

The colophons recorded within the *DG* compositions allow us to locate where and when they were written, and they also indicate the places where the Guru held his court. The mythological and didactic compositions, *Rām Avatār*, *Krishnā Avatār*, and *Srī Charitropakhyān*, have colophons within them, but the readily accepted devotional compositions such as *Jāp Sāhib*, *Svaiye*, and others do not. The devotional compositions have always been considered by most Sikhs as being authored by Guru Gobind Singh but the mythological and didactic compositions were first debated by Sikhs early in the last century.[46] The aforementioned colophons in the *DG* provide us with information that will also be considered in conjunction with some of the early manuscripts of the *DG* later in this chapter.

The Relics of the Tenth Guru

In addition to the scripture itself, we need to assess whether the relics of the Tenth Guru shed any light on the compositions of the *DG*. After all, the authenticity debate has centred on the scripture, without a discussion of the material heritage that provides a novel angle of discussion. Relics associated with the gurus are always considered sacred, but weapons are considered much more profound in Sikh theology. This notion itself can be traced back to the martial spirit that echoes throughout the *DG*, as weapons are considered to represent the power and protection of Akal Purakh. The inscription of *gurbāṇī* (Divine-inspired poetry of the gurus) on weapons suggests that this scripture was both for inspiration and protection in war, and not just limited to the confines of the gurdwara.[47]

We shall begin by discussing a set of weapons which were brought to the UK after the annexation of Panjab and the Anglo-Sikh wars (1845–9).[48] A famous owner of Sikh relics was Lord Dalhousie, the Governor General of India (1848–56), who, upon becoming the guardian of Maharaja Duleep Singh, brought the Royal Treasury of Lahore, or *toshekhānā*, under the possession of the British.[49] It was on the advice of Lord Dalhousie that the arms and other relics from the toshekhānā were sent to England. The treasury included the famous Koh-i-noor diamond or 'Mountain of Light', which was later cut and incorporated into the crown jewels of Queen Elizabeth.[50] There were also two swords that belonged to Guru Gobind Singh in this 'treasury', which are now referred to as the 'Toshekhānā' and 'Raekote' swords.[51] The second sword has more history available regarding it and is said to have been an heirloom of the family of Rai Kalah of Raekote. It was given to Rai Shabaz Khan and his brother-in-law Rai Fateh Khan by Guru Gobind Singh in 1705.[52]

Henry Brereton, the deputy commissioner of Ludhiana, noted in 1854 that the sword's owner was Guru Gobind Singh.[53] He states, 'The sword is an ordinary looking blade with a gilded hilt, and a scabbard newly covered with red velvet.'[54] The letter of H. Brereton describing the sword of the Guru is given in Figure 1.1.

He also states that on the right side of the blade there are inscriptions in the Gurmukhi script:

Akāl Purakh kī rachhā hamanai.
Ik Oaṅkār Satigur Prasādi Utār Khāse Pātshāhī 10.
Sarabaloh kī rachhā hamanai.

The Immortal Being protects me.
One Creator–Destroyer–Preserver, realised through the grace of the True Guru, copy of the manuscript with authentic signature of the Tenth King [Guru Gobind Singh]
The All-Iron protects me.[55]

The script on the left side of the blade was inscribed with the following:

Sarabkāl kī rachhā hamanai Sarab[loh] jī kī rachhā hamanai.

All-Death protects me; All-Iron always protects me.[56]

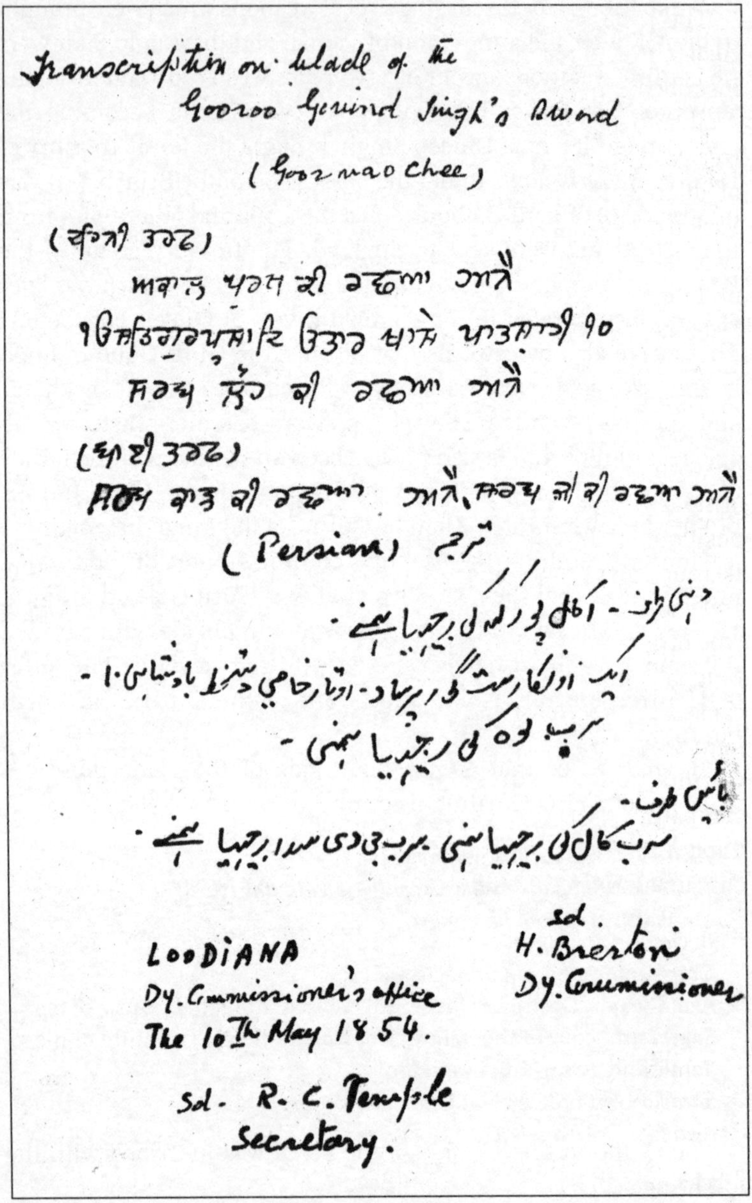

Transcription on blade of the
Gooroo Govind Singh's Sword
(Goorwao Chee)

(ਸੱਜੀ ਤਰਫ)
ਅਕਾਲ ਪੁਰਖ ਕੀ ਰਛਿਆ ਹਮਨੈ
੧ਓਸਤਿਗੁਰਪ੍ਰਸਾਦਿ ਉਤਾਰ ਖਾਸ ਪਾਤਸ਼ਾਹੀ ੧੦
ਸਰਬ ਲੋਹ ਕੀ ਰਛਿਆ ਹਮਨੈ

(ਖੱਬੀ ਤਰਫ)
ਸਰਬ ਕਾਲ ਕੀ ਰਛਿਆ ਹਮਨੈ, ਸਰਬ ਜੀ ਕੀ ਰਛਿਆ ਹਮਨੈ

(Persian) ترجمہ

دہنی طرف - اکال پرکھ کی رچھیا ہمنے -
ایک اونکار ست گورپرساد - اوتار خاص دستخط بادشاہی ۱۰ -
سرب لوہ کی رچھیا ہمنی -

بائیں طرف -
سرب کال کی رچھیا ہمنی - سرب جی دی سدا رچھیا ہمنے -

Sd.
H. Brereton
Dy. Commissioner

LOODIANA
Dy. Commissioner's office
The 10th May 1854.

Sd. R. C. Temple
Secretary.

Figure 1.1 Letter of H. Brereton Describing the Sword of the Guru
Source: Gurinder Singh Mann.

The inscriptions are from the invocation of the composition *Akāl Ustati*. It is highly significant that the Guru's verses are inscribed on the sword itself. More importantly, the lines refer to Akal as being the 'All-Steel', and as a result, the sword symbolizes Akal Purakh in battle. This inscription is related to the notion of dharam yudh, clearly to inspire struggle for noble causes.[57] Various attempts were made to locate the Raekote and Toshekhānā swords after they were taken to the UK, but unfortunately they can no longer be traced. In 1965 some of the artefacts from the Lord Dalhousie collection were returned to Panjab.[58]

We now turn to the body armour commonly known by the Persian term, *chārāinā*, which means 'four mirrors'.[59] This type of body armour consists of two side plates, with the other two to be worn on the front and the back. In the *DG*, the term to describe armour is *kavach* which appears frequently throughout the compositions. From the same period, armours from both Hindu and Islamic armies in India were decorated with elaborate designs and verses from scriptures like the Bhagvad Gītā and Qur'an. This type of armour was introduced in India under the influence of the Mughal Empire.[60] Recently, the sale of a chārāinā at Sotheby's caused an outcry in the Sikh Diaspora in the UK in 2008.[61] This item was a single breastplate of a chārāinā with inscriptions in Gurmukhi script.[62] In order to assess its significance we need to compare it with the complete one which is kept with Maharaja Capt. Amarinder Singh of Patiala. The inscription on the Sotheby's chārāinā is again from the *Akāl Ustati* and is as follows:[63]

Ik Oaṅkār....
Utār Khāse Daskhat kā Ustat Akāl Purakh jī kī Pātshāhi 10.
Akāl Purakh kī rachhiā hamane.
Sarabaloh kī rakhhiā hamane.
Sarabkāl jī dī rachhiā hamane.
Sarabloh jī dī sadā rachhiā hamane.
Agai likharī ke daskhat ... Vahīgurū jī.

There is a clear difference in the orthography of the Sotheby's chārāinā and the historical Raekote sword we considered earlier. The calligraphy and *koftgari* of the Patiala chārāinā and the Sotheby's plate are slightly different, and the Patiala armour has thicker koftgari.[64] It appears that the lines are thinner, to the extent that the koftgari looks worn on the Sotheby's chārāinā, probably due to weathering and damage. The inscriptions on the Patiala plates are from the *AG* and *DG*, with the verses from the *AG* composition *Jāp jī Sāhib* commonly known as 'Mūl Mantra' or 'root formula'. The second part of the plate has verses from the *DG* composition, the *Jāp Sāhib*. The third part of the plate has inscribed the *Rakhyā Shabad* (*sir mastak rakhyā pārbrahamaṅ*) from the *AG*.[65] This composition is normally recited for protection and is also seen written on quoits of the Sikhs.[66] The final plate shows the opening verses of *Akāl Ustati*, as described earlier (see Figure 1.2). We can only speculate what the other three plates of the Sotheby's plate had inscribed on them.[67]

The Patiala plate reveals that the Gurmukhi inscriptions were taken from both *Graṅths* which is highly significant. The use of both scriptures is consistently seen in Sikh practices, namely in the *nitnem* and the khaṅḍe kī pāhul ceremony, as well as the enthronement of both *Graṅths* at two of the Sikh *takhts*. This could also be seen to conform with Sikh theology, namely *mīrī–pīrī*, which is the combination of the saintly and the martial traditions.

The history of the Patiala plate appears to be mentioned in Guru Gobind Singh's *Bachitra Nāṭak*.[68] There is a reference to this armour being used in battle.[69] The Guru narrates how he was attacked by Hari Chand:

> The enraged Hari Chand took his bow and aiming at my horse he shot his first arrow. The second arrow he shot whilst aiming at me. God saved me as the arrow skimmed away past my ear. The third arrow he shot at my belt which pierced through it. Its tip pricked my skin but no wound occurred. The Lord of Time saved the life of his humble servant.[70]

The Patiala armour has an entry hole that could be the battle mark mentioned earlier. In conclusion, the two chārāinās are significant pieces of Sikh material heritage and show that inscriptions of gurbāṇī were present on the armour. With a strong history and their supporting features, the Patiala plate certainly would have belonged to Guru Gobind Singh. It is more likely that the single Sotheby's plate belonged to another Sikh warrior, as there is no historical evidence joining it to the Tenth Guru.

FIGURE 1.2 *Chārāinā* of Guru Gobind Singh[71]
Source: Reproduced from *Anandpur: The City of Bliss* by Dr Mohinder Singh and photographs by Sondeep Shankar. In the collection of Capt. Amarinder Singh of Patiala.

There are also copper plates which bear signatures and inscriptions attributed to the Tenth Guru. In ancient India, inscriptions were written on palm leaves, but a need for a more permanent epigraphical method led to the *tamar patar*, or copper plate, for royal seals, important lineages, and legal deeds. Interestingly, a number of different institutions of various religions have recorded pronouncements or edicts on these types of plates. This relatively new discovery in Sikh material heritage poses new questions about the impact of such plates on the propagation of prayers and edicts by the Guru.[72] There are at least three notable copper plates in separate locations, which we are currently aware of. The prevalence of Sikh relics at important Hindu sites is more than previously thought, and Mann[73] notes that Guru Gobind Singh presented them to the custodians.[74] More importantly, the plates are an important symbol of the Guru, as they show that he acted as a sovereign, who granted his authority to his subjects and gave his blessings. At that time, such an honour would have become widespread news, and would have made the custodians prominent in their communities, which would have clearly benefited the mission of the Guru.

The first plate is located at the temple of Naina Devi and bears the signature of the Tenth Guru.[75] The second plate could be found at Kurukshetra and is no longer extant. This plate was stolen in the 1980s from the gurdwara where it was on display. There is not much information about its contents from its previous owners.[76] The third copper plate is very significant as it provides us with evidence about how the ardās was employed at the time of the Tenth Guru. This plate is located at the Shiva Temple, Kapal Mochan, which is near Paonta Sahib.[77] Local history narrates that the Guru came to Kapal Mochan after the battle of Bhangani. The Guru and the Khalsa army cleaned and washed their *shastras* at this location. The erection of the Gurdwara Kapal Mochan marks the commemoration of his visit.[78] The training in *Shastravidiā* is also said to have taken place here in preparation for future battles.[79] The custodians of the plate state that it was bestowed on their family when the Guru visited Kapal Mochan in AD 1679, and again in AD 1688 when the Guru presented a decorated *hukamnāmā* to their ancestors.[80] This plate records a decree in Gurmukhi script that is identical to the opening lines of the ardās (*Chaṇḍī dī Vār*). This stanza is recited daily by Sikhs, and is a very significant feature of this plate. It also bears the date 14 October 1679 and states this has been given to Jawala Das Braham, and that any of his Sikhs who follows this *hukam* will be blessed.[81] See Figure 1.3 for the hukamnāmā and tamar patar at Kapal Mochan.

FIGURE 1.3 *Hukamnāmā* and *Tamar Patar*, Kapal Mochan
Source: Gurinder Singh Mann.

This is yet another example of where the compositions of the Guru were propagated in a form other than manuscripts.

In addition, it is plausible that the plates were used as stamps, and would then make the edicts and prayers accessible to the *sangats* (congregations) in the surrounding areas. We also know that the Guru kept many scribes with him and it is possible that other copies of hukamnāmās were made.[82] This also provides us with crucial information about the creation of the composition *Chaṇḍī dī Vār*, that is, it was written prior to AD 1679. It may have been written at Paonta Sahib as the tradition of the gurdwara states.[83]

The Transmission of *Dasam Granth* Manuscripts

The major transmission of the scriptures was via manuscripts, so in this part of the chapter we will consider only those with colophons before the nineteenth century, and with a verifiable history. A limitation of studying the *DG* is locating some of the earliest recensions. In our research we have considered new manuscripts that have early colophons.[84] Many scholars have categorized the *DG* as the secondary scripture of the Sikh canon, and this is clear when we examine Sikh liturgy and praxis.[85] A number of scholars have examined the manuscripts of the *AG*, the primary canon, but in comparison there has been little consideration of the *DG*.[86] There have been brief examinations of manuscripts by Trilochan Singh,[87] Randhir Singh,[88] P. Sehgal,[89] and Piara Singh Padam.[90] R.S. Jaggi[91] is an exception as he wrote a substantial portion of his thesis on extant *DG* manuscripts. The scholars of *AG* have given useful insights on how the second Sikh scripture could be examined, as their work has a comprehensive methodology concerning the transmission of the *AG*. The most important factor to consider is that many of the historical sources which narrate the compilation of the *AG* also support the creation of the *DG*.[92]

A description of important *DG* manuscripts is provided by Giani Gian Singh in his *Panth Prakāsh*.[93] He states that there were only four main recensions of the *DG*; however, when we examine colophons in available *DG* manuscripts, we see that this is an incorrect assessment.[94] Jaggi's research[95] is based around the brief details of manuscripts provided by Giani Gian Singh, but

Piara Singh Padam has provided details of other extant manuscripts, which then contradict that research.[96] It is also interesting to note that the Sodhak Committee, which was tasked with making a standard of the works of Guru Gobind Singh in AD 1897, was able to track over thirty-two manuscripts but Giani Gian Singh could only locate a handful. We can conclude that Jaggi's study is very narrow as he has not considered the plethora of manuscripts that are actually available. Many other manuscripts have colophons from AD 1698–1740, and it is the opinion of the authors of this book that they are just as significant in the transmission of the scripture. One only has to take into account the geographical mobility in Giani Gian Singh's time to see why locating other recensions was a barrier to research. One obvious flaw is overlooking numerous manuscripts at Takht Hazur Sahib, which have not been considered or mentioned by writers in Panjab.[97] This is the location of Guru Gobind Singh's *jotī jot* (ascension) and where the *AG* was given the final status of Guruship.[98] The Sodhak Committee also faced the same problem as they did not have the original extant manuscripts available, apart from the 'Anaṅdpurī' recension, as the other volumes were in daily use at the Sikh takhts.[99] There are two significant recensions that are referred to as the 'Anaṅdpurī bīṛhāṅ'. One is said to be written in the *daskhat* (handwriting) of the Guru from beginning to end, which was discovered, examined, and photographed by Manohar Singh Marco in 1963. It was badly damaged with torn pages and broken binding, but this manuscript has been restored and digitized recently. This *biṛh* (which we shall refer to as the 'Marco' biṛh) is of great significance as it contains annotations on *bāṇī* and the calligraphy matches the *khās patre* of the Tenth Guru. The khās patre are individual folios attributed to the Tenth Guru found in the earliest autograph manuscript copies of the *AG* and *DG*. In our research we have come across a number of photographs of these folios which were actually taken from this particular biṛh, and with the restoration of this *Granth* we can now see how the handwriting of the folios match the 'Marco' biṛh. We initially believed that the folios were part of the other 'Anaṅdpurī' biṛh but it is more likely that they come from the 'Marco' biṛh. Some of the folios from this manuscript were published for the first time in 1975.[100] One of the folios read, 'This recension of mine', and seems to have annotations made by the author.[101] Scholars seem to be divided on what this manuscript actually contains, but if this manuscript contains the first compositions or even small verses of the *DG*, then it would be the 'Ur' manuscript. In addition it may also contain important details about the *DG*, but at this early stage it is uncertain as to what the scripture actually contains. Nonetheless, the 'Marco' biṛh sheds light on the compilation of gurbāṇī at Anandpur Sahib by Guru Gobind Singh, but most notably, the writing style is similar to the khās patres found in other *AG* and *DG* recensions, and other smaller liturgical pothīs.

A manuscript of the *Bachitra Nāṭak* from AD 1688 claims within it that it was written from even older pothīs. It consists of 330 folios with black ink and red headings throughout. There is a lot of *haṛtāl* (corrections) throughout the volume, and the contents are given at the beginning. On folio 27 there is a heading in blue ink that reads, '[T]his *pāṭh* was written in *Saṅmat* 1752 *Phagan* 28/1695 AD and completed from the *Bachitra Nāṭak Graṅth* composition in reference to a *pāṭh* of a *Saṅmat* 1742/1685 AD [volume].' On folio 26, it states, '[O]ther volumes were mixed to become a part of this *Mahān Graṅth*. It was also written from another older *Pothī*.' There are also some blank folios throughout the volume. It begins with the *Jāp Sāhib* but with the heading *Srī Akāl Purakh jī de Prasādi Jāpu Pātashāhi 10* and ends with 'the recitation *Yudh Prabaṅdh Graṅth* is auspiciously completed. 1688. The total of the *Dasam, Rāsi Maṅḍal* and *Briha Nāṭak, Yudh Prabaṅdh*. 2520.21..5072. *Aṅg*.' If the colophons are correct then we can safely conclude that this is a very significant manuscript.[102]

Another recension of the *DG*, also referred to as the 'Anaṅdpurī' bīṛh, has not been elaborated on in much detail.[103] An exception to this is the unpublished report by Mahan Singh about the manuscript.[104] Piara Singh Padam explains the importance of this recension especially with regards to the khās patre and the internal corrections of the scribes.[105] Mann also considers some features of the text but again does not elaborate on the development of the *Graṅth* or the daskhat folios.[106] This recension also contains other documents of historical importance within it; for example, in the opening folios of the recension there is a letter from the court poet Mangal to the Guru's wife, Mata Jito, in which he writes that he is sending blessings to the family of the Guru.[107] It also contains an encyclical edict which is a hukamnāmā addressed to Bhai Mohkam Singh and Arjun Singh.[108] There are also two paintings depicting the Guru, one of which portrays him sitting on a *singhāsan* (throne), draped in red clothing next to luxurious cushions and weapons.[109] The second one shows the Guru shooting arrows and killing a lion.[110] These features would indicate an early date, and are of great historical value. The recension itself is 12 inches by 5 inches and has a leather binding cover with a repair of denim cloth. It was bound on a number of occasions and the contents page changed accordingly. This shows that the *DG* was created over time and would explain why the first seven entries have been changed in the contents. The manuscript has two internal dates of AD 1695 and AD 1696, placing this in the lifetime of the Guru. The scribes have recorded their names in the sections they have written, including Darbari, Nihala, Bala, Darbari Singh Chhota, and Haridas. Interestingly, early manuscripts of the *AG* were also scribed by Bhai Haridas, the grandfather of Jassa Singh Ramgharia, and this is likely to be the same person.[111] More importantly, there are eight khās patre folios contained within this recension. Some scholars have claimed these types of folios are forgeries and also appear in other *DG* manuscripts;[112] however, some scholars who have examined the Guru's hukamnāmās state that there are similarities between the two styles of calligraphy. Bhai Randhir Singh came to this conclusion in his publication *Shabad Mūrati* and Dharam Pal Ashta in *The Poetry of the Dasam Granth*.

The 'Anaṅdpurī' manuscript has many amendments and changes, which suggests that it is a working draft. There are unique features in this particular manuscript including the margins containing extra line numbering, which would not be included in a completed *graṅth*. This was a preventative measure to ensure that extra material could not be added in by the scribes. Padam notes the *shudh* (corrections) on the folios of *Srī Charitropakhyān*, which he states were made by the Tenth Guru in his own hand.[113] Pashaura Singh notes that the idea of shudh was started by Guru Arjan Dev and is recorded in early *AG* manuscripts.[114] Then the most plausible explanation is that the Guru dictated his own compositions to the scribes but also wrote the corrections with his own quill and scribed his own renditions sometimes covering several folios.[115] Further evidence to corroborate this is in the aforementioned composition *Akāl Ustati*, which states that the opening verse is in the hand of the Guru and the rest was written by the scribe. The khās patre have been given little attention by scholars and, as a result, a void has been created in understanding the textual development of the *DG*. The folios in question provide us with several important pieces of information, including details about the compositions of the *DG* and how the khās patre follow on sequentially, even in different recensions.[116]

It is now necessary to turn our attention to early Sikh sources of history about the compositions of Guru Gobind Singh. One of the important historical sources are the 'rahitnāme' or 'letters of injunction' which were based on the Tenth Guru's teachings about the Sikh code of conduct. Chaupa Singh was a Sikh who was in the retinue of Guru Tegh Bahadur and was present in the court of the Tenth Guru, under whose guidance he wrote a *rahitnāmā* (a Gurmukhi record of the *rahit*).[117] Modern scholars date the *Chaupā Singh Rahitnāmā* between AD 1740 and AD 1765, while traditional scholars and Gurmukhi manuscriptologists confirm the date as AD 1700.[118] It is in this rahitnāmā that we find the terms *Avatār Līlā (Bachitra Nāṭak)* as well as *Sāgar Granth*. The second work is accepted in the tradition to have been composed by the court poets and was also known as *Vidiāsāgar*. Chaupa Singh makes it quite clear that *Avatār Līlā* and *Sāgar Granth* were two separate works, and this is clarified further by a hagiography of the Sikh gurus by Sarup Das Bhalla.[119] A close inspection of the rahitnāmā reveals some fascinating details in regard to the *DG* compositions. Chaupa Singh quotes from and mentions virtually every composition, explicitly stating that the 'Master has spoken this', and includes *Jāp Sāhib, Akāl Ustati, Chaṇḍī dī Vār, Chaṇḍī Charitra*, and *Srī Charitropakhyān*, and so on. Whilst other rahitnāmās quote some of the *DG* compositions, this work is by far the most important due to its early date and the mention of many compositions by the author. Furthermore, Chaupa Singh states that the first three pieces orated by the Guru were *Jāp Sāhib, Akāl Ustati*, and *Svaiye*, and the date given for the first two compositions is AD 1677 and AD 1678 respectively. Is there any other evidence that corroborates the *Chaupā Siṅgh Rahitnāmā*? In order to resolve this issue we need to turn to another extant manuscript, which is the 'Takht Patna Sahib' recension that has an internal colophon of AD 1698.[120] Significantly, this manuscript actually begins with the three compositions noted by Chaupa Singh, that is, the first ones spoken by the Guru. The title in the 'Takht Patna Sahib' recension reads as follows (also see Figure 1.4):

> *Ik Oaṅkār Vāhigurū jī kī Fateh Srī Bhagautī jū Sāhaī, Tatkarā Suchī Patar*
> *Srī Graṅth jū kā bāṅī* Pātishāhī Dasveṅ jū kī Graṅth *kī Tav Prasād Pātasāhī Dassa.*[121]
>
> *Ik Oaṅkār*, Vahiguru is Victorious, the Divine-Sword Protects, the Contents List for the Holy Granth of the Hymns, of the Tenth Sovereign's Granth, by the Grace of the Tenth Sovereign.

This provides us with vital information as the colophon clearly places this manuscript at the end of the seventeenth century and there is nothing within the recension to dispute this. It is likely that the manuscript was commenced before AD 1705 as there is no *Zafarnāmah* recorded in the contents folio. Even more importantly, the *Graṅth* bears the words 'Pātishāhī Dasveṅ jū kī Graṅth', which literally means the 'Graṅth of the Tenth Sovereign'.[122] The manuscript notes that it has been prepared by the grace of 'Pātasāhī Dasveṅ' or the Tenth Sovereign, which perhaps suggests that it was written under the orders of the Guru—as we have already noted that the giving of edicts was the preserve of a sovereign. The 'Takht Patna Sahib' manuscript *Tatkārā* also outlines the opening bāṇīs within the *Graṅth*, as follows:

> *Patra 21 Jāpu Nishān Chhaṅd [Jāp Sāhib]*
> *Patra 25 Ustati Akāl jū Chhaṅd [Akāl Ustati]*
> *Patra 31 Svaiye Srī Mukhvāk [Amrit Svaiye]*
> *Patra 38 Ath Bachitra Nāṭak Graṅth*

This clearly shows the correlation between the history recorded about the compositions in one of the oldest *rahitnāme* and an extant *DG* manuscript. This also leads to the possibility of dating the *Chaupā Singh Rahitnāmā* by the colophon in this *DG* manuscript.[123] It is plausible that the first few compositions of the 'Takht Patna Sahib' AD 1698 recension and the 'Anandpurī' AD 1696 recension matched, but the latter was reorganized, which led to the obvious changes in the contents folio. Most parts of the 'Anandpurī' recension were written two years earlier than the AD 1698 recension, which after the completion of the *Charitropakhyān*, was bound on the completion of the *Chaubīs Avatār*.

We will now examine another *DG* recension which is similar to the 'Takht Patna Sahib' recension and also present at the

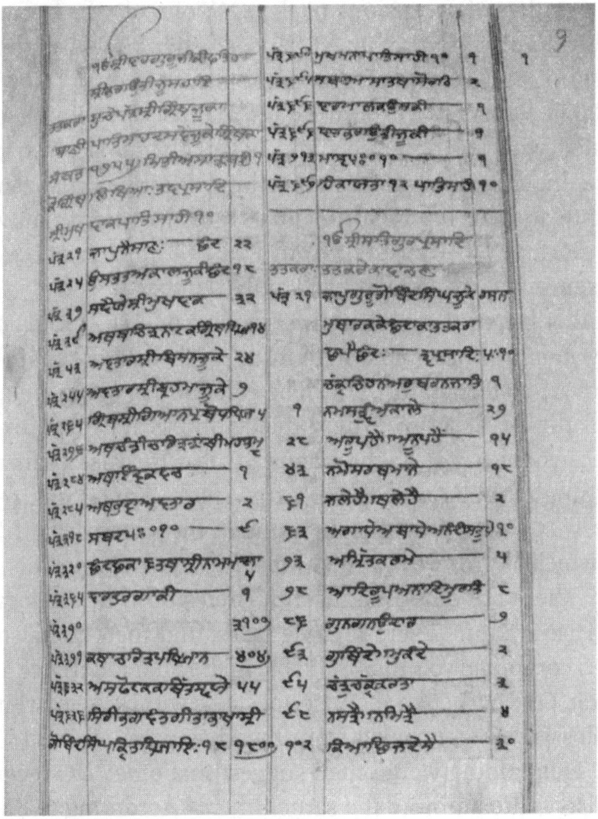

FIGURE 1.4 'Takht Patna Sahib' *Bīṛh*
Source: Gurcharnjit Singh Lamba.

Takht Sahib. Its content folios have identical features with the aforementioned manuscript.

However, there are two noticeable differences: there is no date in this recension and the *Gobińd Gītā* composition is not present.[124] The omission of the *Gobińd Gītā* and other apocrypha could suggest the 'Takht Patna Sahib' recension of AD 1698 was written afterwards.[125] This recension contains mainly floral decorations on some of the pages of the manuscript. If we consider the previous colophon in the aforementioned manuscript to be authentic, then this manuscript was produced in a turbulent period, and as a result copies of it were not made. In the *Sachkhańd* of the Akal Takht, we find a number of recensions of the *DG*, one of which was mentioned by Kanh Singh Nabha.[126] This is better known as the Patna *Misal sarūp* (see Chapter 2). This sarūp has an identical copy which is at Takht Patna Sahib. Both extant manuscripts are beautifully decorated with solar symbols and have colophons of AD 1765.[127] Patna Sahib has a historical connection with the gurus, especially the Ninth and the Tenth Guru, and as a result, many manuscripts of the *AG* and *DG* were sent from Panjab to this location, which was a seminary of the Sikhs even at that time.

Another important manuscript is a joint *AG–DG* recension said to be written by Bhai Mani Singh in AD 1713, which is kept in a family's private collection in Delhi. The colophon is given on an extra folio in the manuscript, which makes it less reliable. Originally this recension was at Takht Hazur Sahib which is confirmed by Kanh Singh Nabha and Akali Kaur Singh. Kanh Singh Nabha provides us with a photograph of one of the khās patre in *Mahān Kosh*, which is from the nine available khās patre in this recension.[128] There are other manuscript copies of it, in the locality of Takht Hazur Sahib where it came from, and there are also other *AG–DG* combined volumes available in the Sikh Reference Library, Amritsar. One particular manuscript states within the margins that the folios have been copied from the khās patre of Guru Gobind Singh. This finding would then suggest that other *DG* recensions were also written around the same time.[129] According to Sikh history, the aforementioned *AG–DG* recension was compiled by Bhai Mani Singh. The story is found in the *Pańth Prakāsh* by Rattan Singh Bhangu ([1841] 2004) and in the *Bansāvalīnāmā* by Kesar

Singh Chhibbar. Chhibbar refers to the handwritten folios of the Guru and, in addition, Bhai Mani Singh's search for them and how he bound them into the recension. In conclusion, this particular recension is mentioned in many historical accounts and in secondary source literature by Singh Sabha scholars, but most importantly, it had its ceremonial place at a takht. This type of recension is no longer printed; in fact, many different versions of this type of recension have been separated or ceremonially cremated.[130] Again, it must be added that there may be other extant recensions of the *AG–DG* recension type which might lead us to different conclusions. It must be mentioned here that the stemma[131] of the *DG* is mostly based around the order of the 'Anaṅdpurī' bīṛh. The standard *DG* follows the sequence of the 'Anaṅdpurī' bīṛh and a key feature of this major archetype is the fact that the *Bachitra Nāṭak* is not in one continuous piece. It was later on, when Bhai Mani Singh recompiled the earlier manuscripts into his joint *AG–DG* recension, that his redaction process involved bringing the *Bachitra Nāṭak* into one continuous chapter.

The Sangrur recension is another manuscript which was part of a binding with the *AG* but was separated.[132] A similar type of manuscript was mentioned in the committee standardization report of the *DG* in AD 1897, and can be identified by its extra compositions which include *Mālkauns kī Vār*, *Ugradantī*, and *Sukhmanā*.[133] According to the report, this volume was with the Buddha Dal. As this type of recension is quite rare and matches the information given by the report, it gives the account added credence. Jaggi[134] also narrates the oral history of the manuscript and associates it with Baba Binod Singh (leader of the Buddha Dal) who may have, at some time, been the caretaker of this *Graṅth*.[135] The 'Sangrur' biṛh could have been another recension compiled by Bhai Mani Singh, as there is always the possibility that he may have written another volume. Its extra compositions also appear in the 'Takht Patna Sahib' manuscripts which were not examined in the AD 1897 standardization. This brings into question whether the modern standard *DG* is representative of the oldest extant manuscripts.[136]

In Aurangabad is a manuscript of the *DG* attributed to Bhai Daya Singh, one of the Paṅj Piāre.[137] This is another manuscript that has gone unnoticed by scholars. This manuscript is written on Arabic paper and contains the *Zafarnāmah* in Persian, as well as the additional apocryphal compositions (see Figure 1.5). It has similarities to the 'Sangrur' manuscript but does not have an adjoining *AG*. Judging from the contents and features of this manuscript, it is probably from the late seventeenth century. There is another recension similar to this in the Ramgharia Bunga at Takht Hazur Sahib which has become too delicate to handle; it also contains the extra compositions.

It is important to note that small anthologies like *Das Granthīs*, *Safarī Biṛhs*, and individual compositions of the *DG* were very popular in the eighteenth and nineteenth centuries. According to the oral tradition of the Buddha Dal, which is also corroborated by Giani Gian Singh, Baba Dip Singh was the head of the *Shahīdī Misal* and also a scribe of many *granths*.[138] According to the same writer, Baba Dip Singh also wrote a biṛh in AD 1747/1804 VS, which ended with the *Asphotak Kabitts*, *Ugradantī*, and other bāṇīs. Padam[139] also records that at Damdama Sahib, the headquarters of Baba Dip Singh, was a granth that exactly matched these features.[140] However,

FIGURE 1.5 'Bhai Daya Singh' *DG* Recension, Aurangabad
Source: Kamalroop Singh.

many others have contested this and say that it does not exist. They are correct, as currently at the takht there is a *guṭkā* which has all the *DG* compositions apart from the *Shastra Nām Mālā*, and there is no volume that matches the features of the other historical recension (see Figure 1.6). On the other hand, the oral tradition of the Nihangs, the Damdami Taksal, and the history of the Damdama Sahib state that this extant manuscript, along with an *AG* manuscript, were the personal manuscripts of the legendry Baba Dip Singh. Both manuscripts are *Safarī Biṛhs*, which are recensions to be carried on expedition.[141]

In addition to this *AG* attributed to Baba Dip Singh, there is another one preserved at Takht Hazur Sahib. This recension was ceremonially taken all over India as part of the *Ādi Guru Granth Sahib* tercentennial enthronement celebrations.[142] After carefully comparing the folios of the two *AG* recensions with the pages from the *DG* guṭkā, we have concluded that the style of handwriting matches. However, this is just an initial examination, because all three manuscripts need to be examined together in situ, to be completely sure. Another notable *Safarī* recension is of *Srī Charitropakhyān*; in fact, there is an abundance of smaller breviaries that can be found in numerous locations.[143]

It is clear that there are several early *DG* manuscripts from the late seventeenth and early eighteenth centuries. There are others which have not been included in our discussion due to the

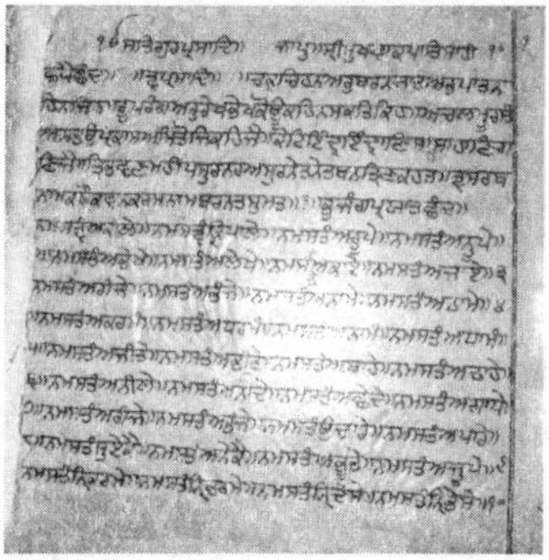

FIGURE 1.6 'Baba Dip Singh' *Gutkā*
Source: Anurag Singh.

limitations of the present publication. There is another AD 1698 manuscript extant in Chandigarh which is likely to have come from the Akal Takht Sahib.[144] There is yet another manuscript dated AD 1698 from Anandpur Sahib that is said to be at a gurdwara in Ayodhya, Uttar Pradesh.[145]

This chapter also dispels the false notion that Bhai Mani Singh was the compiler of the first *DG*, because in actual fact, the 'Anaṅdpurī' and 'Takht Patna Sahib' recensions disprove this. If we take the aforementioned manuscripts to be authentic, then the *DG* as a volume existed at the time of Guru Gobind Singh, and was thus more likely to be authored by him. The textual development and transmission of the *DG* has parallels to the *AG*. For example, the 'Anaṅdpurī' recension is the historical equivalent of the 'Kartārpurī' recension. There are four recensions of the *AG*: the *AG*, the 'Khaṛī' biṛh, the 'Khaṛī' biṛh with the *salok*s of the Ninth Guru, and the *AG* with the saloks of the Ninth Guru (the final recension known as the 'Dam Damī' edition).[146] Similarly, just like the *AG* has different editions, so does the *DG*, as compositions were added to the recensions over time. Jaggi's thesis[147] juxtaposed various extant manuscripts with the standard to show the differences between the texts. This is a fruitless endeavour, as the standard was created as one text out of many, and that would have had slight differences. There are differences in the numbering of verses in some of the recensions. This is a result of the way certain *chhaṅd*s have been defined, as opposed to them being absent.[148] To examine the recensions in comparison to the modern standard is only of benefit if we are trying to find out how the modern version came to be. To disprove the authenticity of original manuscripts based on later editions and, even worse, the standard is obviously a flawed endeavour.

It is vitally important that scholars try to form a historical stemma of the various *DG* manuscripts and employ *only* the oldest scriptures for any future work. This is a major criticism of the 1897 standardization, which is a shame as this methodology has been around for hundreds of years. The *DG* clearly grew as the Guru composed more gurbāṇī, as some of the later copies having the additional apocryphal compositions demonstrate. Recently, Takht Hazur Sahib undertook another process of standardization of the *DG*. The text on the whole is like the standardized *DG* from AD 1897, but with a few negligible alterations in some headings, orthography, and structure. The expert team of traditional scholars from the takht catalogued and compared many of the extant manuscripts at Hazur Sahib, as well from all over India.[149] It was from this extensive task that another new standard was created. In this new version, two metres in *Jāp Sāhib* have been split into *Ardh Bhujaṅg Prayāt Chhaṅd*. The thirty-three *svaiye* or panegyrics have been reduced to thirty-two, leaving out the famous 'Jagat Jot' quatrain. The volume is *larīvār* (all the words are joined), and each new heading is given in different colours, which we find in many of the handwritten manuscripts of the *DG*.

The Myth about the Compilation of the *Dasam Granth*

The relics and colophons of the *DG* manuscripts make it clear when and where it was compiled. A modern-day story which has confused researchers about the compilation of the *DG* began in the early twentieth century. The story centres around Sukha Singh and Mehtab Singh, the legendary Sikh warriors who sought justice for Massa Ranghar's sacrilegious acts at the Harimandir Sahib. Whether their attack on Ranghar was successful would decide if the *DG* would be kept together, but this arbitrary way of settling a theological matter does seem rather fanciful. This story appears to be have been first written in English, in Max Arthur Macauliffe's (1909) six-volume magnum opus, the *The Sikh Religion: Its Gurus, Sacred Writings and Authors*, and then later reproduced by Kanh Singh Nabha in his *Mahān Kosh* or *Encyclopaedia of Sikhism*. Neither author cites the source of this story, and in actual fact, the origins of the story cannot be ascertained. Both scholars were close associates, with Nabha even visiting England at the invitation of Macauliffe, as his six volumes were compiled with the aid of Nabha, as is testified by him.[150] The late appearance of this story means that it has to be treated with suspicion, as it cannot be found in any earlier accounts. Yet, at the same time, this story has been quoted extensively by so-called 'pro' and 'anti' *DG* writers. The Singh Sabha (to whom the *DG* was an anathema) developed their arguments as an antithesis to Hinduism as it was preached by Swami Dayanand. The development of this myth could have been to discredit the authenticity of the *DG*. Continuing with the story, the two warriors came back alive after slaying Massa Ranghar, and, as a result, the *Granth Sahib* was kept in one binding. The most important thing to note here is that the various stories are about the *DG* and the need to separate the *Srī Charitropakhyān*. The stories by Macauliffe and Kanh Singh Nabha find no corroboration with early sources of Sikh history and are just *myths*. Rattan Singh Bhangu was a descendant of Mehtab Singh and therefore he would have been aware of any resolution in relation to any so-called controversy over the *DG*. There are a number of quotations from the *DG* that he includes in his historical account titled *Panth Prakāsh* ([1841] 2004), but there is no mention of a controversy about the *DG* in his book.

In AD 1741, the slaying of Ranghar by Mehtab Singh and Sukha Singh was a gallant act, but the additions by Nabha and Macauliffe seem to differ from the original accounts. In available historical texts, we find the narration of Bhai Mani Singh recompiling a *DG* recension and its relationship to his martyrdom. This story is given by Kesar Singh Chhibbar in 1769, who was a contemporary of Bhai Mani Singh. The original concern of the narration is that when Bhai Mani Singh created his joint version of the *AG–DG*, he changed the order of this *Granth* into Guru order, and as a result, the Sikh sangat stated that he would also be cut from limb to limb (see Figure 1.7).

This story also clarifies the authorship debate as Bhai Mani Singh arranged the *AG* and *DG* into Guru order with *DG* compositions being written in the tenth position, while the *bhagat bāṇī* was separated.[152] It is plausible that confusion with regard to the Bhai Mani Singh story resulted in the myth being created by Macauliffe and Nabha. They may not have understood the cryptic writings of Giani Gian Singh.[153] There is also a possibility that this myth was deliberately propagated.

In the *Panth Prakāsh* of Rattan Singh Bhangu, he too states that the *Granth* was modified, and, as a result, Bhai Mani Singh was cursed by the sangat that he would be cut limb by limb as result of his transgression.[154] According to the oral tradition of the Buddha Dal, after the martyrdom of Bhai Mani Singh, the *AG* and *DG*

FIGURE 1.7 Bhai Mani Singh *AG–DG Bīṛh* Showing *Jāp Sāhib*[151]
Source: Giani Hardeep Singh.

were left in one volume and were taken to Damdama Sahib. It is said that at that time, it was Baba Dip Singh who did the ardās to resolve the issue about the newly formed *AG–DG* volume. After the success of Sukha Singh and Mehtab Singh in slaying Ranghar, it was agreed that the recension should be kept together. Moreover, according to early accounts and manuscripts, the *DG* was already bound at the time of the Guru, and so, in actual fact, Bhai Mani Singh had recompiled the *Granth*—probably to create his own version for exegetical purposes.[155] Therefore, this incident had nothing to do with any composition in the *DG* being considered controversial.

As noted earlier, tradition narrates that *bāṇīs* from both *Granths* were recited at the time of the Khalsa initiation ceremony in AD 1699. This would also correlate with the colophons previously mentioned. In the *Chaupā Singh Rahitnāmā* (1700), the author narrates the history of the *Avatār Līlā* (*Bachitra Nāṭak*) and the *bhog* (completion) of the *DG* in AD 1696, and this also tallies with the account of Chhibbar in the *Bansāvalīnāmā*.[156] The story of the Bhai Mani Singh bīṛh is told in detail by Chhibbar who states that a number of handwritten folios were added into the *Granth*. From the account, it appears that it is in reference to the daskhat folios in the hand of the Tenth Guru. One possibility is that they were collected and inserted into the different recensions at the corresponding points by Bhai Mani Singh. As he was also a close confidant of the Guru, he probably knew most of the details of what the Guru had in mind. He was put in charge of Harimandir Sahib, and this also leads to the distinct possibility that the *DG* was also *prakāsh* at the Akal Takht Sahib. This incident is recorded in the account by Seva Singh ([1800] 1961), although Kesar Singh narrates the events in more detail than Seva Singh as:

> When it was 1782 VS [AD 1725] then Bhai Mani Singh went to Amritsar.
> I heard he was there at Chola Bagh in Amritsar.
> Bhai Mani Singh was ranked high among the Sikhs, many Sikhs with money;
> Came to him, the Sikhs gave him money to find the *bāṅī*.
> Some important handwritten folios came to him.
> In reference to the folios, the *bāṅī* was collected and written.[157]

Bhai Mani Singh obtained some of the important folios, that is, the daskhat or khās patre, from where he was able to establish their position in the compositions of the *DG*. From this he created new recensions: 'He received many chapters, then he separated the *Bhagat Bāṇī*. The Adi Granth and the second Granth he made into one recension.'[158] Chhibbar also narrates how and why the *AG* was created, which also lends credibility to the incident about how the extant *AG–DG* recension of Bhai Mani Singh was created:

> Both of the Granths were bound in one recension, only some Sikhs saw this recension. Then, they said 'why have you put the Bhagat *bāṅī* separate? You have broken the *maryadā* of the Guru, your joints should be cut bit by bit.' Bhai Mani Singh replied to the Sikhs, 'the Bhagats were just people. They should not be equated to the Guru.' [The Sikhs replied] 'God takes a human into his lap and sits the virtuous next to him, but you have taken man from the side of God.' Bhai Mani Singh remained silent.[159]

In essence, Chhibbar states that only after receiving some of the khās patre did Bhai Mani Singh write the *AG–DG* recension.

During this period there were already several recensions of the *DG*, so it seems his primary aim was to preserve the original pothīs and signatures of the Guru, as well as to recompile the *Granth*. The focus of Chhibbar's narration on Bhai Mani Singh's fate was due to him rearranging the order of the bāṇīs and *not* any alleged authorship issues or controversy.[160] From the evidence presented, he must have thought the *DG* was the work of Guru Gobind Singh, as it was included in the tenth chapter under the title '*Mahallā* 10', which was written in Guru order, rather than the *rāg* order of the *AG*. If the work was by the poets, it would have been appended with the work of the *bhagats*.

* * *

It is clear that previous studies on the *DG* have been limited and have not stated anything conclusive. This had led to an assertion that there is no history attached to the *Granth* and its compilation, and has consequently led to speculation regarding its authenticity. We have introduced a small number of relics to show how the writings attributed to Guru Gobind Singh have been utilized. This includes the swords and armour bearing inscriptions from the Tenth Guru's *Granth*. Second, we have introduced a number of unknown manuscripts, some of which bear early dates and others which highlight the similarities and differences between the recensions. Using historical accounts and 'codes of conduct', we have shown that the *DG* was a work written in the Tenth Guru's court. Additionally, the early contents pages make a note that the works within these recensions were written by Guru Gobind Singh. Other important evidence, including the handwritten pages within the recensions, also lead to this conclusion. The dates and locations where the compositions were written are the same as those where the Tenth Guru held court: Anandpur Sahib, Paonta Sahib, and Bhabaur Sahib.

At the beginning of the twentieth century, a partly fictitious story was circulated regarding the authenticity and development of the Bhai Mani Singh's recension. However, its inclusion in Sikh literature was relatively late, and no earlier evidence regarding it has been found. Therefore, based on the new evidence presented, the author of the compositions within the *DG* is none other than

Guru Gobind Singh. The standardization was an important point in the textual history of the *DG*. In the next chapter we will provide the text and translations of the apocrypha that are not present in the standard printed edition.

Notes

1. See R.S. Jaggi, *Dasam Granth dā Kartritav* (New Delhi: Panjābi Sāhitt Sabhā, 1966).

2. The committee was formed to correct differences within different recensions of the *DG*. See Sardul Singh, *Rīpoṭ Sodhak Kommittī Dasam Patāshāhī Srī Gurū Granth Sāhib jī dī* (Amritsar: Vazirchand Printers, 1897).

3. See Daljeet Singh, 'Dasam Granth—Its History', in *Sikhism: Its Philosophy and History*, eds Daljeet Singh and Kharak Singh (Chandigarh: Institute of Sikh Studies, 1997), 710–22, and Gurtej Singh, 'Two Views on Dasam Granth: An Appreciation of Ashta's and Jaggi's Approach', in *Fundamental Issues in Sikh Studies*, eds Kharak Singh et al. (Chandigarh: Institute of Sikh Studies, 1992), 170–86. Also see Jagjit Singh, *Dasam Granth—The Real Issues*, Reprint (n.d.), and his 'Fictional Identity of Dasam Granth', *Sikh Review*, August (1994): 21–4.

4. Louis Fenech, *Darbar of the Sikh Gurus: The Court of God in the World of Men* (New Delhi: Oxford University Press, 2008), 150.

5. Rinehart formulates this discussion on the manuscripts detailed in the thesis of Jaggi (1966), but not by her own assessment of manuscripts. See R. Rinehart, *Debating The Dasam Granth* (New York: Oxford University Press, 2011), 42–3.

6. G.S. Mann, 'Sources for the Study of Guru Gobind Singh's Life and Times', *Journal of Punjab Studies* 15, nos 1–2 (2008): 258. In another recent publication, Darshan Singh, *Poetics of Dasam Granth* (Amritsar: Gurparsad Publications, 2011), the author goes further and states that the author/scribe of the *DG* is Kal the poet. He states Kal has interpolated various sections of the *Granth*, after discounting the other candidates of authorship, namely Ram and Shyam.

7. This includes Panjabi, British, and other European sources from the whole of the nineteenth century.

8. The Sodhak Committee gives the name of the recension as 'Dasam Guru Granth' which tallies with the description by Keshar Singh Chhibbar from the eighteenth century (1767).

9. For example, the Qur'an has many other names. Among those found in the text itself are *al-furqan* (discernment or criterion), *al-huda*

(the guide), *dhikrallah* (the remembrance of God), *al-hikmah* (the wisdom), and *kalamallah* (the word of God). Another term is *al-kitāb* (the book), though it is also used in the Arabic language for other scriptures, such as the Torah and the Gospels. The term *mus'haf* (written work) is often used to refer to particular Qur'anic manuscripts but is also used in the Qur'an to identify earlier revealed books; Seyyed Hossein Nasr, taken from the 'Qur'an', an entry in Encyclopaedia Britannica Online (accessed 2010).

10. The final recension of the *AG* was completed after the *saloks* of Guru Tegh Bahadur were added.

11. The word 'pothī' actually appears in the script of the *AG* itself.

12. Probably the earliest recension of the *DG* is the 'Anaṅdpurī' manuscript dated AD 1695/1696, clearly stating that the volume comprises the auspicious verses dictated by the Tenth Sovereign. Other than the first title, the names we see are mainly in printed *DG* recensions from the late nineteenth century.

13. In many eighteenth-century texts like *Bansavalīnāmā*, the expression 'Srī Mukhvāk Patishāh 10' has been used when quoting verses from the *DG*.

14. Early Sikh historical sources provide us with a number of dates for Vaisakhi which are earlier than the traditionally accepted date of AD 1699.

15. M.A. Macauliffe, *The Sikh Religion: Its Gurus, Sacred Writings and Authors* (Oxford: Clarendon Press, 1909), 5: 261.

16. 'Jāp Sāhib', *DG*, 1.

17. *DG*, 11.

18. Randhir Singh, *Shabadārth Dasam Graṅth Sāhib* (Patiala: Punjabi University, 1973–88), 1: 52. He quotes a line to complete the verse in his footnotes. Scholars have been unaware that Taksals have an oral tradition for the final verse.

19. An example of this imagery is from the *Bachitra Nāṭak*: 'At all times, Lord, the Destroyer of all, protects me. That All-Pervading Lord is my Protector like Steel' (*DG*, 73).

20. 'Akāl Ustatī', *DG*, verses 15:85.

21. *DG*, 13–15. Also see *Chaupā Siṅgh Rahitnāmā* for the specific dates of this as well as the other compositions.

22. The chapter starts with the introduction 'Kāl jī kī Ustatī'.

23. The first reference and paraphrasing of this composition is by the Guru's court poet, Sainapat. His book is dated between AD 1701 and 1711. See Ganda Singh (ed.), *Kavī Saināpati Srī Gur-Sobhā* (Patiala: Punjabi University Publication Bureau, 1987). One of the first complete English translations of any of the Sikh works was undertaken by John Leyden at

the start of the nineteenth century and this included the *Bachitra Nāṭak*. See the 'Anglo-Panjabi Literature and Publishing Initiative' undertaken by the Panjab Cultural Association at http://www.drleyden.co.uk (accessed November 2013), and the forthcoming book by Gurinder Singh Mann on the translations of John Leyden.

24. *Purāṇa* literally means 'old'. The *Mārkaṇḍeya Purāṇa* is one of the eighteen *mahā*-Purāṇas or 'Great Purāṇas'.

25. This composition is also referred to as *Vār Srī Bhagautījī* and *Vār Durgā kī* in some extant manuscripts.

26. See Rinehart, *Debating the Dasam Granth*, 103.

27. *DG*, 99.

28. Mahābhārat or 'The Great (war of the) Bhāratas'. It consists of eighteen *parvas* and is probably the longest epic written in the world.

29. Randhir Singh (1955), 1, is of the opinion that the other chapters of the *DG* are the three missing areas.

30. Vishnu is 'all pervading' according to the Hindu myths, and is worshipped in his many forms and incarnations. Brahma is considered the creator of the universe. Vishnu and Brahma together with Shiva are considered the *tri-muratī* or three forms. Rudra is the 'howler' or 'terrible' and has many names in the Vedas. He is seen as both a destructive deity and also the one who has healing powers.

31. 'Chaubīs Avatār', *DG*, 1133.

32. 'Chaubīs Avatār', *DG*, 156.

33. This is a Hindu practice before starting any task.

34. Jodhi Singh and Dharam Singh, *Sri Dasam Granth Sahib, Text and Translation* (Patiala: Heritage Publications, 1999), 2:409; *DG*, 310.

35. Singh and Singh, *Sri Dasam Granth Sahib*, 2:409; *DG*, 310.

36. 'Rām Avatār', *DG*, 254: verses 863–4. The *hukamnāmās* of Guru Tegh Bahadur also refer to the young Gobind as 'Gobind Das'. See Sabinderjit Singh Sagar, *Hukamnamas of Guru Tegh Bahadur* (Amritsar: Guru Nanak Dev University, 2002), 128–9.

37. At all the takhts, and many other gurdwaras, the weapons of the Guru are on display. The takhts have a daily ritual of displaying and narrating the history of the sacred weapons to the various sangats.

38. We have employed the commonly used term for the composition. However, the name in the text is actually *Pakhyān Charitrā*.

39. In actual fact, if we add all the verses of the *Bachitra Nāṭak* together, it is longer than the *Charitropakhyān*.

40. They are of the opinion that the stories are explicit as they describe sexual imagery. However, in the court of the Tenth Sovereign, the poets wrote on various themes including the *Koka Shastrā*. Kavi Kuvresh wrote

the *Rati Rahas Kok* (The Secret of Love According to Koka), and in this text he writes, 'May the Poet Kuvresh always remain within the court of Guru Gobind.' See Louis Fenech, *Darbar of the Sikh Gurus*, 20.

41. See our book, G.S. Mann and K. Singh, *Sri Dasam Granth Sahib: Questions and Answers* (London: Archimedes Press, 2011), 7.

42. 'Charitropakhyān', *DG*, 1388: verses 402–5.

43. The other sons of Guru Gobind Singh, Sahibzada Zorawar Singh and Sahibzada Fateh Singh, were bricked alive in the same month. This sacrifice is commemorated by an annual festival.

44. 'Hikāitān', *DG*, verse 5.

45. See C.H. Loehlin, *The Granth of Guru Gobind Singh and the Khalsa Brotherhood* (Lucknow: Lucknow Publishing House, 1971), 52–3.

46. Ran Singh, *Dasam Graṅth Niraṅe* (Patiala: Panch Khalsa Diwan, Patiala, 1919).

47. For a discussion of the sacred locations and relics of the Sikhs, see Anne Murphy, *The Materiality of the Past: History and Representation in Sikh Tradition* (New York: Oxford University Press, 2012).

48. This includes *shastras*, manuscripts, and other objects which can be seen in various museums and libraries in the UK such as the British Library, Wellcome Trust, the Victoria and Albert Museum, and others.

49. The treasury also contained arms and other material heritage related to the Khalsa, like Akali *pagris* or *dastārs*, which are now the preserve of the Victoria and Albert Museum. 'Govind's sword is also here; Runjit Singh was in the habit of performing puja to it every morning'; see Colin Mackenzie, *Life in the Mission, the Camp, and the Zenáná, or, Six Years in India* (London: Richard Bentley, 1853), 1: 162. This included the turban of Akali Phula Singh; see Kamalroop Singh and Gurinder Singh Mann, *Akali Phula Singh and His Turban* (Archimedes Press, forthcoming).

50. The Koh-i-noor is a prized possession which many empires have actively sought to acquire. The myth associated with it is that whoever retains the diamond would always rule the world. It has changed many hands, but it was in the hands of the Sikh empire under Maharaja Ranjit Singh before it was taken by the British. See Christy Campbell, *The Maharaja's Box—An Imperial Story of Conspiracy, Love and a Guru's Prophecy* (London: Harper Collins, 2001).

51. In the reports now kept at the National Archives of India, we see the following, 'A set of arms including spear, sword, etc., which Sikh tradition assert to have belonged to the Guru Gobind.' See the letter dated 16 April 1851 in Bhai Nahar Singh and Bhai Kirpal Singh, *Two Swords of Guru Gobind Singh in England (1666–1708 AD)* (Delhi: Atlantic Publishers and Distributors, 1989), 2.

52. Singh and Singh, *Two Swords*, 6.

53. In a letter dated 1 May 1854, by Henry Brereton, the Deputy Commissioner of Ludhiana, to G.C. Barnes, the Commissioner and Superintendent of the Cis-Sutlej States, he provides the mythical background of the sword. He states,

> When Guru Gobind escaped from his enemies at Makhowal he sought refuge and received protection from the Raekote Chief, in gratitude for his kindness he presented him his sword, which was all he possessed with an injunction, that it should not be worn or carried except in battle or in some great emergency. The sword was treasured with religious care, until the time of the late Rae, who took it with him on occasion of a sporting excursion contrary to the earnest remonstrances of his followers. His horse happening to fall with him he drew the sword to cut the stirrup leather by which he was entangled. The struggle of the horse however was violent and the Rao received from the drawn weapon a wound on his thigh, the haemorrhage from which quickly caused his death.

54. Letter dated 1 May 1854, by Henry Brereton, the Deputy Commissioner of Ludhiana to G.C. Barnes, the Commissioner and Superintendent of the Cis-Sutlej States, 10.

55. 'Akāl Ustati', *DG*, 11; S.S. Kohli, *Sri Dasam Granth Sahib* (Birmingham: Sikh National Heritage Trust Publishing, 2003), 29.

56. Kohli, *Sri Dasam Granth* Sahib, 29.

57. Throughout the *DG*, weapons are seen as a crucial deciding factor in readdressing the balance in the world and ensuring that the oppressed have the means to fight tyranny. This leitmotif is expressed throughout the scripture but starkly conveyed by the author in *Bachitra Nāṭak* and *Zafarnāmah*.

58. The weapons had been in the Broun-Lindsay family who returned them to the Indian government in 1966. The weapons were received with great fanfare and are now kept at Takht Keshgarh Sahib, Anandpur Sahib. Several photographs of this historic event can be seen at the British Library, shelfmark Photo 318, and notes of the event can be seen in Mss. Eur. D. 677. One anecdote the authors of this work have heard is that some relics were said to be so treasured by the British Lords that they continued the tradition of *shastra puja* (weapon worship), as it was done by Maharaja Ranjit Singh. We have heard this from several individuals who have been tracing the weapons of the Guru in the UK. One anecdote by Manjit Singh Boparai told to the authors was that he witnessed this when he was invited into the home of a British Lord

who had the swords of the Tenth Guru, before they were sent back to Anandpur Sahib.

59. Another chārāinā from the nineteenth century can be seen in Susan Stronge, ed., *The Arts of the Sikh Kingdoms* (London: V&A Publications, 1999), 136. Also see a sketch of Sikh armour in W.G. Osbourne, *The Court and Camp of Runjeet Singh* (London: Henry Colburn Publishers, 1840), 49.

60. H.R. Robinson, *The Arms and Armour Series: Oriental Armour* (New York: Walker and Co., 1967), 107.

61. See Y. Rana, 'SGPC [Shiromani Gurdwara Parbandhak Committee] Slams Auction of Guru's Relic', http://articles.timesofindia.indiatimes.com/2008-03-30/chandigarh/27766624_1_body-armour-avtar-singh-makkar-sotheby-s-arts (accessed 30 March 2008). The description of the armour was as follows: Lot 269, A Rare Sikh Steel Armour Plate, North West India/Pakistan, 18th Century Arts of the Islamic World, Sale L08220. This listing was removed by Sotheby's after the item was sold to a private buyer. Sotheby's issued a statement saying it was not the armour of Guru Gobind Singh.

62. See Amandeep Madra, 'Guru's Relic under the Hammer', http://news.ukpha.org/2008/03/gurus-relic-under-the-hammer/ (accessed 25 March 2008).

63. *Akāl Ustati, DG*, 11.

64. Persian term meaning the 'koft' (beating) and 'garī' (trade). The practice of creating ornamental work by inlaying steel with gold.

65. See *AG*, 1358–9. It is normally recited when Sikhs tie their turbans and is also contained in Buddha Dal Nihang Singh *guṭkās*.

66. See Chapter 4 of this book, 'The Seed of the Khalsa Raj'.

67. One answer is that the breakup of the chārāinā may have been intentional so that the trader could make more money by selling individual parts of it. Alternatively, only one part is available and the rest is no longer extant. The inscriptions on the other parts of the Sotheby's plates may (have) help(ed) in deciphering whether or not it is/was a copy of the Patiala Plate.

68. We learn from one anecdote that the Guru wore armour. One *sākhī* refers to the formation of Damdama Sahib, where the Guru placed down his armour and asked for the hill to be levelled. The Sikhs duly obliged with his request and it was only after the armour was placed on the ground that the Guru declared the sanctity of the location. The notion of putting down armour or weapons before the creation of a gurdwara is an important concept which needs further investigation. See Attar Singh, trans., *The Travels of Guru Tegh Bahadar and Guru Gobind Singh*

(Lahore: Indian Public Press, 1876), 83. This is translated from Panjabi: *Sāhib Srī Gurū Tegh Bahadar Jī ate Sāhib Srī Gurū Gobind Singh jī de Malwā Desh Rattan dī Sākhī Pothī* (early eighteenth century).

69. See Trilochan Singh and Anurag Singh, *A Brief Account of Life and Works of Guru Gobind Singh* (Amritsar: CSJS, 2002), 6.

70. For another translation with the original Gurmukhi verses, see Jodhi Singh and Dharam Singh, *Sri Dasam Granth Sahib*, 173. Sardul Singh, 'Bachitra Nāṭak', *DG*, 61–2.

71. This is one of the many Sikh relics kept with Capt. Amarinder Singh of Patiala. For more pictures of the chārāinā, see Bhayee Sikandar Singh and Roopinder Singh, *Sikh Heritage: Ethos & Relics* (New Delhi: Rupa & Co., 2012), 142–5.

72. See the research on the plates in Gurinder Singh Mann, 'Sources for the Study', 2008. Professor G.S. Mann shared this information with Gurinder Singh Mann (Leicester) on his visit to Santa Barbara in February 2008.

73. Gurinder Singh Mann, 'Historical Sources on Sri Guru Granth Sahib and Sri Dasam Granth', *Sant Sipāhī*, March 2010.

74. To the relics we can add a hukamnāmā given to Pandit Chetan Ram by the Tenth Guru on his way to Nanded. This is located at Pushkar and is kept with Pandit Nanak Ram. See Amanpreet Singh Gill, '1708—Remembering the Last Journey of Dasam Guru', in *The Nishaan* (New Delhi: Nagaara Trust, Issue III/2008).

75. Kamalroop Singh examined this copper plate in March 2010. It is small and hand-sized with calligraphy inscribed into the copper with a sharp implement, said to be an arrow. The style of calligraphy matches the other epigraphical evidence of the time, as the daskhat of the Tenth Guru has the sword emblem which also appears on many items attributed to him.

76. For information regarding the dates of the Guru's visits to this location, see Fauja Singh, *Atlas Travels of Guru Gobind Singh* (Patiala: Punjabi University Publication Bureau, 2002).

77. The location of Kapal Mochan is revered as being auspicious according to the Purāṇas. The location is a pilgrimage centre, and people gather in larger numbers at the time of *pūran māshī* or full moon. Every year a fair takes place in November.

78. The small shrine was recreated between 1947 and 1951.

79. In recent times, a museum of martial arts was created at the village of Aharwala, in memory of the Tenth Guru at Kapal Mochan, presumably to mark the martial activities that took place. This is adjacent to the *sarovar* (lake) where the Guru is said to have cleaned his shastras.

80. Gurinder Singh Mann, 'Sources for the Study', 241.

81. Jawala Das Braham wanted something which was everlasting and, as a result, the hukam presented to him by the Guru was made out of copper. The name appears as Gobind Singh, which, according to the tradition, was only given to the Guru after AD 1699. Interestingly, a hand-held weapon of Guru Gobind Singh known as a 'kaṭār' or 'tiger knife' has inscribed in Persian the name of the Guru as 'Gobind Singh'. This weapon carries a date of AD 1695/1752 VS, and is kept at Quila Mubarak, Patiala. Clearly this was also several years before the accepted date of AD 1699, the creation of the Khalsa, when the Guru was assigned the name Gobind Singh.

82. One example is a fragment of the ardās which appears to be written in the handwriting of the Tenth Guru. This is kept in the collection of Dr Gurpal Singh Bhuller.

83. Visitors to Gurdwara Paonta Sahib are met with a sign stating that Guru Gobind Singh composed several compositions of the *DG* there. This includes the *Chaṇḍī dī Vār*.

84. Kamalroop Singh was unable to locate one of the manuscripts detailed by Jaggi (1966), which was lost during Operation Blue Star, said to be taken from Sangrur.

85. Tara Singh Narotam, *Srī Gurmat Niraṇe Sāgar* (Lithograph, 1877); W.H. McLeod, *Textual Sources for the Study of Sikhism* (Manchester: Manchester University Press, 1984), 6–7; W.H. McLeod, *The Evolution of the Sikh Community Five Essays, The Sikh Scriptures* (New York: Oxford University Press, 1976), 79; W.H. McLeod, *Essays in Sikh History, Tradition, and Society* (New Delhi: Oxford University Press, 2007), 55.

86. Pashaura Singh, *The Guru Granth Sāhib: Canon, Meaning and Authority* (New Delhi: Oxford University Press, 2000); Piar Singh, *Gathā Srī Adi Granth* (Amritsar: Guru Nanak Dev University, 1992); Professor Sahib Singh, *Srī Gurū Granth Sāhib Darpaṇ* (Jallandhar: Raj Publishers, 1972); Gian Singh 'Nihang', ed., *Srī Gurū Granth Sāhib jī* (Amritsar: Shiromani Gurdwara Prabandhak Committee, 1977).

87. Trilochan Singh, 'History and Compilation of Dasam Granth', *Sikh Review* 3, no. 4 (1955).

88. Randhir Singh, *Shabad Mūrat: Dasave Pātishāh ke Granth dā Itihās* (Amritsar: SGPC, 1962).

89. P. Sehgal, *Gur Govind Singh unkā Kaviyā* (Lucknow: Hindi Sahit Mandir, 1965).

90. Piara Singh Padam, *Dasam Granth Darshan*, 2nd ed. (Patiala: printed by the author, [1968] 1982).

91. R.S. Jaggi, *Dasam Granth dā Kartritav* (New Delhi: Panjābi Sāhitt Sabhā, 1966).

92. The textual history of *AG* was examined by Professor G.S. Mann in *The Making of Sikh Scripture* (New York: Oxford University Press, 2001), and he published historical research on the *Goindval pothīs*. The same historical sources can be employed to form an identical model of the creation, compilation, and transmission of the *DG*. Also see Gurinder Singh Mann (Leicester), 'Historical Sources of the Guru Granth Sahib and the Sri Dasam Granth', *Sant Sipāhī*, March 2010.

93. Gian Singh Giani, *Navīn Paṅth Prakāsh* (1888; repr., Patiala: Bhasha Vibhag, 1987).

94. Gian Singh, *Navīn Paṅth*, 4: 286.

95. Jaggi, *Dasam Graṅth dā Kartritav*.

96. Jaggi, *Dasam Graṅth dā Kartritav*. Also see Padam, *Dasam Graṅth Darshan*.

97. Trilochan Singh mentions some of them but does not elaborate on them in his *The Turban and The Sword of The Sikhs: Essence of Sikhism* (Amritsar: Chattar Singh Jivan Singh, 2001).

98. The extant manuscripts at the takht and surrounding gurdwaras were examined by Kamalroop Singh in 2005.

99. They examined 32 *sarūps* of the *DG* within the locality of Panjab itself. See Sardul Singh, *Rīpoṭ Sodhak Kommittī, Dasam Pātashāhī Srī Gurū Graṅth Sāhib jī dī* (Amritsar: Vazirchand Printers, 1897). Hereafter, *Sodhak Committee Report*.

100. See Manohar Singh Marco, *Srī Anaṅdpurī Bīṛh* (Delhi: Delhi Gurdwara Parbandhak Committee, 1975).

101. Marco, *Srī Anaṅdpurī Bīṛh*.

102. *DG* (Amritsar: Guru Nanak Dev University, MS. 740, AD 1688).

103. The recension has been moved to many different locations in the last 100 years and so accessibility has been greatly limited.

104. Mahan Singh, *Dasam Granth dī Hazūrī Bīṛh dī Ripoṭ* (Dehradun: Dr Balbir Singh Sahitya Kendra, MS. 269, 25/1/1957).

105. Gurinder Singh Mann (Leicester) studied a copy of the 'Anaṅdpurī' biṛh in 2008 in California, USA. We would like to thank Dr Joginder Singh Ahluwalia, California, for sharing copies of this important manuscript with us.

106. G.S. Mann, 'Sources for the Study', 242, 257–8, 285–300.

107. Mahan Singh, *Dasam Granth*, 5. The court poet, Mangal, was from Sialkot.

108. Mahan Singh, *Dasam Granth*, 7. The Guru addresses them, 'You are my Khalsa. Repeat Guru Guru. Send offerings by yourself and not by the *masands*. AD 1701/1758 vs.' This follows the pattern of other hukamnāmās written by the Guru. See Ganda Singh, ed., *Hukamnāme:*

Guru Sāhibān, Mātā Sāhibān, Bandā Singh ate Khālsā jī de, 2nd ed. (Patiala: Punjabi University Publication Bureau, 1985).

109. This picture can be seen on the back cover of our book, *Sri Dasam Granth Sahib: Questions and Answers*. Another picture, which depicts the Tenth Guru in red regalia, is kept in the inner sanctum or *Angithā Sāhib* at Takht Hazur Sahib.

110. This picture can be seen on the cover of the book by J.S. Grewal, *History, Literature, and Identity: Four Centuries of Sikh Tradition* (New Delhi: Oxford University Press, 2011). There are several anecdotes to the Guru protecting villagers from the threats of animals including lions.

111. Bhai Haridas, a devotee of Guru Gobind Singh, prepared an *AG* manuscript dated AD 1682 at Damdama Sahib. This was one of the earliest manuscripts to contain the saloks of Guru Tegh Bahadur. It was kept at Sikh Reference Library, Manuscript No. 511, with the description *Srī Guru Gobind Singh jī de Likharī Bhāī Hardās vālī Biṛh*. It also contained a *Nishān* of the Tenth Guru. It was lost in Operation Blue Star in 1984. See Anurag Singh, 'Sardar Jassa Singh Ramgharia—Servitor of Guru Panth', in *Smriti Granth*, Mahahraja Jassa Singh Ramgharia Janam Samagam Committee, 2010. This new information was discovered by Gurinder Singh Mann (Leicester). The late Dr Chan, Coventry, UK, was also purported to have manuscripts scribed by Bhai Haridas in his possession.

112. Jaggi, *Dasam Granth dā Kartritav*.

113. Piara Singh Padam, *Srī Gurū Gobiṅd Siṅgh jī de Darbārī Rattan* (Patiala: New Patiala Printers, 1976), 17. The text is interspersed with haṛtāl or corrections. Gurinder Singh Mann (Leicester) also noticed this in many of the pages throughout the recension of the xerox copies he inspected.

114. Pashaura Singh, *Life and Works of Guru Arjan* (New Delhi: Oxford University Press, 2006), 160–1. Also see Louis Fenech, *Darbar of the Sikh Gurus*, 67–8, where he discusses the Mughal influence on Sikh manuscript preparation.

115. At Gurdwara Paonta Sahib there are two pens which are said to belong to Guru Gobind Singh and are said to be the pens with which the Guru wrote his compositions. The colophons in the compositions, historical evidence, as well as other internal parameters in the *DG* point to the view that some compositions were indeed written at this location, including the descriptions of the battles at Paonta Sahib.

116. A close inspection of the khās patre in the various *DG* manuscripts show that they originate from the same source as the numbering continues consecutively. The folios seem to have been shared out.

117. See Piara Singh Padam, ed., *Rahitnāme* (Amritsar: Singh Brothers, 2000) and W.H. McLeod, ed., *The Chaupa Singh Rahit-nama* (Dunedin: University of Otago Press, 1987).

118. W.H. McLeod, *Sikhs of the Khalsa: A History of the Khalsa Rahit* (New Delhi: Oxford University Press, 2003), 70. There is a transcribed copy of a manuscript written by the house servant of Guru Gobind Singh. It is surprising that McLeod and Padam (2000) missed a manuscript as important as this. Mann, in his examination of the *rahitnāmā*, believes the date 1700 written in the text to be correct. See Gurinder Singh Mann, 'Sources for the Study', 249–50.

119. Sarup Das Bhalla, *Mahimā Prakāsh*, 2 vols, eds Gobind Singh Lamba and Khazan Singh (Patiala: Bhasha Vibhag, Panjab, 1971), verses: 10:11:5–10, 2:795.

120. This manuscript is kept at Takht Patna Sahib, Bihar. See Jeevan Deol, 'Eighteenth Century Khalsa Identity: Discourse, Praxis and Narrative', in *Sikh Religion, Culture and Ethnicity*, eds Christopher Shackle, Gurharpal Singh, and Arvindpal Singh Mandair (Richmond: Curzon Press, 2001), 25–6. The author claims there are only five major variants of the *DG* based on manuscripts noted in literature. There has been some ambiguity about this manuscript with some scholars naming it as the 'Sukha Singh' recension. This ambiguity is due to one simple reason that there are several early copies of the *DG* located at Takht Patna Sahib. It is likely that scholars who have examined extant manuscripts at Patna Sahib have looked at different recensions. This has been confirmed to Kamalroop Singh, when he examined the manuscripts at the takht, by the present head, Jathedar Iqbal Singh.

121. *DG*, Takht Patna Sahib, AD 1698, *f.* 1. It is also pertinent to add that the title 'Tav Prasad' or 'By Thy Grace' is found in many of the compositions in the *DG*.

122. In the *Jāp jī* of Guru Nanak, it is written as 'the one who is graced with the praise of God, is the King (*Pātasāhī*) of Kings (*Pātshāh*)' (verse 25).

123. The information about this recension is contained in the hukamnāmā issued to Ragi Darshan Singh, by Takht Patna Sahib, 2008. A copy of this can be seen at http://www.sridasamgranth.com/#/dasam-granth-hukumnamas/4529143581 (accessed December 2008).

124. The *Gobiṅd Gītā* composition does not appear in the standard edition of the *DG* and is therefore generally seen as being apocryphal.

125. The AD 1698 recension contains the handwritten pages purported to be by Guru Gobind Singh, and as the second recension does not, it would seem likely it is a later copy of the original. The comparison of the

orthography of both recensions, by the authors of this essay, suggests that this is very likely.

126. This was narrated to the authors by Anurag Singh, who had inspected many manuscripts at the Sikh Reference Library and the Akal Takht during his tenure as the Director of the Sikh History Board of the SGPC.

127. This manuscript was written in Jammu and was inspected by Kamalroop Singh in 2003 at the Sikh Reference Library.

128. Akali Nihang Kaur Singh, *Hazurī Sāthī* (Lahore: Akali Patrika Press, 1934), 143–4; Kanh Singh Nabha, *Mahān Kosh* (Patiala: Bhasha Vibhag, [1930] 1999), 419.

129. This manuscript is at Mata Sahib Kaur Gurdwara, Nanded. This manuscript was photographed and catalogued in 2000 by Kamalroop Singh. In the margins, the scribe records that the page is a reproduction of the signature folios of the Guru.

130. One manuscript is still present at the Bhai Santokh Singh Library, Amritsar. This manuscript was examined by Kamalroop Singh in 2003. In 2009, there were objections by some quarters to a combined printed recension of the *AG* and *DG*. The objections were started by the banned but functional newspaper *The Spokesman*, which was published from Chandigarh. Some even stated that the *AG* and *DG* parts of this recension should be separated. See the response of Gurinder Singh Mann (Leicester) to this matter and the historical narrations of combined recensions of both Granṅths, 'A Historical Analysis of the Combined Recensions of the Guru Granth Sahib and the Sri Dasam Granth', available at http://www.sridasamgranth.com (accessed June 2012).

131. A stemma is a diagram showing the transmission and relationship of manuscripts to a standard text.

132. See Jaggi (1966) and Padam (1968).

133. See the translations and history of the apocrypha in Chapter 2 of this book.

134. Jaggi, *Dasam Granṅth dā Kartritav*.

135. The oral history of the Buddha Dal also confirms this claim, as the late Akali Baba Santa Singh mentions this in Akali Baba Santa Singh (2002). However, Dr Trilochan Singh inspected another recension of the *DG* which he also attributes to Baba Binod Singh. According to him, this biṛh also contained the khās patre which numbered 28 in total, and the descendants of Baba Binod Singh received a *jagīr* from the Patiala Darbar until 1947. See his 'History and Compilation of Dasam Granth', *Sikh Review* 3, no. 4 (1955), 51–60; 3, no. 5 (1955), 34–41; 3, no. 6 (1955), 44–52; 3, no. 7 (1955), 23–9. This recension was last seen at Moti Bagh Library, Patiala.

136. In Sangrur there was a *DG* manuscript from AD 1732 in the possession of Giani Pratap Singh. It is unclear if it is still extant.

137. This manuscript was inspected by Kamalroop Singh in 2005.

138. See Giani Gian Singh, *Navīn Panth*, 4:319.

139. Padam, *Dasam Granth Darshan.*

140. See Sant Gurbachan Singh Bhinderawale, *Gurbāṇī Pāṭh Darpaṇ* (Amritsar: Print Well, 1996), 41, who states that it contained the apocrypha. Kamalroop Singh was told by a close associate of Padam that when Padam had returned to Takht Dam Dama Sahib to re-examine this volume, it had disappeared. Padam was of the opinion that it was taken to the Sikh Reference Library, and was therefore lost during Operation Blue Star in 1984.

141. See Mann, *Making of Sikh Scripture*, 124–5.

142. This recension was carried in an enormous procession, on a large float, together with the weapons of Guru Gobind Singh. A link can also be made with a chakkar of Baba Dip Singh which bears inscriptions written in gold from the *Jāp Sāhib, Akal Ustat,* and *Rām Avatār.* It is present at the Sri Akal Takht Sahib.

143. A *Charitropakhyān* manuscript with a colophon of AD 1723 is also a *Safarī* recension. This recension contains the *Kabio Bāch Benatī Chaupāi.* At the end of this recension there is a reference to it being a 'Tarkas kī Pothī' which can be referred to a small volume to be carried in a quiver. The size of the pothīs shows the development of gurbāṇī and its purpose in battle. This manuscript faithfully records that it was copied from the 'Quiver Scripture' of Bhai Sangat Singh who may be the same legendary martyr at Chamkaur Sahib. See a picture of this manuscript in our *Sri Dasam Granth Sahib: Questions and Answers*, 9. Interestingly, a copy of *Kabio Bāch Benatī Chaupāi* in the hand of the Guru was also known to have existed and was kept with the descendants of the Guru (the Sodhi family at Anandpur Sahib). This is not suprising as another pothī of *Charitropakhyān* is written in hand of the Tenth Guru. This has been kept in the private custody of Raja Hanumant Singh (Nabha).

144. For a photograph, see Chapter 4 in this book.

145. See Gurmukh Singh, *Historical Sikh Shrines* (Amritsar: Singh Brothers, 1995), 323. It is not clear whether this manuscript is extant. The same reference also notes an *AG* manuscript dated AD 1781 at the same location.

146. Kanh Singh Nabha and Avatar Singh Vahiria, along with other scholars, considered all of the different editions as being the *AG.*

147. Jaggi, *Dasam Granth dā Kartritav.*

148. For instance, in *Jāp Sāhib*, the splitting of one line of *Bhujaṅg Prayāt* to *Ardh Bhujaṅg Prayāt* will add one more verse, but in actual fact the text remains the same.

149. An unpublished report by Takht Hazur Sahib, in which there is the examination of many *DG* manuscripts in India.

150. See M.A. Macauliffe, *The Sikh Religion: Its Gurus, Sacred Writings and Authors* (Oxford: Clarendon Press, 1909), 5:260, and Kanh Singh Nabha, *Gurumat Mārtaṇḍ* (Amritsar: SGPC, [1962] 1978), 2:568; it also appears in *Mahān Kosh*.

151. In this extant recension the *AG* and *DG* are bound together, with the compositions written in Guru order.

152. The Buddha Dal also narrate this story as an oral tradition; however, they also state that the *DG* was a part of this *Granth*, as Bhai Mani Singh was present when it was dictated by Guru Gobind Singh, as well as written by hand in some parts (daskhat). Furthermore, the compositions of the Tenth Guru were added in the Bhai Mani Singh recension in Guru order under the entry '*Mahallā* 10'. This story is recounted by Kesar Singh Chhibbar (1769) who was present in the court of the Tenth Guru. If the *DG* was written by the court poets, Bhai Mani Singh would have surely added it with the *bhagat bāṇī*.

153. Giani, *Navīn Panth Prakāsh*.

154. Rattan Singh Bhangu, *Srī Gurū Panth Prakāsh*, ed. Balwant Singh Dhillon (Amritsar: Singh Brothers, [1841] 2004), 219.

155. The Buddha Dal oral tradition states that Bhai Mani Singh was intending a standard edition which can be the reason why a number of *sarūps* are similar in nature. This is likely, as in this period Bhai Mani Singh possibly could have written more than one volume of the *DG*, on top of the *AG–DG* recension. Manuscript evidence also indicates this assertion of the Buddha Dal; also see Trilochan Singh (1955).

156. Piara Singh Padam, ed., *Bhaī Kesar Chhibbar Krit Bansāvalināmā Dasāṅ Pātshāhiāṅ kā* (Amritsar: Singh Brothers, [1769] 1997), 164.

157. Padam, *Bhaī Kesar Chhibbar Krit Bansāvalināmā Dasāṅ Pātshāhiāṅ kā*, verse 383.

158. Rai Jasbir Singh, ed., *Bhaī Kesar Chhibbar Krit Bansāvalināmā Dasāṅ Pātshāhiāṅ kā* (Amritsar: Guru Nanak Dev ji University, 2001), 101.

159. Rai Jasbir Singh, *Bhaī Kesar Chhibbar*.

160. According to the oral tradition of the Buddha Dal, this sākhī refers to the rearrangement of the *AG* into Guru order and joining it with the *DG*. This is recorded in Akali Baba Santa Singh, 'Mukh Shabad', in *Srī Dasam Granth Darpaṇ*, ed. Harbans Singh (Patiala: Gurbani Seva Parkasan, 2002).

The Apocryphal Compositions of the *Dasam Granth*

This study involved researching the *Dasam Granth* (*DG*) 'apocrypha' with the title of Guru Gobind Singh. After referring to entries in the *Encyclopaedia of Sikhism*, a search for the apocrypha was undertaken.[1] In the United Kingdom, both the British Library and Wellcome Trust have comprehensive collections of extant Gurmukhi manuscripts. However, some compositions were not available and subsequent research trips to India, Pakistan, and Canada were necessary to locate the material. Originally, the following scriptures were noted to be written with the title of Guru Gobind Singh, in addition to the *DG* apocrypha:

1. *Gobiṅd Gītā*
2. *Sarabaloh Graṅth*
3. *Sudharam Mārag Graṅth*
4. *Mukat Mārag Graṅth*
5. *Prem Sumārag Graṅth*
6. *Parchīā Prem Bhagatā kī (Prem Aṅbodh)*[2]
7. *Prichīā*

By 'apocrypha' we are referring to other compositions in the extant *DG* manuscripts that are not in the standard printed *DG*. The term 'apocryphal' has had various meanings in Western thought and was a term originally employed for Biblical compositions to mean secret or non-canonical.[3] In recent times it has been employed for religious compositions that are spurious or non-canonical. In this regard, all of the traditional Sikh institutions consider the *DG* apocrypha to be the *gurbāṇī* of the Tenth Guru, but the apocrypha are rarely engaged in Sikh studies, and therefore, this research hopes to address this.

There have been several translations of the *DG* in recent times, including a complete five-volume Gurmukhi translation undertaken by Rattan Singh Jaggi and Gursharan Kaur Jaggi in 1999,[4] and a partial two-volume translation by Jodh Singh and Dharm Singh, also published in 1999.[5] There are also translations of select compositions available including Pritpal Singh Bindra's *Chitro Pakhyaan: Tales of Male-Female Tricky Deceptions from Sri Dasam Granth* and *Hikayaat—Tales in Persian from Dasam Granth,*[6] S.S. Kohli's three-volume *Sri Dasam Granth Sahib,*[7] and Piara Singh Sandhu's two-volume *Selections from Sri Dasam Granth Sahib.*[8] None of the aforementioned scholars have translated the *DG* apocrypha, and therefore the complete translation of the apocrypha presented in this book is a unique project. However, as we shall see later on in this chapter, one composition, the *Ugradantī*, has been translated at least three times. We have also included a discussion of the content of the apocrypha, and we conclude with a discussion of why they were excluded from the standard edition of the *DG*.

The *AG* was also compiled during the Tenth Guru's reign, and its historical accounts tell us about its creation and compilation. However, there has been some controversy about certain parts of the *AG* like the *Rāgamālā*, which is also considered by some scholars to be apocrypha.[9] Likewise, there has also been controversy about some of the compositions of the *DG*. This debate has parallels with the Bhasauria scrutiny of the *AG*, as the Panch Khalsa Divan also wrote literature questioning the authorship of the *DG*.[10] Nonetheless, Sri Akal Takht has adjudicated on many occasions that the *DG* is the work of Guru Gobind Singh.

Translating the Apocryphal Compositions

From the examination of the earliest manuscripts we find that the following compositions are not in the present standard edition, but they feature in manuscripts and anthologies like *pothīs* and *guṭkās*, with other *AG* and *DG* compositions:

1. *Lakhī Jangle Khālsā*
2. *Nishān-ī-Sikhī*
3. *Vār Srī Bhagautī jī kī*
4. *Vār Mālakaus kī*
5. *Srī Bhagautī Asatotra*
6. *Ugradantī Chhakkā*
7. *Sansāhara Sukhamanā*
8. *Rāg Āsā/Rāg Soraṭh*
9. *Asphotak Kabitt Svaiye*
10. *Gobind Gītā*
11. *Indra Kavach*

Composition 10 is very lengthy and appears along with 11 in the Patna Sahib manuscript from AD 1698, and since we have only found them in one other anthology in the Buddha Dal, they have not been included in this study. The primary research and translations were undertaken by Kamalroop Singh and the analysis of the texts by Gurinder Singh Mann. After locating the apocrypha and photographing manuscripts, the separation of the script was required. It was split during word-processing, as it was continuous (*larīvār*), which literally has no spaces between words.[11] The translation was completed using the *Mahān Kosh* and *Anekāth Kosh* dictionaries by K.S. Nabha.[12] *The Sacred Language of the Sikhs* by C. Shackle, published in 1983, was useful for the grammar and transliteration method, and was supplemented with R. Snell's *A Braj Bhāsā Reader*, published in 1991.[13] As this publication offers the first translations of all the apocrypha, we are certain that there will always be room for improvement. We shall now consider each composition in turn.

Table 2.1 Table for Transliteration

Consonants:

Latin	Gurmukhi
o	ੳ
a	ਅ
e	ੲ
s	ਸ
h	ਹ
k	ਕ
kh	ਖ
g	ਗ
gh	ਘ
ṅ	ਙ
c	ਚ
ch	ਛ
j	ਜ
jh	ਝ
ñ	ਞ
ṭ	ਟ
ṭh	ਠ
ḍ	ਡ
ḍh	ਢ
ṇ	ਣ
t	ਤ
th	ਥ
d	ਦ
dh	ਧ
n	ਨ
p	ਪ
ph	ਫ
b	ਬ
bh	ਭ
m	ਮ
y	ਯ
r	ਰ
l	ਲ
v	ਵ
ṛ	ੜ

Vowels:

i	ਿ
ī	ੀ
u	ੁ
ū	ੂ
e	ੇ
ai	ੈ
o	ੋ
au	ੌ
ā	ਾ
āṁ	ਾਂ
ṁ	ੰ
ṁ	ਃ

Source: Authors.
Note: The first three consonants are normally combined with vowels.

Lakhī Jangle Khālsā

mājha srī mukhabāka pātasāhī 10.
In Rāg Mājh, the Holy Oration of Verse by the Tenth Sovereign.

lakhī jaṁgala khālasā dīdāra āi lagā taba ucāru hoiā.
In the Lakhi Jungle the Khalsa is coming and giving its Divine audience, and at this time this was spoken.[14]

suṇi kai sadu māhī dā mehī pāṇī ghāhu muto ne.
Hearing the call of her beloved the she-buffalo has stopped eating grass and drinking.
[The Khalsa has put aside mundane worldly activities to see the Tenth Guru.]

kise nāla nara līā kāī koī sauku payone.
This thought has entered her mind not to meet anybody, being in the pain of separation.
[The Khalsa has rushed to see the Guru out of Divine separation.]

gaiā phirāku miliā mitu māhī tāhī sukaru kīto ne.1.
On meeting the herdsman, the pain has gone and she is thankful to the Divine.[15]
[The Khalsa on meeting Guru Gobind Singh feels peace and gives thanks.]

The *Lakhī Jangle Khālsā* bears the ascription *Srī Mukhvāk Pātashāhī Dasvīṅ* denoting that the composition is the holy verse orated by the Tenth Guru. The name of this composition appears as *Mājh Pātishāhī 10* in the manuscripts. This is present in the 'Takht Sri Patna Sahib' AD 1698 recension as well as other manuscripts. It does not appear in the standard edition of the *DG*, and, due to its length, may not have been included in the *Tatkārā*, and subsequently missed by scholars. In AD 1705, after the battle of Chamkaur, the Tenth Guru reached the location of the Lakhi Jungle or 'the forest of a hundred thousand trees' in the area of Bhatinda, which is near Talwandi Sabo (Damdama Sahib). Sikh tradition narrates that the Guru recited certain verses of the *DG* in this period, like the famous verse 'Mitar piāre nū hāl murīdāṅ dā kehiṅā' (Go tell the beloved friend, the condition of his devotee). This verse is included in the *Shabad Hazāre* composition in the *DG* and is referred to as *Khīyāl*.[16] It is important to orthodox Sikhs that it bears the word Khalsa, as this term only appears in the 33 *svaiye* in the standard *DG*.[17] It will become clear later in this chapter that other apocrypha compositions also contain the word 'Khalsa'. This would appear to suggest that these particular compositions could have been written after the Khalsa was initiated.[18]

This verse is said to have been recited when the Guru reached the Lakhi Jungle.[19] The Khalsa heard about the arrival of the Guru, and they longed to gain sight of him, just as on hearing the call of the herdsman, the water buffalo leave their water and feeding. In their joy they all ran, each trying to pass the other to see their Beloved. Their anxieties were dispelled when they met their herdsman, the Guru, and so in deep gratitude, they thanked him. Historical accounts also corroborate this and tell us that the Lakhi Jungle was the stopping point before the Guru journeyed to the Deccan, and as a result, the Khalsa flocked to see the Guru.[20] Some scholars have commented that a poetic symposium took place before the journey to the Deccan.[21] The love of the Khalsa by the Tenth Guru is echoed in the simple Panjabi verses, with a musical measure from this area, Majha. In Sikh tradition this *rāg* is attributed to Guru Nanak, who developed it from a Panjabi folk tune. *Mājh* was the mode employed by Guru Nanak, Guru Angad, Guru Amar Das, Guru Ram Das, and Guru Arjan in their *bāṇī*.

Nishān-i-Sikhī

srī mukhabāka pātasāhī 10.
The Holy Oration of Verse by the Tenth Sovereign.

nishān i sikhī īṁ paṁja haraph i kāph.
These five letters beginning with *K* are the emblems of Sikhism.

hargez nabāshad azīṁ paṁaz muāph.
A Sikh can never ever be excused from the great five *K*s.

kaṛā kārd o kac-cha kaṁghā bidāṅ.
The Bangle, Sword, Shorts, and a Comb.

bilā kesa hec ast jumalā nishān.
Without unshorn Hair the other lot of symbols are of no significance.

Haraph hāi kāt asat iṅ paṅj kāph.
The emblems of the five *K*s described above are praiseworthy.

Bidā nand bāvar na goyam khilāph.
What has been said above is not against faith.
[There is no excuse against wearing them.]

Hukkā hajāmat halalo harām.
To smoke, shave, eat halal, and adultery.
[Are against the Sikh faith]

Bāchīshe hinan karad rū syāh phām.
To dye the hair is like blackening one's own face.

This small composition forms a part of the *Asfotak Kabitt Svaiye* in the exegesis of the *DG* by Pandit Narain Singh published in 1932.[22] It is important to note that this composition was excised from the standard, by the committee of standardization (this is discussed later in this chapter). Some scholars have attributed the verses to Bhai Nand Lal, the famous Persian poet of the Tenth Guru's court, but there is no evidence to point to this assertion.[23] On the other hand, in Sikh tradition, the composition is attributed to Guru Gobind Singh. The *kārdo* is small hunting knife and not the same as the *kirpān*. This is seen in the tradition where one small *kārd* is kept normally on the body, or underneath the clothes, whilst a three-foot sword (kirpān) is kept on a thicker sword belt (*gatrā*). The *kaṛā* is a wrist bangle, made from steel. It is mainly a defensive guard but also known to be a wrist weapon (*vīnī shastra*).

In recent times the history of the symbols of the Khalsa has been debated especially in regard to the Khalsa codes of praxis/*rahitnāmā*. The Sikh tradition asserts that at the first initiation ceremony on Vaisakhi, the five *K*s were to be adorned by the Khalsa. The five symbols are the *kesh*—uncut hair, including a beard for men, as a symbol of God's creative power, *kaṅghā*—a wooden comb to properly groom the hair as a symbol of cleanliness, *kachherā*—specially made cotton underwear as a reminder of the commitment to purity; kaṛā—steel bracelet worn on the hand, and the kirpān—sword worn to stand for grace, truth, and justice.[24] Some scholars are of the opinion that the five *K*s are a later development and that early Sikh history points to five weapons (*pañch hathiyār*).[25] At first glance, another late seventeenth-century work, the *Sarabloh Granth* (also attributed to Guru Gobind Singh), would support this view, due to a passage about the three jewels:

'Adorned with the kachh, kesh and kirpān they worshipped the Guru.'[26] However, the codes are also clear that the kaṅghā must be used twice daily, and an iron wrist kaṛā worn. Some scholars argue that there was a development of the five *K*s at a later period, but they do not consider the praxis that suggests five were always worn. For example, Kuir Singh lists three of the *K*s mentioned above but then in the next stanza the kaṅghā.[27] The *Nishān-i-Sikhī* verses in Persian from the *DG* shed more light on the five *K*s and is a very early reference to how they were prioritized.[28]

According to sermons by the Damdami Taksal, this composition appeared in the lost *DG* written by Baba Dip Singh, and as a result this hymn is popular within the Taksal. Piara Singh Padam (2000) writes that this composition was on a loose folio in Jind (state next to Patiala), and Pandit Narain Singh included it as a part of the *Asphotak Kabitt Svaiye*. To reiterate, the traditional institutions or *samprādayā* believe it to be authentic, and if we take Padam's account to be true, then this position has some merit, while on the other hand, others believe it to be a later creation.

Vār Srī Bhagautī jī kī Pātashāhī 10.

ika oaṁkar srī vāhigurū jī kī phate.
One Universal Creator, Victory Belongs to the Holy Wondrous Guru.

vāra srī bhagautī jī kī pātashāhī 10.
The Ballad of the Holy Bhagautī [sword] by the Tenth Sovereign.[29]

doharā.
Couplet.

bhagata bhagautī tisaha kī jo rana dhīra dharai.
The Divine Bhagautī assists the one who remains composed in battle.

aṁga saṁga hauṁ lāgahūṁ pāchai paga na karai.1.
You are side by side [the Singh] who never retreats.1.[30]

savaiyā.
Quatrains.

bhagata bhagautī sājakai, prabhu jaga āraṁbha racāi hai.
Creating the Bhagat and Bhagautī, God created the beginning of the universe.[31]

rana rūpa bhabhūta caṛhāi kai, ḍapha ḍaurū ḍaṁka bajāi hai.
By razing the battlefield to ashes, by playing the large and small drum with strikes.

kala nārada haṛa haṛa hasiā, rana sābata jujha macāi hai.
In Kaliyug Nārada calls and laughs, the eternal battle is created.[32]

duladula khiṁga bigsiā, rana ruhara kahara barakhāi hai.2.
The courageous mules and horses are present, in the battle the blood is flowing like a furious torrent.2.

ghara sutā siṁgha jagāiā, khaṛa dharatī hāka calāi hai.
The sleeping Singh was awakened at home, the earth stopped spinning and called out.

mānukha pakaṛa bhakaliā, kara jaga ghamaṁḍa macāi hai.
Mankind was seized by madness, the ego of the world was increasing.

bhakala bhagautī durajanā, phaṭa ṭhuṁṭhura miṁjha kaḍhāi hai.
The Bhagautī has cut the evil people into pieces, smashing the corpses, releasing the bone marrow.[33]

hatha khapara phaṭakaṇa ḍamaracū, kaḍha kaṁgala kholi balāi hai.
[Sword] in hand, the scalps are being broken like a drum, taken out of the armour and the [warriors] subdued.[34]

uthal phuthala ghapan ghor kar, bhakarūlaha dhudha macāi hai.
Up and down [in chaos], around and around in the complete darkness they go, they turn continuously in the dust.

lutha palutha dhara nāla, dhaṛa piṁjara kuṁtaka khai hai.3.
The bodies are lying on each other randomly, headless corpses and corpses, skeletons are being eaten by dogs.3.

lapaṭa jhapaṭa le teganā, lara sūrā ghanā ghatāi hai.
Holding tight to the sword, the brave fighters are sent in dense [formations].

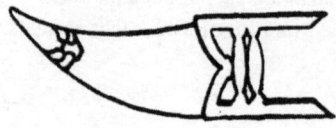

FIGURE 2.1 *Jamdhar*—Death Bearer[35]
Source: Kamalroop Singh.

khacaka khapana jahi jamadhaṛe, raṇa lutha palutha luṭhāi hai.
They have fastened tightly their *jamdhar* swords and sent to kill, in the battle the bodies are piled on each other, laying all over the ground.

rakata paleṭī jogaṇī, huṇa durajana kheta khapāi hai.
The witches are covered in blood, now the wicked in the battlefield are destroyed.

ruṁḍa muṁḍa ghamasāṇa kheta, raṇa jaṁbuka girajha aghāi hai.
So many headless bodies, and heads on the field of battle, hyenas and vultures are eating to their full.

dhama dhamāko jabajarajaṁga, gaṛha koṭana koṭaka ḍhāhi hai.
The sounds of canons can be heard in the thick of battle, millions of fortresses have been pulled down in millions of places.

kaṛa dhaṛade paṛasana bheṛa, kara sailahi saila bhiṛāi hai.4.
The explosions of guns cause roasting of bodies, warriors that are facing each other are fighting like two mountains hitting each other.4.

gagana kaṛkī bījulī, paralau paraloka khapāi hai.
The sky is thundering and lightening, it is end of the world, the heavens are resounding.

utalaka dhumaṁtala ḍhāianubahu, muṁḍaka muṁḍa bhiṛāi hai.
Hundreds of thousands of other worlds and galaxies are destroyed, many heads are everywhere.

barahara kaṁpai dharamarāi, raṇa sūrā ghāna ghatāi hai.
Dharam-Rāj is shaking seeing this scene, dense bodies of brave warriors are sent to battle to kill.[36]

saje bohitha dhakiā, kara khabe khaṛaga macāi hai.5.
On the right the boats are being pushed, on the left the double-edged swords are being used.5.

niberā hiṁdū turaka dā, raṇa madhe khaṛaga cukāi hai.
This is the conclusion of the conflict between the Hindus and Turaks, in the middle of battle the double-edged sword is raised.[37]

jaga araṁbha tih juga huṇa, māsa mānukha vica ghatāi hai.
In the beginning of the world, in this age now, the human made of flesh has been sent.

rakata khapara bhara jogaṇī, raṇa masata maṁgala guṇa gāi hai.
The scalps are filled with blood by the witches, they sing happily and intoxicatedly about the virtues of this final battle.

kesa binā sira kaṭīai, ciṁghāvai kavaṇa choḍāi hai.
The heads are being cut without kesh, they cry, who is there to free them?

hukama maṁne prabhu bakhasale, nigurāṁ nūṁ iho sajāi hai.
Believe in the Divine order and God will forgive, this is the punishment for those without a Guru.

fate jaṁga gobiṁda siṁgh, dala kokaṭa koṭa khapāi hai.6.
Gobind Singh is victorious in war, where millions of armies are cut down and destroyed.6.

doharā.
Couplet.

āsā nā karu brahamanā nā parase paga jāi.
Do not have hope Oh Brahmin, do not fret.

āpa taoāga dūje lage kuṁbhi naraka mahi pāi.7.1.2.
By forsaking your conscience and going after another, you will be in the most terrible hell.7.1.2.[38]

This composition also bears the ascription *Srī Mukhvāk Pātashāhī Dasamī* denoting that the composition is the holy verse orated by the Tenth Guru. This composition should not be confused with the similarly titled composition from the standard *DG*.[39] It appears in the 'Takht Patna Sahib' AD 1698 recension, the 'Sangrur' recension, and the 'Bhai Daya Singh' Aurangabad recension (see Figure 2.2). It also appears in Piara Singh Padam's publication, *Puṅjabī Vārāṅ*.[40] References are made to the angel Gabriel because it describes the Judgement Day. The description of the 'great war' is narrated by Gobind Singh, again pointing to a date close to the creation of the Khalsa. The *vār* is written in Panjabi, in the metric unit of the *pauṛī*. This composition shares similarities to *Chaṇḍī dī Vār*, as it has the same flow and expression. *Chaṇḍī dī Vār* continues on sequentially after two *Chaṇḍī Charitra* compositions in the standard *DG*. It is the essence of the *Mārkaṅḍeya Purāṇa Durgā Sapatashatī*. In this shorter composition, unlike the *Chaṇḍī dī Vār*, the name of Guru Gobind Singh appears in the text as he is narrating the great war. As there is a reference to Brahmins at the end of this composition (concluding doharā), it may be related to the *havan* incident where the Brahmin was exposed and tried to run away: 'Do not have hope Oh Brahmin,

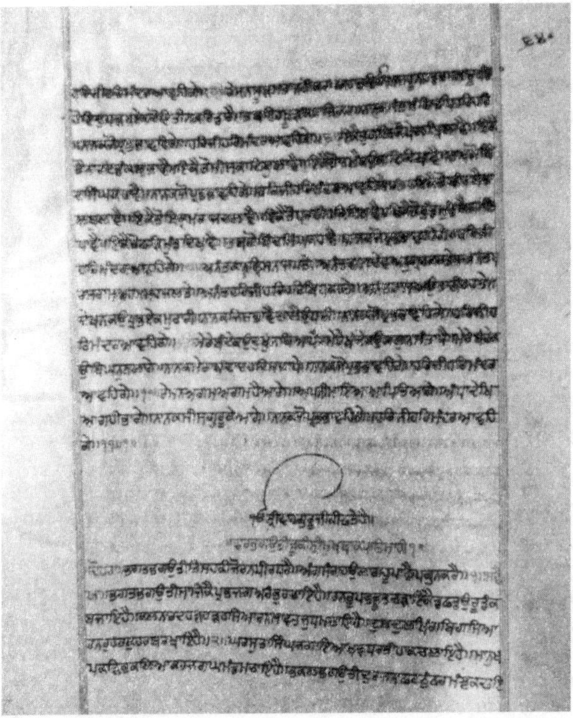

FIGURE 2.2 A Photograph of a Folio Showing the Opening of the *Vār Srī Bhagautī jī kī Pātashāhī 10* from the 'Takht Patna Sahib' AD 1698 *DG* Manuscript
Source: Giani Hardeep Singh.

do not fret. By forsaking your conscious, and going after another, you will be put in the most terrible hell.'

Vār Mālakaus kī Pātisāhī 10

ika oaṁkar vāhagurū jī kī phate hai.
One Universal Creator, Victory Belongs to the Wondrous Guru.

vāra mālakausa kī pātisāhī 10.
The Ballad of Rāg Mālkauns of the Tenth Sovereign.[41]

mālakausa dhuni bimala banāī.
The sound of *Mālkauns* is made sublime.

alakha nāma sacā khudāī.
By the indescribable name of the true Creator.

jaba dono hadā eka rakhāī.
When both are harmonized into one.

nānaka iha bidhi sace kau baṇi āī.
Says Nanak, in this way the true One can be known.

nānaka jo prabhu bhāvahige.
Says Nanak whatever [happens] is the Lord's will.

hari jī harimaṁdari āvahige.1.
Hari will come to Harimandir.1.[42]

jaba nīlā ghoṛā nīlā joṛā.
When [he comes] with a blue horse with blue robes [*bānā*].[43]

pakaṛi khaṁḍā kupharu hai toṛā.
Holding tight to a double-edged sword to annihilate the false.[44]

jaba dula dula ghoṛā āni phaharāiā.
When [he comes] to assist, on the horse *dula-dula* and does reining spins.[45]

taba jīa jūna aṁga lapaṭāiā.
Then all creatures' and life forms' limbs will hang [after being slain].

jaba sīkha pāu hoi jāi.
When the horse rears upright.

caurāsī lakha jīa bhrami bhrami bilalāi.
The eighty-four million life forms will wander and wander weeping in bodies.

nānaka ūhā nāma dhiāi.
Says Nanak in that place meditate on the Name.

nānaka jo prabha bhāvahige.
Says Nanak whatever [happens] is the Lord's will.

hari jī harimaṁdara āvahige.2.
Hari will come to Harimandir.2.

jaba nihakalaṁka nirūpa samānā.
When *Nihkalank* without any form merges.[46]

jaba eka rahā eka disaṭānā.
The One will remain then One will be seen.

āpanī joti āpahi rale.
He will merge in His own light.

taba māta pitā saṁgī nahīke.
There mother and father are of no aid.[47]

nānaka ūhāṁ nāma bhajile.
Says Nanak in that place meditate on the Name.

nānaka jo prabha bhāvahige.
Says Nanak whatever [happens] is the Lord's will.

hari jī harimaṁdara āvahige.3.
God will come to Harimandir.3.

jaba kāma teja jāne nahī aṁdhā.
When lust is so intense, it has blinded all.

lobhu teja suāda kā baṁdhā.
When greed is so intense, it has enslaved all.

haṁ teja bhūpa bikha khādhā.
When ego is so intense, the King eats this poison.

bhūkhana teja bhūpa bilabaṁdhā.[48]
That hunger blinds and binds the King sublimely.

niṁdrā teja asarakā jaṁdā.[49]
When gossip is so intense that creates doubt about scripture.

moha teja kāla kā phaṁdhā.
When attachment is so intense, it is like a noose of death.

agama agocara prabha niraṁkār.[50]
The deep formless Lord who does not take birth.

nanaka jisa bhāvai tisa le udhār.
Says Nanak who reaches Him is saved by Him.

nānaka jo prabha bhāvahige.
Says Nanak whatever [happens] is the Lord's will.

hari jī harimaṁdara āvahige.4.
God will come to Harimandir.4.

jaba agana teja āge dukhu pāe.
When the fire will be so intense, it will cause pain.

jibhiā teja suādi lapaṭāe.
When the tongues are so hungry for tastes, they hang out.

jaba jala teja kā aṁtu na pāvai.
When the waters will run with no end.

nānaka uhā hari hari nāmu dhiāvai.
Says Nanak at that time repeat Hari's name.

nānaka jo prabha bhāvahige.
Says Nanak whatever is the Lord's will.

hari jī hari maṁdara āvahige.5.
Hari will come to Harimandir.5.

re mana mūṛa matā nahī kara.
Oh foolish mind do not philosophize.

kahā bhaio ajahū naha ḍar.
That even now you are not afraid.

mārū khaṁḍā hoi dudhaṛa.
The killer double-edged sword that is sharp on both sides.[51]

eka doi tīna kari ḍārai.
From one is made two, into three and thrown.

taba iha mūṛa kahā jikar.
What will this fool do then.

nānaka saṁta saṁgi japi hari hari.
Says Nanak in the company of Saints remember God.

nānaka jo prabha bhāvahige.
Says Nanak whatever [happens] is the Lord's will.

hari jī hari maṁdara āvahige.6.
Hari will come to Harimandir.6.

ikai to kala ko khela khilāvai.
From One came the play of time.

ikai to nārada ḍaṁka bajāvai.
From One came Nārada beating his drum.

ikai to sīsa kāṭi bulāvai.[52]
From One came the order to take head.

ikai to jamahi kau kāṭi dikhāvai.
From One came the order of birth, and the other to be killed.

taba gobiṁda siṁgha kahāvai.[53]
Then says Gobind Singh.

nānaka jo prabha bhāvahige.
Says Nanak whatever [happens] is the Lord's will.

hari jī hari maṁdara āvahige.7.
Hari will come to Harimandir.7.

ikai to bīra baitāla bulāvai.
From One the warriors and spirits speak.

ikai to bikrama rāja calāvai.
From One came the Kingdom of Vikram.

ikai to dharatī haki dikhāvai.[54]
From One the Earth shows its truth (dharam).

ikai to ruṁḍa muṁḍa lai gali pāvai.
From One the demons *Ruṅḍa* and *Muṅḍa* strangulate.

hāk ikai to phaṛi muṁḍa dikhāvai.
From One they capture and shave the heads.

taba gobiṁda siṁgha kahāvai.
Then says Gobind Singh.

nānaka jo prabha bhāvahige.
Says Nanak whatever [happens] is the Lord's will.

hari jī hari maṁdara āvahige.8.
God will come to Harimandir.8.

anaṁta kānra kisanā japate.[55]
Unlimited angels, Krishnas meditate.

anaṁta vāsadeva anugraha karate.
Unlimited Vishnus show mercy.

anaṁta parasarāma ahaṁa maha jalate.
Unlimited Parasrams burn in ego.

anaṁta hari jī hari hari bidha kahate.
Unlimited people meditate on Hari and speak of his ways.

anaṁta rāma autārī rahate.
Unlimited Rams take *avatār*.

dekhana kau prabha eka murārī.
See that they are all the One Lord *Murārī*.

nānaka jisa bhāvai tā lai udhārī.
Says Nanak who reaches Him is saved by Him.

nānaka jo prabha bhāvahige.
Says Nanak whatever is the Lord's will.

hari jī hari maṁdara āvahige.9.
God will come to Harimandir.9.

mere baṁde kau dukha na biāpai.
My slave will not suffer any pain.

mere baṁde kau kālu na saṁtāpe.
My slave will not suffer death.

mere baṁde kau bighanu na lāge.
My slave will not suffer misfortune.

nānaka merā baṁdā daha disa jāpe.
Says Nanak my slave will have the fortune to see all the worlds.

nānaka jo prabha bhāvahige.
Says Nanak whatever is the Lord's will.

hari jī hari maṁdara āvahige.10.
Hari will come to Harimandir.10.

re mana agama agama hai āge.
Oh mind the Unfathomable is ahead.

apanī māiā āpi tiāge.
He detaches Himself from His own illusion.

aṁdhā dekhiā gahī bhāge.
The blind see it and get lost.

nānaka sīsa gurū ke āge.
Says Nanak my head is offered to the Guru.[56]

nānaka jo prabha bhāvahige.
Says Nanak whatever is the Lord's will.

hari jī hari maṁdara āvahige.11.1.
Hari will come to the Harimandir.11.1.[57]

The composition again starts off with the ascription to Guru Gobind Singh as the author of the composition. It is written in the Rāg Mālkauns from where it receives its title, 'The Ballad of Rāg Mālkauns from the Tenth Sovereign'. The composition is in reference to a future *avatār* coming down to the world on a horse wearing the *bānā* (dress) of the Guru.[58] It is a narration of apocalyptic events when the world has been consumed by the darkness of

Kaliyug. It indicates that God will come to the Harimandir, which could be a reference to the famous temple or, on a personal level, that God will come to those who have Hari in their heart. Again references are made to Gobind Singh within the text, who paraphrases the thoughts of Guru Nanak. This composition appears in the 'Takht Patna Sahib' AD 1698 recension, 'Sangrur' recension, 'Bhai Daya Singh' Aurangabad recension, and the 'Baba Atal' recension, which was examined by the corrective committee of AD 1897 (see Figure 2.3). A striking verse that could be seen to be the thoughts of the Tenth Guru at the first Khalsa initiation is: 'From One came the order to take a head.'

Srī Bhagautī Asatotra

ika oaṁkar srī vāhigurū jī kī phatiha hai.
One Universal Creator, Victory Belongs to the Holy Wondrous Guru.

srī bhagautī jī sahāi
The Holy Bhagautī Protects.

asatotra srī bhagautī jī kā pātisāhī 10.
Panegyrics of the Holy Bhagautī by the Tenth Sovereign.

bhuyaṁga prayāta chaṁda
In the metre of the swift moving Cobra.

namo srī bhagautī baḍhailī sarohī.
Obeisances to the Holy Sword, that cuts the *Sarohī*.[59]

namo eka te davai subhaṭa hātha sohī.
Obeisances to the One who makes two, in the hands of a brave warrior.

namo loha putrī achohaṁ rahaṁtī.
Obeisances to the Steel, that is the form of large enemies.[60]

namo jībha javālā mukhī jiu bolaṁtī.
Salutations to the fiery-tongued volcano that explodes.

mahāṁ māna kī bhāna gaṁgā taraṁgī.
The supremely respected waves of the Ganges.

bhire sāmuhe mokha dātī abhaṁgī.
The Eternal One that grants liberation.

namo tega taravāra srī khaga khaṁḍā.
Salutations *Tegh*, Sword, the Holy double-edged Sword, and Broad Sword.

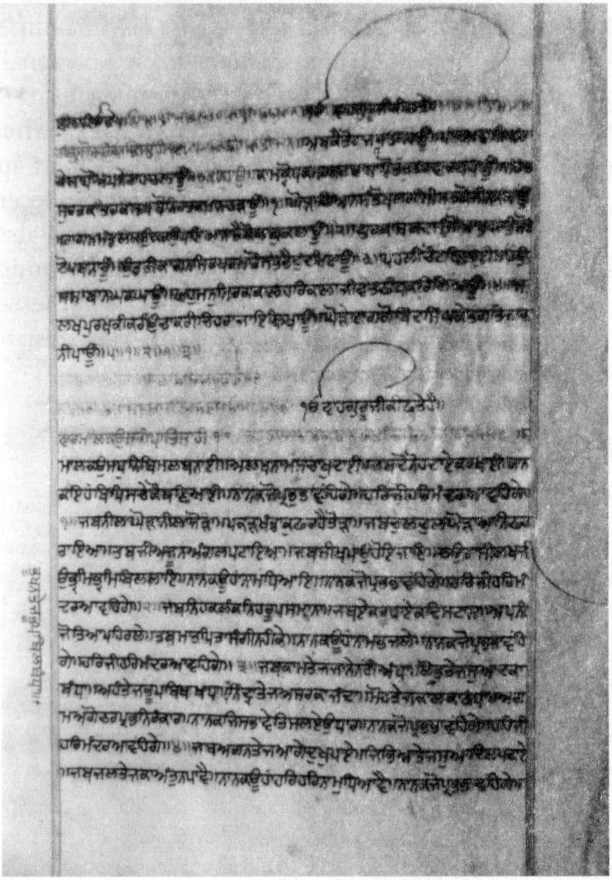

FIGURE 2.3 A Photograph of the Opening Folio of *Vār Mālakaus kī Pātisāhī 10* from the 'Takht Patna Sahib' AD 1698 *DG* Manuscript
Source: Giani Hardeep Singh.

FIGURE 2.4 A *Kharagh*—Broad Sword
Source: Kamalroop Singh.

mahāṁ rudra rūpā birūpā pracaṁḍā.
The greatly furious form, the formless blazing light.

mahāṁ teja khaṁḍā dukhaṁḍā dodhārā.
The great sharp-edged *khaṅḍā*, the double-edged Sword.

mahāṁ satra bana ko mahāṁ bhīma ārā.
The great killer of enemies, the great dreadful teeth for adversaries.

mahāṁ kāla kī kāla kā kāla kradhaṁ.[61]
The great Death of death, the fury of death.

mahāṁ bigrahī bridha dā sidha udhaṁ.
The great giver of perfection to the battlefield.

mahāṁ pātaṇī tūṁ palai kāla kārī.
The great ripper, You are death in action.

mahāṁ asatra tūṁ hī tūṁ hī stradhārī.
The great missile are You, You are donned in weapons.

mahāṁ kāla kī lāṭa bikrāla bhīmaṁ.
You are the great death that dreadfully slices the enemy.

bahī tacha muchaṁ karai satra kīmaṁ.
With your arms, You slice into pieces and kill enemies.

mahāṁ teja kī tejatā teja vaṁtī.
Great sharper than sharp, the sharpest One.

prajā khaṁḍanī daṁḍanī satra haṁtī.
The creative and destroying double-edged sword of the world, killer of enemies.

mahāṁ bīra bidiyā mahāṁ bhīma rūpaṁ
The great teacher of the science of war, the great form of dread.

mahāṁ bhīra mai dhīra dātī anūpaṁ.
The great beautiful giver of patience in the crowded battle.

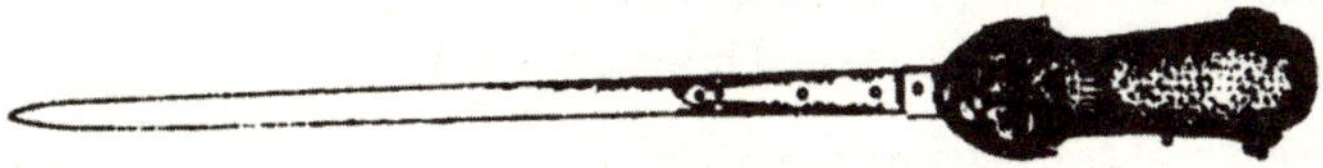

FIGURE 2.5 The *Patas*—Indian Gauntlet
Source: Kamalroop Singh.

tuhī saipha paṭā mahāṁ kāla kātī.
You are the *saif*, the *patas*, the Great Death—*kati*.[62]

anugu āpaṇai ko abhaidāna dātī.
To Your followers, You are the giver of the gift of fearlessness.

jabai miyāna te bīra to ko saṛkai.
When the warriors in the battle are martyred.

paralai kāla ke siṁdha bake kaṛkai.
They go to the great perfect heaven [of the Lord] with jubilation.

dhasai kheta mai hātha lai tuhi sūre.
When the brave warriors clash in the field and are [martyred] by Your hand.

bhire sāmūhe sidha sāvaṁta pūre.
Before those [*shahīds*] are the heavenly perfect realms.

karai hātha daphai kāḍha kai miyāna maiṁ te.
With their two hands they fight in the battle.

phatahi pāi hai bīra maidāna maiṁ te.
They win their victories because of You.

kaṭaka shatra ke agra hoi phaṭa bāhai.
They wipe out all of the enemies.

barai deva kaṁniyā teū kaṁta cāhai.
With Your favour virgin Mother, it is Your wish.

mahāṁ samara maiṁ jo karai hātha jete.
Whosoever You bless with Your hand.

suraga bāsa maiṁ bhogavai barakha tete.
They get all the pleasures of the heavens and happiness.

samara sāmuhe sīsa to pāhi caḍhāvai.
With Your power they slice the heads of their enemies.

mahāṁ bhūpa havai autarai rāja pāvai.
They win the Kingdoms and heavenly worlds.

mahāṁ bhāva so jo kare tora pūjaṁ.
Those who with great love worship You.

samara jīta kai sūra havai hai adūjaṁ.
Are the great victorious warriors with no comparison.

tujai pūja hai bīra bānaita chatrī.
You are worshipped by infinite warriors.

mahāṁ kharaga dhārī mahāṁ teja atrī.
[You] the carrier of the great Kharag, the great radiant Warrior.

parai prīta so prāṁta asatotra yāṁ ko.
Whoever reads this panegyric of Yours early in the morning.

kare rudra kālī namasakāra tāṁ ko.
Even Rudra and Kali will bow to them.

rudra maṁjanī biṁjanī hai agautī.
The cleanser of falsehood, lightening Sword.

sadā jai sadā jai sadā jai bhagautī.
Forever hail, forever hail, forever hail, the Sword.

sadā dāhane dāsa dāsa ko dāna dījai.
To Your slave of slaves give this blessing.

gurū shāha gobiṁda kī rakha kījai.
Protect the Guru-King Gobind as you wish.[63]

This composition also bears the ascription *Srī Mukhvāk Pātashāhī Dasavīṅ* denoting that the verses are from the mouth of the Tenth Guru. It is intended for battle which is consistent with the *vīr ras* (warrior essence) theme of the *DG*. This composition appears in the 'Takht Patna Sahib' AD 1698 recension and the 'Bhai Daya Singh' Aurangabad recension. It also appears in an early *AG* and *DG* anthology from AD 1736.[64] The scribe (Megh Singh) must have had great knowledge of both *Graṅths*, as he selectively uses gurbāṇī from both in his manuscript.[65] The formalization of a daily liturgy from both scriptures at a much earlier period should not be discounted, especially as we see anthologies from the *AG* and the *DG* appearing more frequently. In addition, the rahitnāme also give credence to this argument.

In historical sources the *Bhagautī Asatotra* appears frequently, including in the *Sikhāṅ dī Bhagatmālā*, which is an early eighteenth-century text ascribed to Bhai Mani Singh. In one *sākhī*, Bhai Mani Singh is asked the purpose of the compositions of the *DG* in relation to the *AG*. He states,

The martial scripture [*DG*] was written so the ones who grasp the scripture of devotion [*AG*] can also engage in war. They are to read the martial *Istotar* [*Asatotra*] of the Devi [*Chaṇḍī*] and they will be thus be aided in the wielding of their weapons.[66]

The *Asatotra* makes mention of numerous weapons in the same style and manner as *Shastra Nām Mālā*. The double-edged sword is given centre stage as 'the great killer of enemies, the great dread of adversaries'. The term 'sword' or 'bhagautī' is given praises and a boon is requested to protect King Gobind. This composition has become famous by *kirtanī* (singers of *kirtan*) reciting the lines 'sadā jai sadā jai sadā jai Bhagautī' (Forever hail, forever hail, forever hail, the Sword).[67] This composition is also referenced by Giani Gian Singh in his *Srī Gurū Paṅth Prakāsh* where he readily quotes from the *Bhagautī Asatotra* as well as other apocryphal compositions. According to Sikh tradition, this verse was said before Bhai Daya Singh offered up his head to the Guru.

Chhaṅd Chhakkā Srī Bhagautī jū kā (Ugradantī)

ika oaṁkara srī vāhigurū jī kī phataha.
One Universal Creator, Victory Belongs to the Holy Wondrous Guru.

srī bhagautī jī sahāi.
The Holy Bhagautī Protects.

srī mukhavāka pātashāhī 10.
The Holy Oration of Verse by the Tenth Sovereign.

bhagautī jī kā chaṁda chakkā pahilā.
The First Bhagautī Stanza of Six.[68]

namo ugradaṁtī anaṁtī svaiyā.
Obeisances to the One with sharp teeth, limitless and unrestrained.[69]

namo joga jogesavarī joga maiyā.1.
Obeisances to the Queen of all Yogas, the Mother of Yoga.1.[70]

namo keharī bāhanī satru haṁtī.
Obeisances to the rider of the lion and killer of enemies.

namo sāradā brahama vidiā paṛhaṁtī.2.
Obeisances to the Mother Sarada who teaches about the Creator.2.

namo ridha dā sidhi dā budhi dainī.
Obeisances to the one who bestows magical powers and wisdom.

namo kāla ke kāla kau kāla chainī.3.
Obeisances to the death of deaths, the one who has triumphed over death.3.[71]

namo kāla ajāla hai hera tero.
Obeisances to the one who cannot be caught in the web of death.

namo tīna hū loka kīno ahero.4.
Obeisances to the one whose are the three worlds.4.[72]

namo joti javālā tumai beda gāvaiṁ.
Obeisances to the glowing flame that the Vedas sing praises of.

sur āsura rikhīsavara nahīṁ bheda pāvaiṁ.5.
The demi-gods, demons, sages cannot fathom you.5.

tūṁhī joga jogatana tuhī kharaga dhāre.
You are the essence of yoga, you are the bearer of the double-edged sword.[73]

tuhī jai karaṁtī asura gahi pachāre.6.
You are victorious, having slayed the demons.6.

tuhī jogaṇī khapara bharaṇī adokhaṁ.
You are the faultless female ascetic holding the entire expanse of stars in an alms bowl.

rakata bīja ke prāṇa ko pakaṛa sokhaṁ.7.
You intelligently took the life of Rakat Bīj.7.[74]

tuhī jala thale parabate giri nivāsī.
You reside in the oceans, rivers, earth, hills, and mountains.

tuhī sabha ghaṭana nirālama prakāsī.8.
You are all existence, the detached Divine radiance.8.

tuhī dusaṭa dāhina tuhī saraba pālī.
You destroy the evil and take Motherly care of all.

tuhī bricha puhipā tuhī āpa mālī.9.
You are the plants and flowers and the Gardener.9.

tuhī visava bharaṇī tuhī jaga prakāsī.
You are the expanse of stars in the universe and Your radiance lights the world.

tuhī alakha baraṇī tuhī bhu akāsī.10.
You are the Infinite Invisible power, You are the earth and the sky.10.

namo jālapā devi durage bhavānī.
Obeisances to the giver of speech, enlightened, destroyer of suffering, material existence.

tihū loka navakhaṁḍa maiṁ tuma pradhānī.11.
You are the Master in the three worlds and the nine realms.11.[75]

aṭala chatra dharaṇī tuhī ādi devaṁ.
The bearer of the Eternal canopy You are the Primal Deity.

sakala munajanā tohi nisa dina sarevaṁ.12.
All hermits and men pray to You day and night.12.

tuhī kāla akāla kī joti chājai.
You are the splendid light that is Timeless and in time.

sadā jai sadā jai sadā jai birājai.13.
Always Your victory, always Your victory, always Your victory and reign.13.

yahī dāsa māṁgai kripā siṁdhu kījai.
This slave begs for Your compassion, which is limitless like an ocean.

saṁvaya brahama kī bhagata sarabatra dījai.14.
Bestow on all the devotion to *Braham*.14.

tuhī jāgatī joti jāvalā sarūpaṁ.
You are the awakened Light the embodiment of the flame.

tuhī jaga sakala mahi ramaṁtī anūpaṁ.15.
You are immanent in the whole world and none can eulogize You.15.

mahāṁ mūṛa haūṁ dāsana tihārā.
I am a great fool and slave of Your slaves.

pakaṛa bāṁha bhaujala karahu bega pārā.16.
Hold my arm and take me across the ocean with Your power.16.

phatahi ḍaṁka bājai kripā yau karījai.
May the drum of victory resound, bestow that grace.

yahī bāratā dāsa kī nita suṇījai.17.
Daily hear this plea of Your slave.17.

karahu hukama apanā sabhai dusaṭa ghāūṁ.
Give Your command to destroy all the enemies.

turaka hiṁda kā sakala jhagarā miṭāūṁ.18.
To completely terminate the feud between the Hindu and Turak.18.

agama sūrabīre uṭhahi siṁgha jodhā.
Mountain-like brave warriors will rise, the valiant Singhs for battle.[76]

pakaṛa turaka gana kau karai vai nirodhā.19.
They will pounce on the hordes of Turaks and and make them defenceless.19.

sakala jagata mo khālasā paṁtha gājai.
Throughout the entire world the Khalsa Panth will thunder.

jagai dharama hiṁduka turakana duṁda bhājai.20.
Dharam will enliven India; the Turaks will flee in commotion.20.[77]

japauṁ jāpa ekai hare hari akālaṁ.
Every one will repeat *Hare–Hari Akal.*

havai taba dunīāṁ sabha chinaka maiṁ nihālaṁ.21.
Then the entire world will immediately be blissful.21.

suṇahu tuma bhavānī hamana kī pukāre.
Beauteous Mother please listen to my plea.

karahu dāsa para mihara aparaṁ apāre.22.
Bestow great blessings upon Your slave.22.

doharā.
Couplet.

dāvara tumāre ṭhāḍha hauṁ ika bara dījai mohi.
I stand at Your door, give me one boon.

paṁtha calai taba jagata mai dusaṭa khapāvahu tohi.1.
The Panth prevails in the world, may you destroy the evil forces.1.

bhagavatī chaṁda dūjā.2.
The Second Bhagavatī Stanza.

namo kālakā kāla rūpī kripānī.
Obeisances to the Death of deaths, the embodiment of the Sword.

namo suṁbha nisuṁbha nāsani bhavānī.23.
Obeisances to the Beauteous Mother, the destroyer of Sumbh and Nishumbh.23.

namo caṁḍa ara mūṁḍa saṁghāra kārī.
Obeisances to the slayer of Chand and Munḍ.

namo rakata bījāna ke prāna hārī.24.
Obeisances to the one who took the life of Rakat Bīj.24.

namo veda vidiyā namo jagaya rūpā.
Obeisances to the giver of knowledge of the Veda, and Obeisances to the form of the holy fire.[78]

namo aṁjanī pūranī bhūpa bhūpā.25.
Obeisances to the one with completely enthralling eyes, who is the King of Kings.25.[79]

namo jai aṇaṁtī bhadrakālī abāhaṁ.
Obeisances to the boundless possessor of power, destroyer, with infinite arms.

namo bhagavatī tejavaṁtī aḍhāhaṁ.26.
Obeisances to Bhagavatī, possessor of great splendour subjugated by none.26.

namo sakati rūpaṇa agaṁmaṇa aḍolā.
Obeisances to the embodiment of power, unborn, and unyielding.[80]

namo khaṛaga dhārana achedaṇa atolā.27.
Obeisances to the Invincible bearer of the sword, undivided and immeasurable.27.

namo garaba gaṁjana sirī joga māyā.
Obeisances to the obliterator of ego, the holy creator of illusion.

sabhai thaka rahe marama kinahūṁ na pāyā.28.
All gave up as nobody can understand or attain You.28.

tuhī jala agani pavana tūṁ hūra nūrā.
You are water, fire, and air and the Angels and nymphs.[81]

tuhī joti uḍagana tuhī caṁda sūrā.29.
You are the light of stars, moon, and the sun.29.

tuhī khecarā bhūcarā jodha bīre.
You are the brave warriors on the earth and in space.

tuhī rachanī srisaṭi rūpana gahīre.30.
You are the protector, the adorned form of creation.30.

tuhī jagata jananī anaṁtī akālaṁ.
You are the Mother of all living beings and are endless and eternal.

tuhī aṁna dainī sabhana ko samālaṁ.31.
You provide nourishment and nuture all.31.

tuhī khaṁḍa brahamaṁḍa bhūmaṁ sarūpī.
You are the form of the dimensions, universe and earth.

tuhī bisana siva brahama iṁdarā anūpī.32.
You are the unsurpassed splendour of Vishnu, Shiva, Brahma, and Indra.32.

tuhī sītalā totalā bāka bānī.
You are the cooling and warming speech.[82]

namo caṁḍakā maṁgalā srī bhavānī.33.
Obeisances to *Chandakā*, the blissful Holy Bhavānī.33.[83]

nahīṁ tuma binā koi rachaka hamārā.
There is no one else but You who can protect me.

tuhī ādi kuāra devī apārā.34.
You are the primal chaste infinite Goddess.34.

tuhī devakī krisana mātā kahāyaṁ.
You were known as mother Devakī, the mother of Krishna.

tuhī naiṇā devī alakha jaga sahāyaṁ.35.
You are the beautiful-eyed Goddess, the invisible protector of the universe.35.

tuhī thaṁbha siuṁ nikasa narasiṁgha hoī.
You transformed into Narsingh and manifested from the pillar.[84]

udara haranākhasa kā nakhahu kara paroī.36.
With Your nails You tore open the belly of Harnaksh.36.

tuhī kacha hui daita madhukīṭa jāre.
You manifested as Kachh the turtle, and destroyed Madhu and Kītabh demons.[85]

tuhī hoi bairāha hiranāchaya māre.37.
You manifested as Bairāh the boar and killed Hirankashyapa.37.

tuhī hui bāvana mahāṁ chala dikhāyo.
You manifested as Bāvan the dwarf and performed a great deception.

pakaṛa rāje bala ko patālai paṭhāyo.38.
Seizing and banishing Raja Bal to the nether world.38.

tuhī hoi parasarāma jaga mahi prakāsī.
You were Parasram who manifested in this world.

sakala chatrīana kau karai chai bināsī.39.
Who destroyed, obliterated all the Kshatriyas.39.[86]

tuhī phira bhī rāmacaṁdra apārā.
You were then manifest as the great Ram.

pakaṛa laṁka sau daita rāvaṇa pachārā.40.
Seizing Sri Lanka he destroyed the demon Rāvana.40.

tuhīṁ mukati dāiṇī sadā subha karaṁtī.
You are the bestower of liberation and are always doing good.

tuhī sūra balabīra dusaṭaṇa dahaṁtī.41.
You are a brave warrior with great strength, annihilating the demons.41.

tuhī rādhakā rukamaṇī tūṁ kushilā.
You are Rādhikā, Rukamanī and you are Kaushalyā.[87]

tuhī aṁjanī renakā tūṁ ahliā.42.
You are Anjanī, Renukā and you are Ahalyā.42.[88]

tuhī bharaṇa pokhaṇa sabhana para kripālī.
You are the compassionate Mother who nourishes and protects all.

karahu mohi mukatā kaṭahu bharama jālī.43.
Grant me salvation, cut this net of illusion.43.

namo dukha haraṁtī anaṁdata sarūpā.
Obeisances to the reliever of suffering, the embodiment of bliss.

apana dāsa para mihara kījai anūpā.44.
Unsurpassed One, bestow Your grace on Your slave.44.

doharā.[89]
Couplet.

dāsa jāna kara āpanā kirapā kījai mohi.
Make this being Your slave, bestow Your grace on me.

ihai benatī dāsa kī suṇahu bhavānī tohi.2.
This is the plea of Your slave, hear me Beauteous Mother.2.

bhagavatī chaṁda tījā.3.
The Third Bhagavatī Stanza.3.

tūhī kalapa brichaṇa tuhī kāmadhenā.
You are Kalpavriksha, You are Kamadhenu.[90]

tuhī asaṭa sidhaṇa tuhī nūra nainā.45.
You are the eight miraculous powers, You are the brilliant eyes.45.

tuhī suraga pātāla baikuṁṭha dharaṇī.
You are the support of the earth, heavens, underworld, and paradise.

tuhī pāpa khaṁḍaṇa udara jagata bharaṇī.46.
You are the destroyer of sin, the world, and constellations are inside You.46.

tuhī brāhamaṇī beda pāṭhaṇa savitrī.
You are the creative Mother who gave birth to the verses of the Vedas.

tuhī dharamaṇī karaṇa kāraṇa pavitrī.47.
You are the Mother of dharam whose intent and action are pure.47.

tuhī gorajā pārabatī joga dharaṇaṁ.
You are Parvati in meditative union in the Jungle.[91]

tuhī lachamī alakha rūpī avaraṇaṁ.48.
You are Lakshami whose invisible form is ineffable.48.[92]

tuhī sabha jagata kau upāvai chapāvai.
You give birth to the universe and remain hidden in it.

tuhī bahuṛa āpe chinika mau khapāvai.49.
Then in an instant, You destroy all.49.

tuhī bhagata karatāra kī sakati rāṇī.
You are the devotion and powerful consort of the Creator.

tuhī hari simari kara bhī joga dhayāṇī.50.
You are the remembrance of Hari, and the absorption of yoga.50.

agamakhela tumarā kahā ko bakhānai.
Who can explain Your unfathomable play.

tuhī bheda apanā apanu āpa jānai.51.
You only know Your own mystery.51.

sagala ḍhūṁḍa thāke lakhiyo kicha na bhedā.
All have searched to find you and given up, but no one can explain Your mystery.

tuhī īsarī dukha bināsana achedā.52.
You are the Mother Creator who destroys eternal suffering.52.

karahu mehara apunī carana dhūri pāvauṁ.
Bless me that I might receive the dust of Your feet.

tumana duāra para sīsa apanā ghasāvauṁ.53.
At Your door, I bow my head and pay homage.53.[93]

yahī dāna māṁgau karahu jai hamārī.
I beseech You for this charity, make me victorious.

sabhai dusaṭa daitā khapai china majhārī.54.
May all enemies and demons be destroyed within a moment.54.

tuhī ḍākaṇī sākaṇī sūrabīre.
You are the *wākaṇī, sākaṇī*, and the brave warriors.[94]

tuhī rūpa nārāiṇī hari sarīre.55.
You are the embodiment and dwelling place of all beings, You are the body of Hari.55.

tuhī alakha duragā jagata karanahārī.
You are invisible, unreachable, the cause of the world.

sakala choḍa kara oṭa pakaṛī tihārī.56.
I have left all and hold onto Your protection.56.

tuhī macha hoi siṁdhu bhītara khilaṁtī.
You manifested as Matsya and played in the ocean.

tuhī daiṁta saṁkhāsure kau dalaṁtī.57.
You destroyed the demon Sankhasur.57.[95]

tuhī krisana hoi kaṁsa kesī khapāyo.
You were born as Krishna and killed Kans and Keshī.[96]

tumana mala caṁḍūra gahi kara uḍāyo.58.
You got the wrestler Chandūr into a hold and killed him.58.[97]

jagana nātha hui daita gayāsura biḍāre.
You were Jagan Nāth and killed Gayāsur demon.

tuhī nihakalaṁkī bhī khaṛaga dhāre.59.
You are Nihakalank bearing the double-edged sword.59.

tuhī daiṁta kilākāsure kau saṁgharaṇī.
You annihilated the demon Kilkasur.

tuhī sabha jugaṇa bīca avatāra dharaṇī.60.
You are manifest as an avatār in every age.60.

jugo juga sakala khela tuma hī racāyo.
In all ages after ages you have created this play.

tumana khela kā bheda kinahūṁ na pāyo.61.
No one has fathomed the secret of Your play.61.

FIGURE 2.6 *Ashtbujā Dhujā*—Eight-pronged Spearhead[98]
Source: Kamalroop Singh.

tuhī ashaṭa durage bhavānī akālaṁ.
You are the Eternal eight-armed Durga Bhavanī.

tuhī sakala brahamaṁḍa ūpara dayālaṁ.62.
Your benevolence is over all creation.62.

tumana kudaratī khela kīno apārā.
You enact as nature and perform wondrous marvels.

tumana teja sau koṭi ravi sasi ujārā.63.
It is with Your eminence that millions of suns and moons yield radiance.63.

tuhī nija vajīrana prabhū dara suhaṁtī.
You are the Almighty Lord's personal minister and adorn His abode.

tuhī nisa dinā jāpa hari hari japaṁtī.64.
You meditate day and night on the Lord.64.

niraṁjana purakha shāha shāhana apāre.
You are the pure being, King of Kings and are immeasurable.

tuhī sakati haiva nikaṭavaratī murāre.65.
You are the might of Krishna with which he destroyed the Mura demon.65.

suṇahu dāsa kī benatī hari bhavānī.
Please heed my request O Hari Bhavānī.

daiā dhāra muhi lāja rākhahu nidānī.66.
With Your benevolence, save my honour till the end.66.

doharā.
Couplet.

dāno māre rohile deva bacāe tohi.
You have killed the angry demons and saved the demi-gods.

siṁgha tumāro raṇa gaje hāka na jhālasa koi.3.
Nobody could endure the roar of Your lion in the battlefield.3.

bhagavatī chaṁda cauthā.4.
The Fourth Bhagavatī Stanza.4.

tuhī jota javālā mukhī hoi dikhānī.
You reveal Yourself as the flame of the Volcano.

parabata phoṛa lāṭāṁ agana jaga magānī.67.
Shattering the mountains with flames of fire, the Universal form of sacrificial fire.67.

tuhī haraṇa bharaṇī tuhī āpa māe.
You fill the expanse, You, Yourself are the Mother of all.

tuhī saraba ṭhaurana rahī āpa chāe.68.
You reside as the shade in all places.68.

tuhī utabhujā setajā sukha nidhānī.
You are the earth and sweat, the treasure of happiness.

tuhī aṁḍajā jerajā catara bānī.69.
You are the egg and womb, the four types of life.69.[99]

tuhī tīra taravāra kātī kaqārī.
You are the arrow, sword, knife, and dagger.

tuhī saṁkha padamaṇa gadā cakradhārī.70.
You are the bearer of the conch, lotus, mace, and the quoit. 70.

tuhī topa baṁdūka golā calaṁtī.
You fire the shot from the cannon and gun.

tuhī koṭa gaṛha kau dhamaka siu uḍaṁtī.71.
You destroy castles and large fortresses with loud explosions.71.

tuhī baḍa ajītaṇa sagala dokha haraṇī.
You are greatly invincible and the obliterater of all misery.

tuhī hari aḍolaṇa agama khela karaṇī.72.
You are the unwavering Hari, the activator of the profound play.72.

tuhī ati balisaṭaṇa catura bhuja bhavānī.
You are the four-armed Bhavānī with very immense power.

tumana saraba dusaṭā kīe māra phānī.73.
You are the killer and annihilator of all the enemies.73.

tuhī gupati paragaṭa sabhana mo khilaṁtī.
You are the invisible and the visible force animating in all.

tuhī suṁbha mahikhāsurai kau dalaṁtī.74.
You reduce to nothing Sumbh and Mahisasur demons.74.[100]

tuhī jagata maṁḍaṇa daiāvaṁta bhārī.
You are the most gracious embellisher of the Universe.

sakala sida muni jana le taiṁ ubārī.75.
You are the liberator of all perfected beings and silent sages.75.

lakhai nāhi koū ajaba khela terā.
Nobody can grasp Your play that is beyond comprehension.

tuhī dharaṇa dhara kai karahi phira niberā.76.
You create the earth and then again You finish it.76.

tuhī bijala hoi gagana caṛha jhilamilānī.
You are the lightning, which rises, flashing in the sky.

tumana carana para surata hamarī lagānī.77.
My awareness is joined to Your lotus feet.77.

tuhī alakha karatāraṇī siva sarūpā.
You are the indescribable creative Mother, the liberated form.

tuhī ghaṭa ghaṭe deva durage anūpā.78.
You are in each and every heart, the radiant Durga that cannot be expressed.78.

tuhī hai sabhana bīca sabha te nirālī.
You reside in all and are separate from all.

tuhī sabha jagata kī karahi pratipālī.79.
You are the sustainer of the entire universe.79.

tuhī khāsa bhagataṇa hare hari japaṁtī.
You are the special devotee repeating *Hare–Hari.*

tuhī hara caraṇa para apuṇa sira dharaṁtī.80.
You lower Your head at the feet of Hari.80.

tuhī hari kripā siu agama rūpa hoī.
With Hari's grace You became the infinite form.

sabhai paca mūe pāra pāvata na koī.81.
All have expired but none could comprehend You.81.

tuhī sūra balavaṁtaṇī guṇa gahīre.
You are the mighty warrioress with unparalleled genius.

tumana davāra ghura haiṁ anahada naphīre.82.
At Your doorway trumpets sound the unstruck melody.82.

niraṁjana sarūpā tuhī ādi rāṇī.
You are the immaculate form, the primal Queen.

tuhī joga bidayā tuhī brahama bāṇī.83.
You are the yogic wisdom and You are the utterance of God.83.

niraṁjana prabhū nātha kādara murāre.
The immaculate Lord, Master, all powerful Murāre.

tahāṁ tū kharī kudaratī rūpa dhāre.84.
Wherever you stand, You manifest as Mother nature.84.

tuhī aṁbhake sakati durage bhavānī.
You are the life Mother, bestowing power, Durga Bhavānī.

tumana kudaratī jota ghaṭi ghaṭi samānī.85.
Your Eternal light is prevalent in every particle in nature.85.

dharana pavana ākāsa kudarati sarūpā.
You manifest as the earth, wind, sky, and embody the creation.

tuhī kudaratī alakha devī anūpā.86.
You are the indescribable, incomparable, Goddess of nature.86.

nahī bhākha sākau mai mahimā tuhārī.
I cannot possibly describe Your glory.

lakhayā nāhi kinahūṁ tumana aṁta pārī.87.
No one has been able to comprehend Your end or limits.87.

yahī dāsa tumarā carana dhūri pāvai.
This slave longs for the dust of Your feet.

tumana dāvara ṭhāḍhā sadā dhuni lagāvai.88.
I stand at Your door always engaged in singing.88.

doharā.
Couplet.

mukha pasārai kālakā daita cabāvai dāṁta.
With an opened mouth Kalikā with her sharp teeth grinds the demons.

paṁtha calāvai jagata mai judha karahi taba sāṁti.
The Panth will appear in this world that conducts war to bring peace.4.

bhagavatī chaṁda paṁjavāṁ.5.
The Fifth Bhagavatī Stanza.

namo devisā kuṁbharī hiṁgulājā.
Obeisances to the the Queen of demi-gods, Kumbhari and Hingulaja.

tuhī sabha jagata ke karahi sidha kājā.89.
You perfectly complete the functions of all the universe.89.

tuhī alakha javālā kamachiā pradhānī.
You are the indescribable Javala and chief Kamakhya.[101]

tumana jasa sakala jagata kara hai bakhānī.90.
The entire universe sings Your glory, Mother.90.

tuhī hari niraṁkāra ṭhākura japaṁtī.
You are the repetition of Hari, the Formless Master.

tuhī rāchasana kau pakaṛa kara dahaṁtī.91.
You grab the demons and destroy them.91.

hamana bairīana kau pakaṛa ghāta kījai.
Get hold of my enemies and annihilate them.

tabai dāsa gobiṁda kā mana patījai.92.
Then Your slave Gobind's mind will be assured.92.

tuhīṁ āsa pūrana jagata gura bhavānī.
You are the fulfiller of all wishes, the Universal Guru Bhavānī.

chatra chīna mugalana karahu bega phānī.93.
With force quickly destroy the royal canopies and symbols of Mughal sovereignty.93.

sakala hiṁda siuṁ turaka dusaṭā bidārahu.
Drive all the Turaks and enemies from Hind.

dharama kī dhujā kau jagata mai jhulārahu.94.
Fly the flag of dharam all over the world.94.

duhūṁ paṁtha maiṁ kapaṭa vidayā calānī.
Both paths are propagating deceitful knowledge.

bahuṛa tīsarā paṁtha kījai paradhānī.95.
Come and elevate a supreme third path [Khalsa].95.

jo upajai marai tāhi simarana na kījai.
Do not meditate on the one who is subject to birth and death.

aṭala purakha akāla kā nāma lījai.96.
Meditate on the name of the eternal Akal Purakh.96.

maṛī gora devala masītāṁ girāyaṁ.
Demolish the graves, the shrines of the demi-Gods, and mosques.

tuhī eka akāla hari hari japāṁyaṁ.97.
So that only Your one eternal name Hari Hari is recited.97.

miṭahi beda sāsatra aṭhārahi purānā.
The Vedas, the Shastras and the eighteen Puranas have been forsaken.

miṭai bāṁga salavāta sunaṁta kurānā.98.
The *azan, salavat, sunnat* (Islamic call to prayer, honorific praise of the Prophet Mohammed, and circumcision), and the Qur'an have been forsaken.98.[102]

sakala srishaṭa ika barana hoi kara bhulānī.
All the people of the world have forgotten to praise the One.

dharama nema kī jugata kinahūṁ na jānī.99.
The lifestyle of dharam is no longer comprehended by humanity.99.

kaṭhina duṁda varatai jagata mahi gubārā.
The thick mist [of ignorance] is causing darkness in the world.

dayā dhāra kara mohi lījai ubārā.100.
Manifest Your kindness, and liberate me from this.100.

tuhī kudarata sakati durage bhavānī.
You are the Creator's power Durga Bhavānī.

tuhī jagata mātā sakala bidha nidhānī.101.
You are Mother of the universe, the treasure of precepts.101.

tuhī biāsa gorakha agasataṁ kabīre.
You are Vyas, Gorakh Nath, the sage Agast and Kabir.

tuhī rikha munīsara tuhīṁ gauṁsa pīre.102.
You are the Rishi, silent sage, You are Ghaus *pīr* [Highest Sufi saint].102.

niraṁjana purakha kau sadā tūṁ dhiāvaiṁ.
You always meditate upon the unblemished Being.

prabhū davāra ṭhāḍhī vajīrana kahāvaiṁ.103.
You stand as the minister at Prabhu's doorway.103.

nahīṁ tuma bināṁ koī dūsara hajūre.
Other than You, none else is as close [to Akal Purakh].

tuhīṁ alakhaṇī hoi rahī jagata pūre.104.
You are indescribable and reside in the entire universe.104.

apuna jāna kara mohi līјai bacāī.
Make me Yours and save me.

asura pāpīana māra devahu uḍāī.105.
Kill the demons and the wicked, uplift the righteous.105.

sakala jagata kau sukha basāvahu anaṁdā.
Bestow peace and bliss to the whole world.

tuhī darada meṭaṇa srī hari mukaṁdā.106.
You are the remover of suffering and the Holy Hari, bestower of liberation.106.

yahī deha āgiā turakana gahi khapāūṁ.
Give me this command to destroy the Turaks.

gaū ghāta kā dokha jaga siuṁ miṭāūṁ.107.
To eliminate the stain of the killing of the cow from the entire world.107.

chatra takhata mugalana karahūṁ māra dūre.
To destroy the canopies and thrones of the Mughal.

ghurahi taba jagata mahi phataha dharama tūre.108.
The victorious call of dharam will again resound in the world.108.

tumana dara kharā dāsa kara hai pukārā.
Standing at Your door, this slave implores to you.

turakana meṭa kījai jagata mahi ujārā.109.
Destroy the Turaks and illuminate the world.109.

tabahi gīta maṁgala phatahi ke sunāūṁ.
Only then can I sing the songs of victory.

tumana kau simara dūkha sagale miṭāūṁ.110.
By Your remembrance I will eradicate all suffering.110.

doharā.
Couplet.

kirapā kījai dāsa para kuṁṭa nivāūṁ cāra.
Have grace on Your slave, to enable [him to make] the four corners of the world pay obeisance [to Your feet].

nāma tihāro jo japai bhe siṁdha bhava pāra.
Whoever recites Your name crosses over the ocean of existence.5.

bhagavatī chaṁda chevāṁ.6.
The Sixth Bhagavatī Stanza.6.

namo kasaṭa haraṇī duragā sakati māe.
Obeisances to the destroyer of difficulties, the powerful Mother Durga.

sabhai dusaṭa dāno pakaṛa tai khapāe.111.
You have seized all the evil demons and annihilated them.111.

tumana bhavana trai loka mahi birājai.
Your realm is in all the three worlds where you dwell.

tahāṁ nūra tumarā agama rūpa chājai.112.
There Your eternal form is ever prevalent.112.

tuhī dhaula gira koṭa kāṁgaṛa basaṁtī.
You reside in the many Dhaula mountains, and Khangara hills.

tuhī achala anāda devana anaṁtī.113.
You are beyond deception, the endless eternal Divine.113.

raṭoṁ nisa dinā jāpa tumarā bhavānī.
With focus repeating Your name day and night O Bhavānī.

tumana carana moṁ prīti hamarī lagānī.114.
My love is only directed to Your feet. 114.

karahu hari bhavānī jagata kī saṁbhāre.
Hari Bhavānī you should sustain the world.

hamana dushaṭa dokhī sabhana hohiṁ chāre.115.
All my enemies and the wicked should be reduced to ashes.115.

sadā sarabadā caraṇa tumare dhiāūṁ.
I should always, forever, contemplate Your feet.

tumana mihara siuṁ dusaṭa sagale khapāūṁ.116.
With Your mercy all the wicked with be destroyed.116.

yahī āsa pūrana karahu tuma hamārī.
Fulfil this wish of mine, please do this for me.

miṭai kasaṭa gaūana chuṭai kheda bhārī.117.
Relieve the cows of suffering and all ailments.117.

phataha satigurū kī jagata siuṁ bulāūṁ.
The victory of the Satiguru, I will declare to the world.

sabhana kau sabada vāhi vāhi driṛāūṁ.118.
To all, I shall impart Vahiguru Vahiguru.118.

karahu khālasā paṁtha tīsara pravesā.
The Khalsa will be designated as the third path. [103]

jagahi siṁgha jodhe dharahi nīla bhesā.119.
The Singh warriors shall rise and wear the blue dress.119. [104]

sakala rāchasana kau pakaṛa vai khapāvaiṁ.
They will capture and destroy all demons.

sabhai jagata siuṁ dhuni phataha kī bulāvaiṁ.120.
The tune of victory will resound in the world.120.

tuhī sāradā beda gāyaṇa surasatī.
You are Sarada, Saraswati singing the Vedas.

tuhī deva durage niraṁjana parasatī.121.
You are the Divine Durga who is in constant touch with the perfect One.121.

yahī benatī khāsa hamarī suṇījai.
Kindly listen to this important request of mine.

asura māra kara racha gaūana karījai.122.
Annihilate the demons and protect the cow.122.[105]

tuhī sidha nava nidha kau bharaṇahārī.
You are the bestower of perfection, and the nine treasures.

tuhī aṁnadāyaṇa sakala jaga bhikhārī.123.
You are the provider of nourishment, and all the universe is the beggar.123.

tuhī rikhī basisaṭe tuhī hai durabāsā.
You are the sage Vashishta and Durvasa.

tuhī jamadagani saṁta gotama prakāsā.124.
You are the radiance of Jamadgin and Saint Gautama.124.

tuhī kāla ke asura saṁghāra karaṇī.
You are the destroyer of the demon Kāl.

tuhī sevakana para sadā mihara dharaṇī.125.
You bestow eternal grace on Your devotees.125.

kahāṁ lau bakhānau tumana gati apāre.
How can I describe Your transcendent nature?

tuhī jālapā alakha rūpaṇa murāre.126.
You deliver us from entanglements, beyond comparison the form of Murāre.126.

tuhī hari hare hari hare hari bhavānī.
You are *Hari Hare Hari Hare Hari* Bhavānī.

niraṁjana purakha para bhī tūṁ kurabānī.127.
You are also the sacrifice to the immaculate Being.127.

yahī dehi bara mohi satigura dhiāūṁ.
Grant me the boon to meditate on the Satiguru.

asura jīta kara dharama naubata bajāūṁ.128.
Defeat the demons and play the victory drum of dharam.128.

miṭahi sabha jaga siuṁ turakana duṁda sorā.
The dominance of the Turaks will be wiped out from the world.

bacahi saṁta sevaka khapahi dusaṭa corā.129.
The Saints and humble servants shall be saved, the evil thieves will perish.129.

sabhai srisaṭa parajā sukhī hui birājai.
The population of the world will live in happiness.

miṭai dūkha saṁtāpa ānaṁda gājai.130.
All the suffering and fever shall end and ecstasy will abound.130.

na chāḍauṁ kahūṁ dusaṭa asurana nisānī.
I intend not to leave any impression of the evil demons.

calai sabha jagata mahi dharama kī kahānī.131.
The world will operate to the theme of dharam.131.

chatra dhārīana kau karahu bega nāsā.
I will soon destroy those that bear the canopy [Mughals].

apana dāsa kā dekhīahu aba tamāsā.132.
Now witness this spectacle of Your slave.132.

doharā.
Couplet.

taba kharaga tamāsā dekhīai hara durage abināsa.
Now behold the wonder of the sword, Divine Eternal Durga.

pakaṛa tega dusamana hatūṁ karahūṁ dharama prakāsa.133.
By wielding the sword and destroying the enemy I shall radiate the light of dharam.133.

hara bhagata bhagautī tisai kī jo raṇadhīra dharei.
Har Bhagat Bhagautī assists the one who remains composed on the battlefield.

tiha aṁga saṁga tuma lāga rahujo pāche paga na dharei.134.
You are beside the [Singh] who never retreats from the battlefield.134.[106]

chaupaī. [107]
Quartet.

khaqa chaṁda bhagavatī mahāṁ punīte.
These six *chhaṅds* of Bhagavatī are very auspicious.

tisa paṭhavata upajata paratīte.
The recitation of which generates firm belief.

iuṁ nisabāsara durage guna gāyaṁ.
By daily singing these praises of Durga.

tahi sahaje aṭala amara pada pāyaṁ.135.
Then equipoise and the state of eternal salvation is achieved.135.

yahi khasaṭaka chaṁda saṁpūrana bhayo.
The six Bhagavatī chhaṅds are now concluded.

tisa ucarata sagalā bharama gayo.
From this recitation it has expelled all doubt.

hari alakha īsarī bhī kripālaṁ.
The indescribable Hari, the Divine Mother has conferred Her grace.

tina dāsa āpanā kīo nihālaṁ.136.
Only then was Her slave exalted.136.

dūkha roga soga bhai miṭe kalesā.
Eradicating suffering, illness, sorrow, fear, and affliction.

bahu sukha upajai anada pravesā.
With abundant happiness and immersed in blissfulness.

ita bidhi durage kirapā dhārī.
In this way Durga has manifested Her grace.

tiha āpana dāsa kau līā ubārī.137.
Her slave has been taken into Her protection.137.

iti srī gobiṁda siṁgha viracite srī bhagavatī chaṁda khasaṭamaṁ samāpataṁma sata subhama sata.6.
Here the holy Gobind Singh has spoken the holy six verses of Bhagavatī, concluding auspiciously, the truth all truth.6.

The *Ugradantī* is a reference to the Holy Sword and feminine Divine who is 'the One with the fierce teeth', and appears in one of the earliest recensions of the *DG*, namely 'Takht Patna Sahib AD 1698' recension. The title *Devī jī kī Ustati* is also used for this composition. It is highly significant that an early composition from the time period of the Guru has been excised from the standard recension. This recension also incorporates handwritten pages of the Tenth Guru. The actual name of this composition varies and includes *Chhaṅd Chhakkā* and *Chhaṅd Chhakkā Bhagautī jū kā*; however, over time the text has adopted the name of *Ugradantī* which appears as the first line of the main text.[108]

There have been some translation of the *Ugradantī*, including one by Harjinder Singh Kanwal.[109] The author, who is a Namdhari, states that his community venerates this composition. Another brief translation of this text appears by in the *Sikh Review* by Harkrishan Singh.[110] The most recent commentary and translation appear in the *Journal of Punjab Studies* by Ami Shah.[111] The journal mistakingly makes the claim that Shah's version is the first English translation.

The transmission of this composition continues in other several eighteenth-century recensions of the *DG* but not the one attributed to Bhai Mani Singh. A recension known as the 'Sangrur' *bīṛh* also contained this composition. This manuscript seems to be from the early eighteenth century based on the compositions and internal features noted by scholars, but this manuscript is no longer extant. A manuscript of the *Sau Sākhī* dated AD 1714 also has the *Ugradantī* appended to it, which is highly significant. This composition also appears in other nineteenth-century *DG* recensions.[112]

The incident of the Devi in hagiographic texts is often linked with the apocryphal compositions, so we can assume that they were composed in or after AD 1696, and as a result they were not found in the 'Anaṅdpurī' recension but found in the later AD 1698 recension at Takht Patna Sahib (see Figure 2.7). The *Ugradantī* is discussed in detail by Kuir Singh in *Gurbilās Patishāhī 10* and also by Kesar Singh Chhibbar in his *Baṅsavlināmā*.[113] We also see a discussion by Pandit Singh Narotam in his *Srī Gurmat Niraṇai Sāgar*, and Kanh Singh Nabha also quotes this composition in his *Hum Hindū Nahiṅ*.[114]

The apocryphal compositions have verses that have important references to practices that are now only found within the Buddha Dal and Takht Hazur Sahib. The spirit which permeates these compositions is very much situated within their symbolic universe. One such practice is called *shastra pujā* or worship of weapons, and on Dussherā the *Chaṇḍī Pāṭh* was read by the Guru, and was also undertaken at Sri Akal Takht, prior to reform.[116] In Kuir Singh's work, his verses 123–30 read very much like portions of the three *Chaṇḍī* variant compositions and the *Ugradantī*.[117] Kanh Singh quotes a part of the *Ugradantī* in defence of Sikh identity, but he argues that the Guru did not write it.[118] He references Tara Singh Narotam,[119] where the argument about its authorship originates. Narotam was of the opinion that the *Ugradantī* was written by a devoted Sikh who knew Sikh theology, such as the third path, Khalsa, *amrit* (Khalsa initiation—*khaṇḍe kī pahul*), and so on. He believes this to be Sukha Singh of Patna Sahib. However, his theory would not explain the early date in the colophons at Takht Patna Sahib. From Narotam's comparison of language in the *DG*, which is pure Braj, he concludes that this composition

FIGURE 2.7 A Photograph of a Folio Showing the Opening of the *Ugradantī* from the 'Takht Patna Sahib' AD 1698 *DG* Manuscript[115]
Source: Giani Hardeep Singh.

is written by a Sikh. He argues that the Guru uses the words 'hamne' (I/One) and suchlike in *Akal Ustāti*, while in the compositions of the *Ugradantī* the word 'tuman' (You/Thou) is used. He argues that the *Ugradantī* is anti-Hindu and anti-Islam and against the message in the *AG*, and the pen-name 'Das Gobind' is not in context. He asserts that some of the compositions are influenced by Shi'a Islamic prophecies.[120] The manuscript Narotam bases his observation on is, according to him, the 'Sukha Singh' recension at Takht Patna Sahib. Considering that there are at least three extant manuscripts containing apocrypha at the *takht*, a number at Takht Hazur Sahib, and others in Panjab, this makes his argument implausible. Also see a later *DG* manuscript containing the *Chhakkā* commissioned by Maharaja Ranjit Singh (Figure 2.8). From the analysis of the manuscripts it becomes clear that the transmission took place from an early manuscript from the times of Guru Gobind Singh.

Saṅsāhara Sukhamanā

ika oaṁkar srī vāhagurū jī kī phate hai.
One Universal God, the Holy Wondrous Guru is Always Victorious.

srī akāla purakhu jī sahāi.
The Holy Akal Purakh is the Protector.
saṁsāhara sukhamanā.
Ambrosia amidst the World.[122]

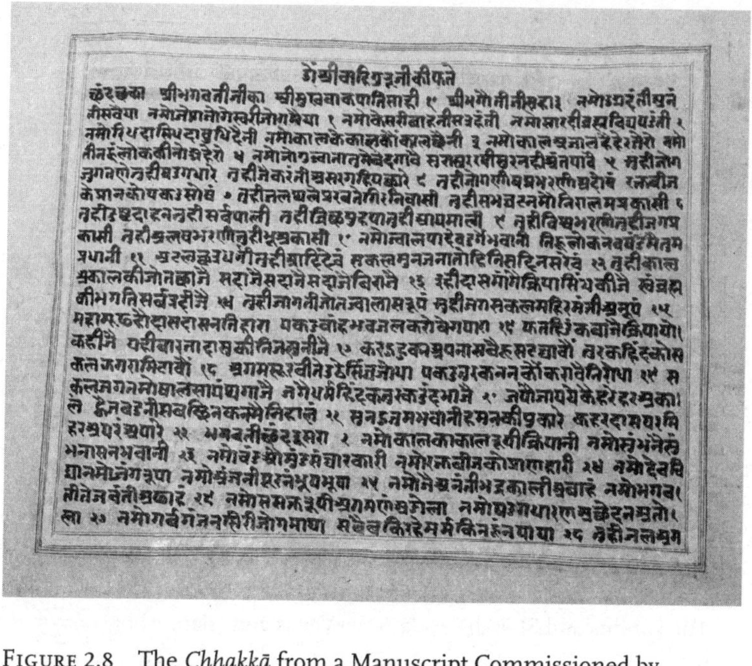

FIGURE 2.8 The *Chhakkā* from a Manuscript Commissioned by Maharaja Ranjit Singh at the British Library[121]
Source: The British Library Board, London, British Library, Mss. Panj. D6.

srī mukhavāka pātisāhī 10 rāga gauṛī.
From the Holy Oration of Verse by the Tenth Sovereign in Rāg Gauṛī.[123]

pauṛī.
[Literally a step, a type of stanza][124]

prithame srī niraṁkāra ko paranaṁ.
Firstly [I will] seek the support of the Holy Formless [Being].

phuni kichu bhagati rīta rasi baranaṁ.
Then the essence of some methods of devotion will be elucidated.

dīna daiāla pūranu atu suāmī.
Merciful to the humble and complete, you are the Master.

bhagati vachalu hari aṁtarijāmī.
[You are] the lover of Your devotees, Hari [You are] the knower of hearts.[125]

ghaṭi ghaṭi rahai dekhai nahī koī.
You reside in every heart, but nobody sees you.

jala thala rahai saraba mai soī.
You reside in the water and ground, and in all.

bahu beaṁtu aṁtu nahī pāvai.
You are without any limit nobody can reach Your end.

paṛi paṛi paṁḍita rāhu batāvai.1.
Reading and reading the Priests [Pandits] explain Your ways.1.

saloku [type of metric poetry].[126]
gahira gaṁbhīra gahīru hai aparaṁ apara apāra.
Deep, unfathomable, untraceable, is [the One] who is beyond all, and needs no support.

jina simariā tina pāiā gobiṁda kisana murār.1.
Whoever meditates on You, will achieve the beautiful Lord of the Universe, Murār.1.

soraṭhā. [A type of metric poetry].[127]
bācahi beda kateba paṁḍata sekha bakhānahī.
The Pandits and Sheikhs explain the Vedas and Islamic holy books.

rāhu japāvai bega manūā hari caraṇī dharahi.2.
The way to gain strength Oh mind is to seek the support of Hari's holy feet.2.

pauṛī.
cāra juga mahi yahi varatārā.
In the four ages was the arrangement.

paṛi paṛi paṁḍata deṁhi bīcārā.
Reading and reading the Pandits give explanations [that].

sīla sacu sati juga mahi boliā.
In the age of truth (*satiyuga*) the truthful conduct was said to be manifest.

daiā dharamu duāpara hoiā.
Compassion and righteousness took place in the second age (Dvapuryuga).

sata saṁtokha sīla sacu jānā.
Know that [in this age] to be truth, contentment, and pure conduct.

satajuga duāpari traitai mānā.
Know there to be the age of truth, then the second age, and the third (Tretayuga).

tīni janamu māhi iha bilāsā.
In the three ages was this tale.

daiā sīla sacu dharamu nivāsā.
That compassion, pure conduct, truth, and righteousness provided shelter.2.

saloku.
saṁtokha sadā sukhī sūrabīra sativaṁtā.
Those who practice contentment are always at peace, and brave warriors imbued with truth.

daiā dharama hari bhajana te bega milahi bhagavaṁtā.1.
Compassion and dharam come from devotion to Hari, will power comes from Bhagavant.1.

soraṭhā.
kisana murārī jānu nisa dina ghaṭi mai raci rahio.
Krishan Murārī is the very life, day and night, He resides in the hearts.

caraṇī rākhahu dhiāna gahira gaṁbhīra gaṁhīru hai.2.
Keep focus on the feet, of the One who is deep, Unfathomable, and Untraceable.2.

pauṛī.
kalijuga racio yahi varatārā.
In the dark age (Kaliyuga) the following is dealt.

dharama chāḍi adharama piārā.
Abandoning righteousness, unrighteousness is loved.

nāmu chāḍi āna kau rācahiṁ.
Abandoning the name [of God] there is repeated rowdiness.

dharama tiāga pāpa mahiṁ khācahiṁ.
Renouncing righteousness, people are absorbed in sin.

sacu kiṁcata jhūṭhu paradhānā.
There is less truth, falsehood is the chief.

kāma krodha lobha kā giānā.
There is much interest in lust, anger, and greed.

saca ḍūbai jhūṭhā tarai.
People who are truthful drown the false swim.

nīca kī sevā brahamaṇu karai.3.
The Brahmin serves the lowly.3.

saloku.
tīna juga muhatāja sata saṁtokh suca dharama ke.
Three ages felt the need for truth, contentment, purity, and righteousness.

aba āio kalajuga rāja jhūṭha lobhu paradhānu hai.1.
The reign of Kaliyuga has come, of greed and falsehood that are the leaders.1.

soraṭha.
daiā dharama ara dānu kalijuga maiṁ paradhānu hai.
Compassion, righteousness, and charity are chiefs in the age of darkness.

kalijuga bhī hairānu mere pahire bītate.2.
The age of darkness has surprised itself, that my age is in decay.2.

pauṛī.
patanī rākhai jīa panānā.
Keeping a wife, the men travel away [keep mistresses].

beṭe lo gahi bāpa hairānā.
The sons have sex, the fathers are surprised.

bhāī bhāva lobha ko jānai.
Brothers are just interested in greed.

rahati sadā jaise loka bigānai.
Their way of life is like they are all outsiders.

kāma krodha lobha hitakārī.
They are in love with lust, anger, and greed.

nārī chāḍi raciā paranārī.
Leaving their own women, they make [love] to another's wife.

isa juga mahi pākhaṁḍa paradhānā.
In this age, false show is leading.

kāma krodha lobha aru pāpa.4.
Lust, anger, greed, and sin.4.

saloku.
sācā sāvaṁī saca mai basai sācā mana kā bol.
True is the Master, in truth does he reside, true is saying [His mantra] of the mind.

aṁtara tere ravi rahiā jiu kasatūrī kol.1.
The Sun resides inside You, like the scent gland in the deer.1.

soraṭhā.
yahi to kalijuga nāhi kalijuga ke paraṁnāva hai.
This is not Kaliyuga itself, but the intention of Kaliyuga.

guṇa kalijuga māhi hātho hāthī niberasī.2.
The virtues of Kaliyuga is that a person is ruined by his own action.2.

pauṛī.
suno saṁtoyahi bacana hamārā.
Listen saints to this instruction of mine!

trai juga mai thāihu varatārā.
In the three ages this was what was given.

jina sevaka ne sevā kīnī.
The servants [of Akal] undertook service.

ūcī padavī tribhavaṇa dīnī.
In the three worlds they were given a high status.[128]

kari tapa sāhai nihacai cīnī.
They did great penance, without any doubt [Akal] graced them.

brahamā bisana mahādeva kīnī.
Brahma, Vishnu, and Shiva did this [penance].

durigama mātā bhī paracaṁḍā.
Durga the Mother was also great shining light.

caudaha bhavanā phirai navakhaṁḍā.5.
The fourteen worlds and nine realms circumambulate [them].5.

saloku.
bisana nāma hirade dhare brahama dharama ati cīn.
Take the name of Vishnu in Your heart, the dharam of Brahma, and its great symbols.

siṁgha bāhanī māta hai mahādeva parabīn.1.
The army of Singhs is [with the] the Mother, the great Divine one knows all.1.

soraṭhā.
ih mahātapasī jana rākhe ūcī ṭhaura hai.
These servants of great penance have a very high place.

kīnī juga paravana cāra juga mahi jānīai.2.
[They] did this in the ages and were the elect, in all four ages they are known.2.

pauṛī.
dasa avatahara prabhū jī kīneṁ.
Prabhu made the ten manifestations [avatār].

bhagatāṁ kārana garabha jūna līneṁ.
For the sake of the devotees, they were conceived and took birth.

bisana rūpa dhara bhagata udhāre.
Vishnu's form ascended and aided the devotees.

bhagatāṁ kārana asura siṁghāre.
For the devotees, the demons were destroyed.

cāra beda brahame ne kīne.
The four Vedas did Brahma make.

patita mahāṁ giāna kara cīne.
Even the fallen were bestowed with great knowledge.

paṛi paṛi paṁḍita rāhu batāvai.
Reading and reading the Pandits tell of the path.

saṭha sākhata giānu na pāvai.6.
These fools are rigid; they do not even gain a little wisdom.6.

saloku.
beda bacana mana mai dharo brahama vāka paravān.
Impart into the mind the instruction in the Vedas; the speech of God is greatest.

jina jana hari jāniā nahī so mahāṁ agiānī giān.1.
That being that does not know Hari, know that person to be greatly ignorant.

soraṭhā.
mūṛi na jānai koi beda bacana paravāna hai.
They do not know anything, the teachings of the Vedas is very great.

majina jana jāniā soi gobiṁda ke hīai basai.2. [129]
Those servants that know Gobind reside in [him].2.

pauṛī.
mahādeva devana ko devan.
The greatest Divinity the Supreme Deity of deities.

nisa dina jana karate vakī sevan.
Day and night the beings are doing his service.

jina seviā tina hī baru pāiā.
The ones that serve him receive the blessings.

pārabrahama prabha nihacai āiā.
[and] Comes the faith in the Lord, *Pārabraham.*

caṁḍī mātā tūṁ carapaṭi nārī.
Mother Chaṇḍī, You are the most esteemed woman.

tīna loka jina prithamī tārī.
The one who uplifts the Earth and three worlds.

suāmī saṁta dhiāvahi dhuna dharaiṁ.
The ascetics and Saints meditate on Your melody.

cāri juga mai jai jai karaiṁ.7.
In the four ages Your victory resounds.7.

saloku.
devī devana pūjate autārana līne sāth.
The Devi and Devas worship You; the manifestations [avatārs] get Your aid.

joga māiā jagatāranī kīnī dīna nāth.1.
The Mother of Divine union, the protector of the world, the shelter of the humble.1.

soraṭhā.
siṁgha bāhanī māta cārajuga mai simarate.
The Mother of the army of Lions, the four ages remember You.

jana devana pūjata yāhi iha māiā jagu tāranī.2.
The angelic beings worship You, You unveil the illusionary world.2.

pauṛī.
pārabrahama beaṁta akāla.
The great Creator is infinite and timeless.

bhagati sudāmā kīo nihālā.
He caused [his] devotee Sudamā to be in ecstasy.

jana dīpana kai griha bhojanu līā.
The one who took food in the house of Dīpan.

dīna daiāla kirapā nidha kīā.
You are merciful to the humble, You are called the merciful treasure.

kabīru bhagatu bhaiā adhikāī.
The devotee Kabir was made great [by You].

nāmadeva kī hari chāna chavāī.
Namdev carefully sieved through Hari's [name].

saṁsā meṭa bhio hari nāī.
[He] eradicated [his] doubt by repeating the name of Hari.

saina bhagati kī paija rakhāī.
The devotee Sain's honour was protected.

ravidāsa dāsa jana kete gunā.
The servant [of God], Ravidas, had so many virtues.[130]

pāra na pāvai hari simarani binā.
The weight [of inner pollution] cannot be lifted without the remembrance of Hari.

cāra juga nihacai nidha pāiā.
In the four ages this is the treasure for those with belief.

nānaka janu hari caranī lāiā.
Says Nanak, those servants get a [place] at the feet of Hari.8.

saloka.
dīna daiāla kirapā karahu sabha bhagatana hoia anaṁuda.
Oh merciful to the humble, be graceful that all devotees are in bliss.

kāraja sabha pūre pavahi pali pali bhaji gobiṁdā.1.
That all their affairs are resolved, and each moment they meditate on Gobind.1.

soraṭhā.
jugata jagata kī dekhu kāma krodha ati lobha mai.
Look, joined is the world to lust, anger, and so much greed.

ṭarai na karama kī rekh āna dhiāna bhūle phirahi.2.
They run away from good deeds, with their attention elsewhere, they wander around lost.2.

pauṛī.
mai adhīna dāsana ko dāsā.
I am the obedient slave of slaves [of Akal].

mai janu gobiṁda kī rākho āsā.
I am the servant Gobind and place my hopes [in You].

bhūle loka mujha prabha jī kahai.
The lost people say I am the respected Lord.

mahāṁ aprādhī pāpa mai rahaiṁ.
They are great criminals, and live in sin.

bhūle loka mujha kahai aṁtarajāmī.
The lost people say I am the knower of hearts.

vā koṁ naraka na hoigā yāmī.
They will find a place in hell, and no other place.

ita uta vā ko dhuna nahīṁ dhiānā.
Here or there they will not meditate on the sound [of the *shabad*].

je kou kahai mujhai jānī jānā.9.
If someone does say it, they know everything.9.

saloku.
jānī jāna karate phirahi samajha tināhi mana māhi.
Saying they know everything they will wander around, but they do not understand inside their minds.

aṁta kāla ve naraka mai nisa dina bemukha pāṁhi.1.
In the moment of death, they who have turned their backs [on the Guru] will be put into hell forever.1.

soraṭha.
mahā aparādhī loka karanahāra aurai kahahi.
The great criminal sinning masses will lose control of their senses and say.

vahu karana karāvani joga e loga joga sabha naraka ke.2.
'We are the ones that do only', these people are worthy of going to hell.2.

pauṛī.
suno loko tuma dharo dhiānā.
Listen people with great attention and focus.

gura apane kauṁ hari janu jānuā.
Know Your Guru as a servant of Hari.

ahi kalajuga yaha kali paradhānā.
In this age of Kaliyuga ignorance is chief.[131]

pākhaṁḍī rāja bhajanī bhomānā.
False Kings will be engrossed in sensuality.

nīca te ūca ūca nahī koī.
The lowly will be high, and nobody will actually have dignity.

kāma krodha lobhi ati hoī.
Lust, anger, greed will affect most of the people.

sabhi saṁto prabhu eko jāno.
All Saints, see the Lord as One.

aurana dūjā koī jāno.10.
There is no other or second [for them].10.

saloku.
bhūle kāhe tuma phiro aru bemukh kāhe hogā.
Lost person why do you wander, why do you turn your back [on the Guru]?

mai dāsana ko dāsaho tuma bhūle kāhe logā.1.
I am the slave of slaves, why are you lost, Oh people.1.

soraṭha.
jo tuma samajhahu aura brahama hatiā tuma koṁ parai.
You try to instruct others, but [it is like] murdering God, you should read.

na pāvo ṭhora darasani te bemukha paro.2.
There will be no place [of rest], and you will not behold the vision [of Akal], as your back is turned.2.

pauṛī.
ika saṁtani pākhaṁḍi ati kīnā.
One saint is greatly pretending, and being false.

dharama āpanā aura ko dīnā.
He gives away his own dharam to another.

nāma chāḍi āna kau miliā.
Giving up the name [he] prefers to meet with the rowdy.

janama khoi kuṭaṁba saṁga galiā.
He loses the [profit] of this life, to [his] family he is attached.

gura rākhe pākhanḍī bāu.
Guru protects us from false love.

loka pujāvai dunā cāu.
People worship falsehood with enthusiasm.

sukha saṁniāsī khuṁḍīā pūjā.
They give comfort to the renunciates, and worship the shaven-headed ones.

koū būjhe ko ūna būjhā.11.
Some understand [this mystery], others do not solve it.11.

saloku.
chai darasana chatīsa pākhaṁḍa hai apanī apanī ṭhaurā.
The six *darshanas* [schools of Indian Philosophy], the thirty-six *smritis* [vast corpus of traditional Sanskrit scripture on various subjects] are pretence, and each has its own place.

rāma nāmu ko japati hai japane mai bhī aurā.1.
By repeating the name of Ram in the mind [you will know].

soraṭhā.
jina kau mile gupāla satigura soī jānīai.
Who wishes to meet Gopal will know this from the true Guru.

sadā rahe kirapāla nisa dina mana ḍolai nahīṁ.
Who always remains merciful day and night; whose mind never loses faith.2.

pauṛī.
isa kala kā suno para vaisa.
Listen to the take of this dark [age].

brahamana chatrī sūdra baisa.
There are the priests, warriors, labourers, and traders.

brahamana chatrī kī kahī na jāi.
Brahmins and warriors cannot be called so.

baisa sūdra mai bisana bhagatāi.
The traders and labourers are the devotees of God.

brahammna chatrī dhūrama kī hīnā.
The priests and warriors are devoid of dharam.

suciā taji asuca pradhāna.
They leave the truth [cleanliness], and make impurity the chief.

brahama chatrī ūca te ūcā.
The priests and warriors [think] they are higher than high.

bhrishaṭa rūpa rahita besūcā.12.
[Even though] they are filthy in form, and live unclean.12.

saloka.
mānasa janam tumo ko dīā nāma dāna rakahu nītā.
This human birth has been given to you, meditate on the name and give in charity daily.

dharama choḍi ānai japahu eha sarīra anītā.1.
By leaving righteousness, and repeatedly blabbering, it is an injustice to this body.1.

soraṭhā.
dharama apane kau chāḍi pūjai jata malecha kī.
By leaving one's own dharam and worshipping the caste of impure invaders [Mughals].

jete hohi dhanāḍi suci kiriā dūnī tajahi.2.
Those who are wealthy have abandoned the two pure actions [compassion and righteousness].2.

pauṛī.
isa kali mai brahamanu gurū kahāvai.
In this [age of] ignorance, people call the Brahmins, the Guru.

karahi pākhaṁḍa brahamaṁḍi dikhāvai.
Who perform false shows to the whole universe.

sikha saṁtana kau deha upadesuā.
They give the order to the Sikhs and Saints.

chāḍoja caukā hohu malechā.
Leave the holy cooking square, you are impure.

aṁdari gaiā bāhari bhī jāvā.
Inside they have lost, as well as outside.

suca asuca nāe ko bhāvā.
Clean and unclean are both treated the same.

daiā dharama tuma chaḍo nāhī.
Do not leave compassion and righteousness.

saṁta milai japo mana māhī.13.
Meet the saints and repeat [the name] inside your mind.13.[132]

saloka.
karatā purakhu hīai dharo aru hīarā rākhahu sudha.
Inside your heart focus on the Creative Being, and keep your heart spotless.

mana mai hari hari hari bhajoṁ harigobiṁda kolu lūja.1.
In the mind vibrate on Hari Hari Hari, fight alongside Hari Gobind.1.

soraṭhā.
tuma kāhe bhūle mūṛa suca kiriā hari bhajana te.
Why have you forgotten Oh fool, the true action is to vibrate on Hari.

tuma mata jānoṁ kūṛe satigura ke parabhā vahai.
Know the construct of your mind [in Kaliyuga] to be false, this [*bhajan*] is known through the true Guru.2.

pauṛī.
kali ke loka hota akaramī.
The people of the Kali [age] perform bad actions.

chatra brahamaṇa hota adharamī.
The priests and warriors are unrighteous.

tīna juga mai suca paradhān.
In the three [other] ages truth is chief.

aba suca kiriā kī hotī hānu.
Then when will the true action come?

jina gura tuma koṁ maṁtaru dīnā.
When the Guru gives to you the *mantra*.

vahu mahā aparādhī prabha hī kīnā.
Those great criminals and sinners, the Lord will do this [purify them].

gur giāna dāna isanānā.
By the Guru's wisdom of charity, and bathing.

sabha te ūcā prabha kā nāmā.14.
Higher than all is the name of God.14.

saloku.
mai manukh deha kāmī kuṭali aparādhī mati hīna.
I gave this body to the human, but they have become lustful, twisted, criminal, and mindless.

mahā narakha mai parata hai loka kahai mujha dīna.1.
The greatest hell is [to sleep with] another's woman, but people say they were weak.1.

sorațhā.
mahā aparādhī patita dāsana kau dāsana kahai.
The great criminals, the fallen, and will say we are the slave of the slaves [of God].

vāke janama na jāta bharama karama bhūle phirahi.2.
All their births are without any status, in doubt, and acting falsely, they wander around lost.2.

pauṛī.
suca asuca kau eko jānai.
See purity and impurity as the same.

eko eke eko hī mānai.
There is only the One alone, believe in only the One.

bhaina bhāī māī aru bāpā.
[Like a] Sister, Brother, Mother, and Father.

eko jānai tribhavani nāthā.
There is only One master in the three worlds.

garī chuhārā jaisā naja.
Like there is a seed in the date, like life in food.

jaisā saṁdalā taisā piājā.
Like sandalwood, so is the onion.[133]

saraba mī kā eko khelu.
All is the grace and play of the One.

karaṇihāra soṁ rākhahu melu.15.
The Great doer, keep us unified with You.15.

saloku.
suci kiriā ati malīna dono eko jān.
The cleansing techniques and great filth know these to be the same.

saraba mī raci rahio hari ke ghaṭi paravān.1.
All is grace that has been made [by Hari], [keeping] inside the [name] of Hari is the greatest.

soraṭhā.
jina jana jāniā eka suci kiriā vāke mana basai.
Those that know the One, is the true cleansing, to keep the mind [on the One].

kachū nā vākoṁ veka mana maiṁ dubidhānā rahai.2.
Do not look at the differences, so that the duality of the mind remains.2.

pauṛī.
vāhagurū japate sabha koī.
Vahiguru is repeated by only a few in many.[134]

yākā aratha samajhai janu soī.
Those servants that repeat it, will understand the meaning as.

vāvā vahī apara apārā.
[the first letter] Va is great, the infinite.

hāhā hiradai hari hari vīcārā.
[the second letter] Ha is in the heart, to understand and contemplate Hari Hari.

gagā gobiṁda simaranu ati kīnā.
[the third letter] Ga, Gobind, is the great remembrance.

rārā rāma nāma mani cīnā.
[the fourth letter] Ra is the name of Ram, is understood in the mind.

ina achara kā samajhana hāru.
If these letters are not understood [by somebody].

rākhai dubidhā hoi khuārā.16.
They will keep in duality, and lose faith.16.

saloku.
cāra akhara tisa kao bhale mana ko dharai uṭhāi.
The four letters are high, keep them in the awareness of the mind.

rāma nāma ke nāma para sadā rahe lapaṭāi.1.
Fill yourself with the name of Ram, and always remain immersed [in it].1.

sorațhā.
cāra achara paradhānā birale hari jana cīnī.
These four letters are the most high, only the rare beings of Hari understand.

ika rāte jana paravāna ikanā pațana subhāva hai.2.
One exalted being is repeating it; one is driven to read it.2.

paurī.
vāhagurū japate hari log.
Vahiguru is repeated by the people of Hari.

vākoṁ harakha na kabahū sogā.
They remain in happiness and never in sorrow.

ika bāhari bhajai aṁdari mana dhrohu.
They vibrate on this [endless] Ocean, inside they are attracted to it.

jhuka jhuka nivahi kahāvai niramohā.
They lower themselves and are humble and when they speak, it is with detachment.

jihabā rațahi laihi hari nāmā.
Their tongues repeat again and again the name of Hari.

aṁdarahu khoțe dhuna nahīṁ dhāmā.
Those who are divided inside, [the mantra] does not sound in them.

phira kai jora lokana bharamāvai.
Again and again they try their strength, these people are in doubt.

bharama bharama pavai janama gavāvaiṁ.17.
In many doubts upon doubts they lose this birth.17.

saloka.
jihabārațiha aṁdara phațahi aru mana mai rākhai dhrohā.
The tongue keeps moving, the mind flies, fluttering like a bird's wing, the mind is satisfied.

vāha gurū vahi japata hai pāra na pāvai koi.1.
Repeating Vahiguru, nobody can know [God's] end or limit.1.

sorațhā.
achara hai iha cāra bāra bāra kahate phirahi.
These are the four letters, again and again say them, then.

kabahūṁ na pāvai pāra jā kai mana dubidhā rahai.2.
Otherwise the other side cannot be reached, while there is duality in the mind.2.

pauṛī.
jāṁ kai mana mai dubidhā rahai.
If in the mind there remains duality.

cāra achara vākoṁ yahi kahai.
Then say all of these four letters [i.e. Vahiguru].

vavā vaira dhana rākhai ṭhāi.
Va [gets rid] of enmity, and gives wealth.

hāhā haumai harakha mai pāi.
Ha [gets rid] of egotism and gives happiness.

gagā guna avaguna sabha khovai.
Ga gives virtues and removes all virtuelessness.

rārā rāma nāma āvana nahī devai.
Ra is the name of Ram and will stop you coming [back into rebirth].

cāra chara dubidhā mai paṛai.
The four letters will put aside duality.

vāṁkī pūrī kabahūṁ nā paṛai.18.
When complete, then there will no more falls.18.

saloku.
pūrī tabahū parata hai mana mai saca nivās.
The way is complete, when the mind becomes the resting place of truth.

ikanā kapaṭi subhāva hai ika kapaṭikī bādhe rās.1.
When there is one true love, then the One great essence comes forth.1.

soraṭhā.
bisavār ghātī mitra dhroha akiratighaṇā niṁdaka ghane.
The killers of faith, false attraction, ungratefulness, and the dark cloud of back-biting.

lālaca ḍūbe moha ita uta vāko kachu nahī.
In greed and attachment they drown, neither here nor there do they have anything.2.

pauṛī.
vāha gurū ke achara cāri.
Vahiguru has four letters.

satasaṁgati mili dharo piār.
In the meeting of the true sangat show your love [of Vahiguru].

sāce mana achara jo paṛai.
With a true mind whoever reads the letters.

vāko kabahū na saṁsā paṛai.
That person can never fall into doubt.

saṁsā paṛai rākhai mana dhrohā.
It keeps the doubts at bay, and protects the mind from false attraction.

vāṁkī pūrī kabahū na hoi.
Otherwise [the mind] can never become complete.

apanī khāi bigānī cita dharai.
You eat yourself up, while being conscious about another.

apane hātha āpa hī marai.19.
From your own hands, you are killing yourself.19.

saloku.
vāhagurū jihabā raṭahi mani mai rākhaiaurā.
While saying Vahiguru with the tongue, and remembering someone else in the mind.

sukha bhāgai dukha mai parai kabahū na pāvai ṭhaurā.1.
Peace leaves, we fill with pain, and can never find a place [of rest].1.

soraṭha.
vāhagurū siu khela mana kī dubidhā dūri karā.
Meet the master Vahiguru, and the duality of the mind is put far away.

sadā raho hari melu hari caraṇī citu lāgi rahai.
Always remain with Hari, and always put [His] feet in your heart.2.

pauṛī.
jo jo kathiā rākhu parasidhā.
Those that recite [Vahiguru] are protected, and are great and famous.

nirāqa bāṇī kī suṇahu navanidhā.
On hearing the profound utterance [that is Vahiguru] one procures the nine treasures.

vāhu niraṁkāra niravairu nirālā.
The wondrous formless One, without enmity, who is completely free from the material creation.

kānana kuṁḍala nainā bisālā.
The One with very beautiful ears, locks, and eyes.

disaṭi na āvai dūra te dūri.
He cannot be seen, He is so far.

samājhi dekha tūṁ rahe hajūri.
Understand and look, you will see He is [also] ever present.

parite parai parai pare hai.
He is further than the four directions, and so far.

hai hajūri dūri nahī nerai.20.
Yet [He is the] everpresent One, He is not near nor far.20.

doharā.
Couplet.

aṁta na kinahī pāiā lakha caurāsī jūni.
Nobody knows the limits of the 8.4 million beings of creation.

jini lāiā tini pāiā hari caraṇī mana pūrā.1.
Who is guided this way they find Hari's feet and become complete.1.

soraṭhā.
kudarati ke bali jāu dūra te dūri hajūri hai
I am a sacrifice to the Creative power, so far, [yet He] is ever present.

saca rākhahu mana māhi hari jana hirakha na rākhī.
Keep purity in the mind, do not speak ill of the servants of Hari [saints].2.

pauṛī.
muṁḍīā muṁḍata hoi kai rahiā.
The shaven-headed one after being shaven, lives like this.

nisa dila rāma nāmi citu gahiā.
Hold day and night the name of Ram in your consciousness.

chudra asaṁta gura lopa rati karai.
The weak fraudulent saints and gurus hide and [commit] murder.

sabha akāratha simarana paraharai.
All is wasted when one does not remember [God] and puts this [contemplation] to the side.

saṁniāsī siva siva hari japai.
The renunciates say Shiva Shiva and meditate on Hari.

dehī sāṛi nagana hoi pacai.
They burn their bodies and stay naked, as an excuse.

choḍi māiā saṁniāsī hoiā.
Leaving materialism they have become renunciates.

māiā mamatā grahasata te khoiā.21.
[However] they are attached to materialism, and take off the householders.21.

doharā.
mumḍīā mamuḍata hoiābāra haqī ke lāi.
The shaven-headed ones are shaved, they set up shop outside [put on a show].

mana kī dubidhā nā miṭai sabho akāratha jātā.1.
The duality of their mind does not go, all is wasted [in vain].1.

soraṭhā.
jaṭādhārī samniāsīāsa ju rākhai eka kī.
Those with matted hair, renunciates, [should] keep hope in the One.

sirajana hari ke pāsi pākhamḍī parama dukha pāvahī.
In front of the Creator Hari, the false ones will suffer immense pain.2.

pauṛī.
ika jogī jugati joga kī rākhahi.
One yogi is joined and keeps in union.

madhama āsana nisa dinu vai bhākhahi.
In the middle posture, day and night they kill the vices.

ridha kī mūrati ridha phailāvahi.
They become the form of perfection, and are in complete absorption.

hari kā nāma nā kabahūm pāvahi.
[but] They can never gain the name of Hari.

eka puja pamtha hari hari mai rahai.
There is one pathway of worship, to keep near to Hari Hari.

apane kesa āpa hī gahai.
They remove their own kesh themselves.

kesa gahehī hari hāthi nā āvai.
They lose their kesh and Hari is never in their hands [realized].

hari simarana binu mukati na pāvai.22.
Without remembrance of Hari there is no liberation.22.

doharā.
jogī jugati na jānīākisa bidhi milai gupālu.
The yogi does not know the way, what way can Gopal be met?

mana kī dubidhā dūri karibega milahi diālu.
The duality of the mind has to be put far away, the strength comes from the mercy of Hari.1.

soraṭhā.
sīla choḍi karitā tātākhahi bāla ukhāṛahi hāth kari.
Leaving good conduct, one has to face the inferno, the strength leaves our hands.

hari jana oi nā milahi una kā milaṇā dūri hai.
The servants of Hari will not be met; to meet them is far away.2.

pauṛī.
ikanā sikha bhaiā biuhārā
One Sikh works hard.

bāṇī gāvahi mili akhara cāri.
Sings bāṇī, and joins the four letters [says Vahiguru].

sikha saṁta sabha ikaṭhe hohī.
The Saintly Sikhs get together.

paṛi bāṇī jhuki pairī pavahī.
They read bāṇī and bow low and touch each other's feet [in humility].

ika sāce sikha sāca mai rahai.
These true Sikhs keep in the truth.

pala pala rāma nāma vai kahaiṁ.
With each and every breath they praise the name of Ram.

ika māri hāṁka ūce paṛahī.
One makes a show of reading out loudly.

aṁdari kapaṭu sāṁcu mukhi kaṛahī.23.
This makes the inner entry to truth, narrower.23.[135]

doharā.
ūcā paṛana kichu nahī ghaṭi aṁdari paṛa nāmu.
There is little in reading loudly, inside you read the name.

jiu machulī jala pīvatī hari hari bhaju mana rāmā.1 .
Like the fish drinks water, vibrate on the name of Hari Hari, and give the mind peace.1.

soraṭhā.
mana hī aṁdari pāpu sācu bhī mana mai rahai.
In the mind there is sin, but in the mind there is also the truth.

aisā japu tūṁ jāpu mana mai saṁsā nā rahai.2.
Recite the [mantra] in such a way that the doubts of the mind cannot remain.2.

pauṛī.
hari jī hari jana kai mani āvai.
Hari, comes into the minds of Hari's being [devotee].
daiā karata kachu bāra na lāvai.
Giving His grace He comes in no time.

jo karanī karatai karī bidha karī.
Whatever He does, the Creator does it in His own way.

apanai hāthi likhi masataki dharī.
With His own hand He writes the destiny and records it on the forehead.

bhāṁvanī pāṁḍa vahi vaṁcali gale.
The hopeful Pandav's got lost in the Himalayas.

harī caṁda nīca jala bhare.
Hari Chand gave the low class some water [filled].

rāvaṇi isatrī jāṁkī harī.
Ravan took the woman [Sita] far away.

kāṭata sīsa nā lāgī gharī.24.
His head was cut off in no time.24.

doharā.
hari jana hari kau arādhiā nāle līno boD.
The servants of Hari remember Hari each moment and also take knowledge.

kichu simaranu kichu asura hui līno hari pramodh.1.
With a little remembrance, there is some effect, taking the [name of] Hari there is joy.1.[136]

soraṭhā.
āndinā parai arathu dharamu na apanā chāḍīai.
Every day read this exposition; do not leave your dharam.

bahuri milai hari tabu jo gatihoi sarīra mai.
Then meeting Hari again, who is manifest inside your body.

pauṛī.
hari simaranu prahalāda udhāre.
By the remembrance of Hari, Prahalad was protected.

prahalāda udhāri harinākasa māre.
Prahalad was protected, Harnakash was killed.

hari simaranu manukha deha pāī.
By the remembrance of Hari, the human body was obtained.

āna japo sabha bhagati gavāī.
By repeating [the name of another], all devotion [and merit gained] is lost.

hari simarani jamadūta na āvai.
By the remembrance of Hari, the messengers of death cannot approach.

hari simarani sata saṁgati pāvai.
By the remembrance of Hari, the true sangat is found.

hari simaranu hota bhagati bilāsu.
By the remembrance of Hari, there is bliss of devotion.

hari jana ke ghaṭi hari karai nivāsu.25.
In the heart of the being of Hari, Hari resides.25.

doharā.
simaranu sabha te ūca hai aru ūca nīca dhari dhiānu.
This remembrance is the highest, think and focus on what is a high or low [practice].

hari guna ghaṭi mai raci rahio hari karanī paravān.1.
Inscribe the virtues of Hari in your heart, the power of Hari is great.

soraṭhā.
japata raho dinu rāti sāce mana so raci rahai.
Repeat [the name] day and night, keep the truth in mind.

hari jana bali bali jāta tisa simarana sukhu pāiai.
I am a sacrifice to the being of Hari, who knows the peace of remembrance.

pauṛī.
hari kai simarani bharamu sabha jāi.
With the remembrance of Hari, all doubts flee.

hari kai simarani sadā sukha pāi.
With the remembrance of Hari, there is always peace.

hari kai simarani anaṁda sukha hoi.
With the remembrance of Hari, there is bliss and happiness.

hari kai simarani maila sabhi khoi.
With the remembrance of Hari, all filth is removed.

hari ke simarani koṭa pāpa jāhi.
With the remembrance of Hari, millions of sins are erased.

hari kai simarani basai mana māhi.
With the remembrance of Hari, [He] will reside in the mind.

hari kai simarani dūta dukha jāi.
With the remembrance of Hari, enemies and pain flee.

hari kai simarani paramagati pāi.26.
With the remembrance of Hari, the highest state is achieved.26.

doharā.
simari simari jana simarate simara tara hai mana māhi.
By remembering again and again, the beings who practise this, find [God in] their being.

ika mani hoi kai simarani sācī padavī pāhi.1.
By having single-pointedness of mind, and remembering, the true state is achieved.1.

soraṭhā.
simarana karahu nisaṁga raṁgu prabhū kā dekhi lehu.
Become detached by remembering, and see the colours of Prabhu.

nā tuma karahu duraṁga hari jana harakhu na rākhī.
Do not become two colours, by having resentment to the beings [Saints] of Hari.

pauṛī.
musalamānu musalamu īmānu.
The Muslims and the Muslims Imams.

kare baṁdagī paṛai kurānā.
Practice devotion and read the Qu'ran.

sidaku rākhi nivāja gujāre.
Keeping faith and reading the *niwaz*.

tīhe roje pharaju utārai.
Keeping fasts and doing their [Islamic] duties.

dīnadāra sidaku āla akīdai.
Being pious, keeping faith, and not drinking alcohol.

pala pala dama dama nāmu mani cīdai.
With each moment, on each breath, taking the name in the mind.

siphata paikaṁbara kī rākhai mana māhi.
Praising the Prophet and keeping him in mind.

cāra yāra para bali bali jāhi. 27.
Forever being a sacrifice to the four friends of Prophet Mohammed.27. [137]

doharā.
musalamāna suī jānīai kalamāṁ paṛai mana māhi.
Recognize a Muslim to be one who recites the *Kalama* within his mind.

dīna mahaṁmmada ke nāma pari hari jana bali bali jāhi.1.
Taking the name of the religion of Prophet Mohammed, who is a sacrifice to the servants of Hari.1.

soraṭhā.
kāphara beīmāna dīna dunīā kai jaradarū.
The non-believers are dishonourable and are pale-faced in this world and the next.

hiṁdū musalamāna sabha karanī paravāna hai.
The actions of the Hindu and Muslim are well known.

pauṛī.
isu kala mai suca kiriā jānu.
In this age of Kaliyuga know the truth about what occurs.

brahamana suca kiriā paravānu.
The Brahmins who are known for their pure rituals.

bakarā mārai jīvatai khovai.
They kill the male goat, and kill life.

lāi premu māsa kau dhovai.
They take their beloved meat and wash it.

jaba vahu māsu bhāga tayārā.
When this meat has been prepared.

taba jevaṇa baiṭhe sabha kuṛiārā.
Then the partakers sit, they are all false!

dekhahu caukā bhiṭai kāi.
Look how they eat in their sacred square.

hāḍa cāmu khāṇe teṁ jāi.28.[138]
Coming to eat the skins and bones, then leave.28.

doharā.
caukā dehi banāi kai brahamana ati balivānā.
The Brahmins and warriors make the sacred square.

hāḍa cicoṛahi kāga jiuṁ lapaṭi rahe jiu suānā.1.
They eat the bones like crows, and their tongues hang out like dogs.1.

soraṭhā.
hāḍa māsu tuma khāhu suca kiriā tuma ḍhūṁḍhate.
Why are you eating meat and bones, you are forgetting pure actions.

hari jana iha suca nāhi dharama apane kau khovate.
For the servants Hari this is not dharam, why lose one's own honour?

pauṛī.
hari kī karanī rākhahu āsā.
By the power of Hari, keep your hopes.

hari kī karanī mani bisavāsā.
By the power of Hari, keep faith in mind.

hari kī karanī rahai niramohā.
By the power of Hari, stay detached.

hari kī karanī rākhai mani dhrohā.
By the power of Hari, keep the mind free from injury.

hari kī karanī japu tapa karai.
By the power of Hari, keep reciting and do penance on [the name].

hari kī karanī naraka so parai.
By the power of Hari, remove us from hell.

hari kī karanī rahai sukha vāsā.
By the power of Hari, allow one to stay happy.

hari kī karanī phirai udāsā.
By the power of Hari, people wander detached.

hari kī karanī jogu kamāvai.
By the power of Hari, practise yoga.

hari kī karanī cita prabha siuṁ lāvai.
By the power of Hari, focus your awareness on Prabhu.

hari kī karanī rāju sabhu bhaiā.
By the power of Hari, all kingdoms are obtained.

binu simaranu akāratha gaiā.
Without the remembrance of Hari, the opportunity is lost.

hari kī karanī jasu saṁsāri.
By the power of Hari, are the enjoyments of the world.

hari kī karanī darada bikāra.
By the power of Hari, are the pains and vices.

hari kī karanī dharati akāsā.
By the power of Hari, are the earth and sky.

hari karanī jala pauna nivāsā.
By the power of Hari, reside water and air.

hari kī karanī bhajanu ati hoi.
By the power of Hari, devotion is perfected.

hari kī karanī paramabudhi hoi.
By the power of Hari, one obtains enlightenment.

hari kī karanī bhaio bhikhāra.
By the power of Hari, some are beggars.

hari kī karanī bhāi upakārī.
By the power of Hari, is there charity.

hari kī karanī mailudhovai.
By the power of Hari, is the filth cleaned.

hari kī karanī bīju dharamu bovai.
By the power of Hari, are the seeds of dharam planted.

hari kī karanī dasa autāra.
By the power of Hari, are the ten avatārs.[139]

hari kī karanī mukati duārā.
By the power of Hari, do we find the door of liberation.

hari kī karanī srisaṭi upajāe.
By the power of Hari, is the creation manifest.

hari kī karanī satigura pāe.
By the power of Hari, we find the true Guru.

hari kī karanī citu caranī lāe.
By the power of Hari, our hearts join to [his] feet.

hari kī karanī suraga mahi jāi.
By the power of Hari, we go to the heavenly realms.

hari kī karanī naraka mahi pāi.
By the power of Hari, we go to the realms of hell.

hari kī karanī kāraju sabhu hoi.
By the power of Hari, our works are accomplished.

hari kī karanī pāpa mailu khoi.29.
By the power of Hari, the filth of sin is removed.29.

doharā.
hari karaṇā paravānu aru karāvana jogu.
Whatever Hari does is known, and [Hari] is capable.

jo kichu kīā su hari kīā nisa dina hari jana bhogu.1.
Whatever is done is done well by Hari, each day Hari joins with his servants.

soraṭhā.
hari jana hari ārādha kāraja sabha pūre pavahi.
The servants of Hari remember him, all their affairs are resolved.

mahā tapasī sādha hari caraṇī citu lāgā rahai.
The great *Sadhus* practising their austerities focus their hearts on the feet of Hari.[140]

pauṛī.
hari kī karanī sādha bhau tajai.
By the power of Hari, the pure feel love.

hari kī karanī sādha hari racai.
By the power of Hari, the pure meditate of Hari.

kali kalesa sādhūbhī hovai.
Ignorance and afflictions of the Sadhus are removed.

ghara ghara tana tana nisa dina jovai.
They enjoy [Hari] in their hearts and bodies, day and night.

sādha kī niṁdā naraka mahi parahī.
Those slandering the pure ones end up in hell.

hari kī karaṇī sira pari dharahī.
By the power of Hari, on one's head is imparted [blessings].

cāri juga saṁgrāmu ati bhaiā.
This is the struggle that takes place in the four ages.

isa kalajuga acaraja māhi rahiā.30.
This Kaliyuga is astonishing.30.

doharā.
rāma nāma hiradai dharahu daiā dharama adhīnā.
In your heart take the name of Ram, be merciful, and obediently follow dharam.

rāju teja saṁgrāmu karahu hari jana iha mati līnā.1.
Fight passionately for kingdoms, servants of Hari, take this advice.1.

soraṭhā.
nāmu dānu isanāna hari kītā cita lāīai.
Take the name, charity, and bath, and accept what works Hari does.

hari karanī paravānu cāra juga mahi jānīai.
Whatever Hari does is right, as known in the four ages.

pauṛī.
ika dhrohī mitra sai karahi prīti.
One becomes loving to treacherous friends.

mitra rākhai dharama kī prīti.
[He thinks that] keeping friends is the love of dharam.

dhrohī dhrohī kare mitra kau khāhi.
They are treacherous and exploit friendship.

mitra kai hari sadā sahāi.
The true friend is Hari who is always present.

dhrohī khāi aura mani gharai.
The treacherous exploit and their mind suffers.

khāta khāta vahu khata mai paṛai.
[The false friends] ruin the reputation, into pieces.

mitra rākhai hari kī āsa.
Keep friendship and hope in Hari.

para khajānā dūnī rāsi.31.
Taking from another's wealth ruins one's security.31.

doharā.
mitra mani ānaṁda dhrohī kai dhroha dhiānā.
Blissful friendly mind, focus your attention on your treacherous [friend].

mitra hari kai mani vasai dhrohī beīmānā.1.
Your true friend is Hari who resides in your mind, your treacherous [friend is] dishonourable.1.

soraṭhā.
akirataghaṇu gaiā nirāsi bisavāsaghātī bhī jāigā.
The ungrateful are hopeless, the faith breakers also go.

niṁdaku jaṁmīna asamāṁniīhā ūhā na hoisī.
The slanders from the earth to sky are not seen neither here nor there.

pauṛī.
satajugi sata sura bhagati kamāvai.
In Satayuga the brave earnt the merit of devotion to the truth.

tretai japa tapa joga liva lāgai.
In Tretayuga penance, recitals, and yoga were used to connect [to the Divine].

duāpari darasanu hari saṁta kā kīnā.
In the Dvapurayuga the Saints of Hari could be seen.

vāhagurū sācā mani līnā.
The true mind takes to Vahiguru.

kalijugi dekhahu hota saṁgrām.
Look at how the age of Kaliyuga is [full of] conflict.

jhūṭhe cita siu japai hari nāmu.
With false hearts people repeat Hari's name.

trai juga thā khaṁwe kī dhārā.
The three ages are like the edge of the khaṇḍā.

kalajuga krodha lobha ahaṁkāra.33.
In Kaliyuga there is anger, greed, and ego.33.

doharā.
satajugi saṁsā nā rahai aru tretai japu mana rāmā.
In Satayuga there were no doubts, and in Tretayuga was meditation on Ram.

duāpara darasana mai rahe kalajuga mai saṁgrāmā.1.
In Dvapuryuga was the [holy] darshana, in Kaliyuga is conflict.1.

soraṭhā.
satajugi sata saṁtokha aru tretai japa tapa cīnī.
In Satayuga there is truth and contentment, in Tretayuga is penance and recital.

duāpari hari kīne coja kalijugi nāma dāna saṁgrāma hai.2.
In Dvapurayuga is the name of Hari, in Kaliyuga the name, charity, and war.2.

pauṛī.
sikha saṁto mukhi bolahu rāmā.
Sikh saints recite Ram aloud.

sādha saṁgi karanī paravānā.
To be in the company of the Holy is highest.

sādha saṁgi kīā prabhu pāiā.
In the company of the Holy, Prabhu is realized.

sādha saṁgi kīā hari jana ihu manu lāiā.
In the company of the Holy, the mind is joined to servant of Hari.

isa kali mahi bhaiou saṁgrāmā.
In this Kaliyuga is terrible conflict.

bidha nai ṭhaṭī karanī paravānā.
[When] nobody knows what action is most high.

satagura kī jo niṁdā karai.
Whoever slanders the true Guru.

māi bāpa kai āgai marai.33.
Will die before his mother and father.33.

doharā.
pūrī vākī nā pavai saṁtā kahiu nā mānā.
It may not be said fully Oh saints do not be proud.

bidha nai cadī suho ihainā choḍai mukha nāmuā.1.
Do not lose this way, do not leave saying the name with your mouth.1.

soraṭhā.
lobha pāpa sabha jhūṭhu hai isa kala mai saṁgrāma.
Greed and sin are false, and are the source of conflict in Kaliyuga.

hari jana hiradai hari basai nā choḍai hari nāmā.
Hari resides in the heart of Hari's servants, do not leave the name of Hari.

pauṛī.
biuhāra calaṇa kala mai hai aisā.
In Kaliyuga this is how day-to-day work is.

aṁdari bahi kai liāvai paisā.
Sitting inside they are getting money.

lai paisā ghari mai jo āvai .
Those that bring money to the house.

mahā aneka anaṁda sukha pāvai.
Will experience all types of bliss and happiness.

mana māna sakoṁ bahu samajhāvai.
[This person will] instruct many people.

joṁ dīsai sā kuṭaṁbṁ kiā khāvai.
People will give to the Kings, but what will their children eat.

sāha ā ekaṁ o saṁḍi ā kīā.
The King comes calling out.

jo kichu thā tumārā hama dīā.34.
This place of yours, I gave it [to you].34.

doharā.
dekhai sāhu paise ge kī jai kau nau pāu.
Look at the King, the money is gone, who will help.

aṁdari bahi pairī pavahi jo sau dāma bhugavāu.1.
Inside and outside, they touch his feet, who listen lose their senses.1.

soraṭhā.
paise tere jhāi daina kau kichu ghara nahī.
Your money will go; giving it away is not hard.

kāṭa bāṭa kara māhi tuma te hama phāraga bhe.2.
It is very unfortunate now you owe it to me, there is a difference.

pauṛī.
asura rāja iha kala mai bhaiā.
[These are the type of] demonic rulers in this Kaliyuga.

jhapa tapa sata chīna hui gaiā.
Truth, meditation, penance are all gone.

thore dina asurana kā jorā.
For a few days is the rule of the demonic.

bhagata paratāpa hota nahīṁ thorā.
The radiance of the devotees is much less.

hui go saṁgrāma saṁta bhī dekhai.
There will be conflict that the saints will see.

karanā prabha kā hoigā lekhai.
The cause is Prabh, based on the accounts.

likhiā lekhu āpana hāthi.
That has been written by [Himself].

dharamu paragāsu jāigā pāpu.35.
[In the end] there will be the radiance of dharam, and sin will leave.35.

doharā.
sādho sidataṁ nā karo aṁt na vāṁkā dekhu.
Oh Sadhu do not forget, you will see the end.

aṁta dekhi dukhu pāvasīkare na karamā kī rekh.1.
At the end will be great pain, no one will be saved by merely trying.1.

soraṭhā.
khela lehu dina cāribahu rina khelanu hoisī.
Play for the four days, the chance will not come again.[141]

uḍanu hoigo chāruḍhūḍhe hathi na āvasī.
In the end you will be ashes, in the darkness nothing will be of use.2.

pauṛī.
isa kali mai japa nāma kā jāpa.
In this Kaliyuga, repeat the name.

nihacai hoi sāca mani thāpā.
Have faith, and firmly place truth in the mind.

binu hari nāma dharamu nahī koī.
Without the name of Hari there is no dharam.

aṁti kāli simarani gati hoī.
At the time of death, remembrance leads to liberation.

nihacai hoi simarahu mana māhi.
Having faith, remember [Hari] in your mind.

carana lāgi pāpa sabha jāi.
Cling to his feet, and all sins will go.

lākha siāna pakari kari dekhai.
I have seen many hundreds of thousands of ways.

binu hari simarana kachū na lekhai.36.
Without the remembrance of Hari, nothing else is of use.36.

doharā.
hari kā milaṇā dūri hai duramati manahu na jāi.
Meeting Hari is far, evil-mindedness will not leave the mind.

duramati jāi tau hari milai hari jana hari ke pāi.1.
When evil-mindedness goes, then Hari is met, the servants of God realize [Him].1.

soraṭhā.
hari kā nāmu tuma lehujiṁu machulī jala pīvatī.
Take the name of Hari like a fish drinks water.

hari siu rākhu saṁnehu jiu nīru mītu machulī karai.
Hari will take you, like the river holds the fish.

pauṛī.
aṁrita velai kari isanānuā.
Wake in the early hours and take a bath.

mana ṭhaharāvahu dhuna dhari dhiānā.
Hold the mind steady and focus on the sound [of the shabad].

aisā japanā japahu re bhāī.
This is the way to recite the name, brothers.

aṁti kāli hari hoi sahāī.
At your last moment, Hari will come to your aid.

hari caranī aisā cita lāvahu.
In this way focus your awareness of the feet of Hari.

manasā dhāri hari nāmu dhiāvahu.
Concentrate and firmly hold the name of Hari in your mind with.

dhiānu lāi nihacai hoi raho.
Concentrate and have faith.

prīta nīta nita citu mai laho.37.
With love and awareness do this daily.37.

doharā.
prīta karahu cita lāi kai ika mani hoi kai jāpā.
Love with awareness, and single-mindedly repeat [the name].

kari isanānu sukhamana paṛo nihacai mana kau thāpā.1.
Have a bath and read *Sukhamana* [this composition] with faith in this way.1.

soraṭhā.
nāmu dānu isanānu binu karamā nahī pāīai.
The name, charity, and bath cannot be gained without good fortune.

saṁta saṁgati paravāna suca dhiānu nahī chāḍīai.2.
The company of the Saint is high, do not leave the pure concentration [on Hari].2.

pauṛī.
jāpahu aparama apāra niraṁkārā.
Repeat the great, limitless, formless One's name.

tū saraba jīā pālanahārā.
You are the nurturer of all beings.

tū alakha alekhu lekha kā dhanī.
You are invisible, indescribable, and of limitless wealth.

tū beaṁta terā aṁta kiā ganī.
You are limitless, who can know Your end.

tū saraba nidhānu pūrana mai gāiā.
I sing that You are the total treasure, complete.

tūṁ sukha deu seva kari pāiā.
You give happiness, and Your own service.

tū bhagata vachala hari aṁtarijāmī.
You love Your devotees, Hari the knower of hearts.

tūṁ hari diālu akāla nihāla jiu dhāmī.38.
You are the merciful Hari, Akal, the house of ecstasy.38.

doharā.
tūṁ si tūnu becamūna mai mūna paṛaṁtīā hoi.
You are colourless, You are the Creator of the moon.[142]

hari jana simaranu simara lehumana kī duramati khoi.1.
The servants of Hari remember him and eradicate their evil-mindedness.

soraṭhā.
lakha caurāsī jāhi terā aṁtu na kina hī pāiā.
The 8.4 million forms cannot fathom Your limit.

japata raho dina rāti satiguri saṁsā meṭiā.
Meditate day and night and the true Guru will remove the doubts.

pauṛī.
tūṁ āpe dātā āpe bhugatā tū āpe mihara karaṁtā.
You are the giver, the enjoyer, and You are merciful.

tūṁ āpe jogī tūṁ āpe bhogī tū āpe bhoga karaṁtā.
You are the renunciate, You are the enjoyer, You enjoy Yourself.

tūṁ āpe alakha alekhu bidhātā tūṁ āpe karahi su hoī.
You are invisible, indescribable architect, and do whatever passes.

tū āpe dari dari phirahi che hāvahitū āpe sukha mai hoī.
You Yourself wander door to door, You are the happiness.

tūṁ āpe sāhu āpe hī tasakara terī kudarati kau bali jāṁu.
You are the king, You are the thief, I am a sacrifice to Your creative power.

tūṁ āpe bāṁdhahi tūṁ āpe choḍahi tūṁ āpe karahi suchāṁu.
You enslave, You release, You do as it pleases You.

tūṁ āpe sāhu āpe kai pārī tūṁ āpe bhaiā bhikhārī.
You are the king, the trader, and You are the beggar.

tūṁ āpe purakhu alekha kahāvahi tūṁ āpe suṁdara nārī.39.
You are called the invisible, You are the beautiful woman.39.

doharā.
tūṁ apane raṁgi āpa hī rātā terī kudarati kaṁu bali jāī.
You are the colour of love, imbued with love, I am a sacrifice to Your creative power.

hari jana hari hari hiradai bhajahu jana nānaka eka manāī.1.
Servants of Hari, meditate on Hari Hari, servant Nanak believes in the One.1.

soraṭhā.
japanā japo mana māhi ika mana hoi kai dhiāīai.
Repeat [the word] that should be repeated in the mind, with one-mindedness and concentration.

bina ika dūjā nāhi hari kā nāmu na choḍīai.
There is no other One, do not renounce the name of Hari.

pauṛī.
jisu rākhahi tū dehi vaḍiāī.
Those that You protect, You grant glory.

jisu rākhahi tūṁ sadā sahāī.
Those that You protect, You are present with.

jisu rākhahi tūṁ rahai sumer.
Those that You protect, You keep in heaven.

simarahi muna jana jachu kumer.
By remembering, the silent sages, beings, slaves, and treasure keepers.

jisa rākhahi tūṁ ādi jugādī.
Are protected by You, in the beginning, in each age.

harinākhasu mārio rākhio prahalādī.
You killed Harnaksh and protected Prahalad.

jisu rākhahi tūṁ apanāṁ jāni.
Those that You protect, You know Yourself.

vāṁ kau kathahu na hovai hāṁni.40.
No one else can explain [their greatness], or can they come to harm.40.

doharā.
hari kā nāma hiradai dharo prabha jī lehu parākh.
Place firmly the name of Hari in Your heart, look with discernment at Prabhu.

kari isanāna sukhamana paṛo nihacai mana kuṁ thāp.1.
Bathe and read the *Sukhamana* with faith, and gain mental strength.1.

soraṭhā.
japa tūṁ ika mani hoi āna nāmu japanā nahī.
Repeat the [name] with one mind, do not meditate on another.

mānasa janamu hai deva binu hari bhajana na pāīai.40.
The human birth is enlightenment but this cannot be gained without devotion to Hari.40.

pauṛī.
na raṭanamai.
[I will] not cry out loud.

na jaṭanamai.
[I will] not keep matted hair.

na ghaṭanamai.
[I will] not make predictions.

na jatanamai.
[I will] not keep celibacy.

na bhiṁḍa ke dikhāimai.
[I will] not show miracles.

na sāsa ke caṛāe mai.
[I will] not raise my breath [like a Yogi].

catara sujāna hai.
[Nor will I be] wise and clever.

isanāna jala dhoi hai.
[Nor will I] continually wash with water.

bahata bāta manu goi hai.
[I will] not please the mind with various riddles.

dehī sāṛi khoi hai.
[I will] not burn this body.

na biḍha ke ḍiḍhāe mai.
[I will] not show heresy.

na aneka bahu gāe mai.
[I will] not keep singing unnecessarily.

na bajaṁtra ke bajāe.
[I will] not keep playing musical instruments.

na dehī dhūṛi nāe mai.
[I will] not bathe my body in dust.

na mālā ke phirāe mai.
[I will] not keep holding onto a rosary.

sāca ke ḍiḍhāe mai.
[I will] show the truth.

hari pāvana kīhe bātā.
[I will] contemplate the mystery of Hari.

suca sācu hīai sāti.
Who is the truth, pure and Eternal.

nahī sovahi je rāt.
Who never sleeps at night.

hari jana hari milahi āpahī.41.[143]
Hari meets His servants himself.41.

ḍakhaṇā.
mana hī aṁdari ḍhāhi binu dekhai mahabūba ke.
This mind gets low without seeing the Lover.

jaba hī hoi nibāhu hari jana sacu mai raci rahe.1.
When the time comes it is continuous, the servants of Hari get absorbed into [Him].1.

pauṛī.
isa jaga mai pāga hātha de rākhai.
In this age the hand of protection on the turban.

nisa dinu rāma nāma yahu bhākhai.
Is to say the name of Ram day and night.

ina māiā munī jana mohe.
But this *maya* even fascinates the silent sages.

iha kala sevaka māiā ke hoe.
Even the humble servants are [attracted] to maya.

māi bāpu bhāī jaba māiā.
The mother, father, brother all [love] maya.

aurata prīti bhaina aru bhāiā.
The wife loves it and the sister are in [maya].

jaba māiā taba ādara hoi.
When you have no maya left.

bina dhana bāta na puchai koi.42.
Nobody will talk to you if you have no money.42.

doharā.
dhanu māiā kiā cahāṁha de māiā mohu sabha kūri.
The greed and love of wealth and maya are all false.

hari jana hari ke nāma binu hota jāṁta sabha dhūra.1.
Servant of Hari, take the name of Hari, and become the dust of all people [humble].1.

pauṛī.
sunahu saṁto tuma sācī bānī.
Listen saints to this true bāṇī.

gura apane kau hari janu jānī.
Through the Guru you will know Hari.

jāṁ hari hovai sadā sahāī.
When Hari is always with you.

dharama bilāsa parama gati pāī.
You will have the bliss of dharam and reach the highest state.

pākhaṁḍa chāṁḍi brahamaṁḍi mana dharo.
Stop all false hypocrisy and turn your mind to the Universal Lord.

āna chāḍi simaranu nita karo.
Renounce everything else and remember [the Lord] every day.

suca kiriā aru hari hari bhajo.
Do pure actions and meditate on Hari Hari.

jhūṭhā pairī pauṇā tajo.43.
Renounce going towards false actions.43.

doharā.
jo tuma sāce sikha hota jahu kubadhī mati.
If you are a truthful Sikh, then give up your evil-mindedness.

hari jana hari kā bhajana bhajo taba hoi tumārī gati.1.
Servants of Hari, meditate on Hari, so that you reach your [highest] state.1.

soraṭhā.
jo tuma rākhahu sācu bacanu hamārā māni lehu.
If you desire to keep pure, then remember these orders of mine.

gura kā hoi sarāpu jo tuma hohu adharama mahi.
You will be cursed by the Guru if you follow the path of *adharam*.

This composition again bears the ascription *Srī Mukhvāk Pātashāhī Dasavīṅ* but has various names.[144] The metre of this composition is Rāg Gauṛī—a metre which is used throughout the *AG*. It is the same metre employed in the *Sukhmanī Sāhib*, and the two compositions share similar names and verses. The composition refers to the coming of Kaliyuga and the perilous times it brings including lust, greed, and anger. There is a prescription that sleeping with other people's wives is a great sin; this cautionary aspect, as we know, runs throughout the *Srī Charitropakhyān*, especially in the Anup Kaur *Charitras* (19–21). The saints and *bhagats* of the *AG* are commented upon including Kabir, Ravidas, and Namdev. The focus on the deeper meaning of Vahiguru is another aspect of this composition, where the term is broken down to each individual letter. This exegesis is similar to the way the term has been discussed in Bhai Gurdas's vārs and also in the *Sarabaloh Granth*. This composition appears in the 'Takht Patna Sahib' AD 1698 recension, the 'Sangrur' recension, Aurangabad 'Bhai Daya Singh' recension, and the 'Baba Atal' recension which was examined by the corrective committee of AD 1897. There are other guṭkās and pothīs where this composition also appears (see Figure 2.9).[145]

FIGURE 2.9 A Photograph of a Folio Showing the Ornate Opening from *Sansāhara Sukhamanā* in the 'Takht Patna Sahib' AD 1698 *DG* Manuscript
Source: Giani Hardeep Singh.

Rāg Āsā and *Rāg Soraṭh*

ika oaṁkara vāhagurū jī kī phate.[146]
One Universal Creator, the Wondrous Guru is Victorious.

rāga āsā pātisāhī 10.
Rāg Āsā by the Tenth Sovereign.

āja hamāre saṁta kāja hai sasatra bādha dari āvahu re.
Today the Saints have been commanded to come to my door adorned in weapons.

hamare saṁgī paṁca bīra hai bacana gurū kā lai jāvahu re.1.rahāu.
My friends are the five warriors who have lived the commands of the Guru. Pause.

saṁta hamāre bhāī bīra hai roma roma samāvahu re.
The Saints are my brothers and warriors who are merged into my very fibre (hair).

bhīra parī saṁta saṁga hoeiā apanā rūpa dikhāvahu re.1.
There is a crowd of Saints who are showing their form.1.

saṁta kāja jagata hau āyo nāvā rūpa dikhāvahu re.
The affairs of the Saints are shown in new ways.

saṁga hamāre saṁta maṁḍalī eiha sīsa gurū kai lai jāvahu re.2.
In my company are a collection of Saints who have given their heads to the Guru.2.

sīsa kā rana jagata hau āeio lai badalā asura khapāvahu re.
The head is needed for the battle of the Earth, it is time to fight the demons.

eka sīsa kā badalā magiu sīsacārau bahuṛi magohu re.3.
For each head we will take a head, and request four more heads.3.

saṁta hamāre putra mitra hai sīla saṁtokha kamāvahu re.
The Saints are my sons and friends who cultivate contentment and patience.

jata sata saṁjama bacana hamāro rahata bacana kamāvahu re.4.
They are restrained, truthful, and disciplined, they live the way of life that has been commanded.4.

aura kete dekhahu bina kesa ke hamarī saina sabala teja hai saraba gurū samāio re.

Look at those that do not keep kesh, in my army they are the form of power and the Guru.

sabha sāka saina tora jagata ke ihu sīsa gurū pai lai jāvahu re.5.
They will break the other armies of this world, for they lay their heads at the feet of the Guru.5.

āgiā kīnī abināsī purakha nai hukama kesa lai āyo re.
The Immortal Lord commanded that kesh be kept.

pragaṭa hona ke dina sa dūra the turaka anīta caṛāiou re.6.
It will be known from this day that the Turak will be defeated.6.

jaṁha jaṁha dekhau taṁha taṁha saṁghārau bacana pāi majaba calāio re.
Wherever you shall look they shall be defeated.

anika hanavaṁta rāma hamare hai kīe tū kisa bidha dekha bhulāio re.7.
There will be many as strong as Hanuman, who will be reminded by Ram to awaken.7.[147]

khabaradāra hui āiu kesa dhārī khaṛaga rūpa jhamakāio re.
It is my strict order you should keep kesh and glisten like the form of the sword.

hamaro nāma gurū kesa dhārī hama apanī saina bulāio re.
My name is the Guru adorned with the hair, I will call my army.

āio vakhata sitāba saina kā saṁtana kamarabaṁdh āvahu re.8.
Come quickly the armies will come, Saints tie your cummerbunds.8.

nānaka gobiṁda eka kara dekhahu hama tījā majaba calāio re.
See Nanak Gobind as one, I will start the third way.

jāta pāta kachu rahana na devau kari ekaṁkāra bulāio re.9.1.[148]
Caste will not remain, as this is the call of *Ik Oaṅkār*.9.1.

ika oaṁkara vāhagurū jī kī phate.
One Universal Creator, the Wondrous Guru is Victorious.

rāga soraṭhi pātisāhī 10.
Rāg Soraṭh by the Tenth Sovereign.

aba kai te rājapūta kahāoaū.
If you say you are a Rajput.

pāṁca mavāsī ghara kae sādho apane rāha calāū.1.rahāu.
Then the five rulers in the home of your body control them.1. Pause.

kāma kradha karama kaṭārā bādho tata travāra baṁdhāū.
Lust and anger are the actions of your tiger knife and sword, tie them close to your body.

sahaja surata kā tarasā bādho nirata kamāna caṛāū.1.
Make your consciousness the quiver of your arrows, and tie it close to you, make the bow your upliftment.1.

ghoṛā giāna saṁtokha lagāmī sata kī jīna kasāū.
Make the horse your knowledge, contentment your saddle, truth your bridle, tie them tightly.

gagana maṁḍala kau karau paeiānā ḍai ko cābaka lāū.2.
Make the heavenly realms your advance in battle and fear your stick.2.

gura kā sabada saṁjoā pahirau sohaṁ ṭopa banāū.
The word of the Guru is your armour, and the word *Soham* your pistol.

uḍatī kāgana sira para māro saba bhai duaṁda miṭāū.3.
The crows that fly in your head, kill these, and all the fear and duality.3.

pahilī coṭa bilīā mārau sasā bāna ghara ghāū.
Firstly strike the cat and kill it with the bow of praises in your inner home.

yaha mana miraga kāla hari kālā jīvata phādha kari liāū.4.
Kill the black deer of this mind, with Hari's name unfasten the noose of death.4.

alakha purakha kī karau cākarī ciharā jāi likhāū.
Come into service of the Indescribable Being, and sign your presence for him.

ghoṛe dāsa gobiṁda siṁgha ke bhagati dādanī pāūṁ.5.2.
The horses of the slave Gobind Singh are his devoted charity.5.2.

The composition again starts off with the ascription to Guru Gobind Singh as its writer. It is written in Rāg Āsā which is recorded in its title, and is a small verse and hence it is unlikely to be recorded in the *Tatkārā* of *DG* manuscripts. The basis of this verse is that the saints have the power to become warriors as long as they subscribe to certain tenants of the Khalsa. A reference is made to the five warriors: a possible description of the Pañj Piāre who live according to the Guru's instructions. The saints who have previously given their head to the Guru (*charan pāhul*) are now needed to fight the demons, and in order to do so they need to give a head like the Pañj Piāre by taking *khaṅde kī pāhul* (Khalsa saint–warrior initiation of the double-edged sword). In order to do this they would need to be adorned in weapons. The author emphasizes the retainment of the kesh or unshorn hair (one of the five *K*s), and perceives them to be fundamental for the success of the Khalsa. The armies of the Khalsa who keep the kesh will become the supreme army and the Turaks will be defeated in battle as a result. The keeping of kesh is not a ritualistic requirement but a direct commandment from God. The Panth as a result will become Hanuman like in strength.[149] The order from the Guru who himself adorns the kesh is to keep the kesh and hence this adornment is to glisten like the sword. The lineage of the Khalsa is that Guru Nanak and Gobind Singh are one and, as a result, a third way or *tīsārā panth* will be started and the shackles of caste will be eliminated, as this is the will of the formless *Ik Oaṅkār*.[150]

Whilst there are many eulogies on the Khalsa, this is not better represented than this verse, which directly connects a Sikh from being a saint to a warrior by adorning themselves in the kesh of God. This composition appears in the 'Takht Patna Sahib' AD 1698 recension and the 'Aurangabad' Bhai Daya Singh recension (see Figure 2.10). The composition Rāg Soraṭh again contains the name of the rāg in the title. This composition is a philosophical take on understanding what constitutes a good living and trying to avoid those thieves who stop an individual from fulfilling this. The verse is a play on words in reference to the Rajput warrior practices which end with one remembering God's name. The final verse states that horses (which are normally a preserve of the Rajputs) also have a charitable association with Gobind Singh.[151] It seems as if the Guru wished to impart a spiritual message like the *AG* in his finalization of the *chhatrī* ideals in the *DG*.

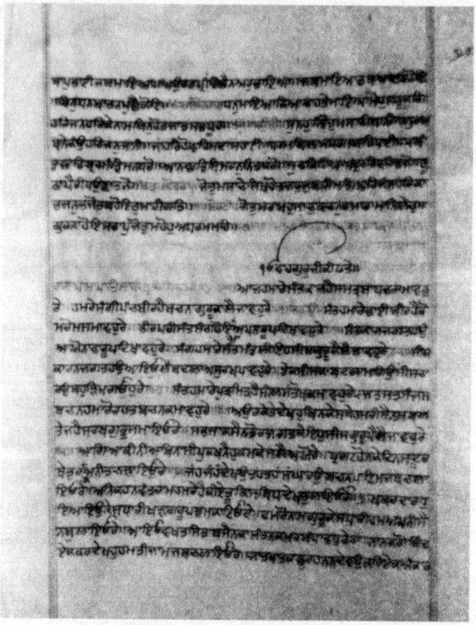

FIGURE 2.10 A Photograph of a Folio Showing the Opening of the *Rāga Āsā* in the 'Takht Patna Sahib' AD 1698 *DG* Manuscript
Source: Giani Hardeep Singh.

Indra Kavach and *Gobind Gītā*

There are other compositions which are attributed to Guru Gobind Singh, namely the *Gobind Gītā* and the *Indra Kavach* which appear only in one *DG* manuscript. These two compositions have not been translated, and the *Indra Kavach* will not be discussed. Although the *Gobind Gītā* is a larger composition which deserves study at another time, a brief synopsis is presented here. In short, it is a translation of the eighteenth chapter of the Mahābhārat, the 'Bhagvad Gītā'. It only appears in the manuscript at Takht Patna Sahib with a colophon of AD 1698.[152] The other undated manuscript does not contain the *Gobind Gītā*. The composition mentions *adhiātamic* sciences and *Shastravidiā*.[153] There are also references to the Sikh tradition throughout, especially with references to the *AG* composition *Sukhmanī Sāhib* and the Khalsa being a *brahamgiānī*.[154] There are descriptions that refer to Guru Nanak as the One Indivisible Lord and the *āratī* composition of Guru Nanak is also cited.[155] There is also an explanation of the name Singh as *parmātamā*; the author also states, 'I Gobind, love the Khalsa.'[156] This is in the tenth chapter or *adhiyaī*. The term 'Akal', which is a common term through the *DG*, is also utilized through the text: 'See the Timeless Being [Akal] as one and the world as the Timeless Being [Akal].'[157] There are also many references to the Khalsa throughout the text.

Asphotak Kabitt Svaiye

The *Asphotak Kabitt Svaiye* or 'Miscellaneous Verses and Stanzas' are quite well known but are not in the standard *DG*, although they do feature in the Panjabi translation by Pandit Narain Singh. They are extra verses that are said to be from various compositions in the *DG*, like the *Salok Vārā te Vadhīk* in the *AG*. It is in most extant manuscripts and it is uncertain why it was removed.[158] As it is well known we have not included a translation of it in this present edition. The no longer extant recension by Baba Dip Singh, as mentioned by Giani Gian Singh, was said to have finished at this composition.

The Standardization of the *Dasam Granth*

The question as to why these compositions do not appear in the standard *DG* will now be considered. In order to do this we need to look at the standardization report of the *DG* by Sardul Singh.[159] In this report they looked at various aspects of the *DG* and what they considered to be authentic and what should be published in a new recension of the *DG*.

The first statement is about the actual contents of the standard *DG* and how they came to the conclusions about the compositions that were not included and thus labelled apocryphal. The report states, '*Devī jī ke Ustati or Namo Ugradantī Anantī Svaiya*; In the old days the Khalsa Singhs read this description of themselves. However, this is not from the Guru, as some aspects of these *bāṇī* are not anywhere noted elsewhere in the *DG*, even though this bāṇī is well known.'[160] He states that the *Sukhmanā* and *Mālkauns kī Vār* were in one extant manuscript at Baba Atal Rai Sahib.[161] In the rest of the thirty-two *granths* (at Amritsar) these compositions do not appear in them.[162] Even though *Gurgaddī* was given to the *AG*, the *DG* was always placed on the same royal canopy. He continues:

> The *bāṇī* written by the Tenth Guru was to infuse honour and the courage to fight the invaders, due to the wars in which so many *biṛhs* were destroyed, means that a *Khās biṛh* (important recension) is no longer available to us. Most of the recensions now are generally the same. In the Buddha Dal *Biṛh* and the *biṛh* of Bhai Mani Singh, the *Sukhmanā*, *Mālkauns kī Vār*, and *Chhakke* [*Ugradantī*] and one or two other *shabads* were present. However these copies are very rare.[163]

This composition is an example of vīr ras bāṇī based on the style of the composition and internal parameters. The praises to Durga within it may have been a factor which led to some unease, but this does not seem consistent with their other comments, for example, the recital of *DG* compositions on the occasion of Dussherā. Then, the actual purging of this composition does not seem to be completely based on antagonism to Hinduism. We need to look at other factors which help us determine the deletion of this composition. Apart from numerous salutations to the Goddess there are also lines which mirror lines in other compositions in the standard *DG* recension. For instance, there are several lines in praise of weapons which mirror that of *Shastra Nām Mālā*. Kanh Singh Nabha in his *Mahān Kosh* does not comment on the *Ugradantī* directly, but it is referenced under the terms 'chhakkā' in his dictionary.[164] He states that it is penned under Guru Gobind Singh's name, but is written by a Devi worshipper. Kanh Singh contradicts himself in *Hum Hindū Nahiṅ* and quotes from the *Bhagauti Asatotra*, and then states that *Ugradantī* was written by Bhai Sukha Singh at Patna.[165] Some writers have confused the *Bhagautī Chhaṅd* (*Bhagauti jū kā Chhaṅd*) with *Ugradantī* and vice versa; this is apparent in Jaggī's PhD thesis on the *DG*. In the *Mahān Kosh*, Nabha says that in a different manuscript of the *DG*, there are some extra scriptures or hymns. He states a pauṛī has been written by a Sikh, and quotes the first pauṛī. In the footnote he writes that it is also in the Sangrur Government Gurdwara recension.

The Apocrypha in Tradition

The Damdami Taksal readily uses the apocrypha in exegesis as stated earlier. One of the senior preachers of the organization Giani Hardeep Singh of the Hazuri Taksal also has some copies of these rare scriptures, as well as having numerous photographic copies of rare folios. He recently published a prayer anthology in 2009 of the prayers of the Tenth Guru which contained the apocrypha in it.[166] *Sukhmanā Sāhib* has a tradition in the Buddha Dal as testified by Akali Baba Santa Singh Nihang and Akali Nihang Ragi Baldev Singh.[167] Nihang Partap Singh recognized the *Bhagauti jū kā Chhaṅd*, as it has been printed by the Buddha Dal. Akali Baba Anoop Singh, a veteran who served at the Akal Takht, mentions that the *Gobiṅd Gītā*, *Sukhmanā Sāhib*, and the *Ugradantī* without the *svaiye* had been read in the early 1900s. This was at the time of Akali Jathedar Baba Sahib Singh Kaladhari before the advent of the Shiromani Gurdwara Parbandhak Committee (SGPC).[168] Baba Daya Singh of the Bidhi Chand Dal has insisted these compositions be read, and tried to persuade Jathedar Kulwant Singh of Takht Hazur Sahib to include them into the new version of the *DG* published by the takht. *Sukhmanā Sāhib* is mentioned in the oral tradition of the Nihangs. The various Nihang Dals possess manuscripts which would be useful for scholarly purposes, but this is an area that most scholars have neglected. Giani Sher Singh Nihang (Ambala) has an early anthology which contains *Bhagautī Asatotra*, *Ugradantī*, and the *Indra Kavach*; though undated, it shares many features with the Patna Sahib AD 1698 *sarūp*. With the accounts in traditional hagiographies, the praxis of the Nihang Singhs, the report of 1897 of the standardization, the position of other traditional Sikhs, and the inclusion in early extant manuscripts and anthologies, it would strongly suggest that these compositions should not have been excised.

The Namdharis or Kukā are another *samprādayā* who accept the *DG* in its entirety as the work of Guru Gobind Singh. Their origins in the middle of the nineteenth century were as a reform to break the idolism penetrating into Sikhism. They based their values on the Khalsa but now have their own living Guru, *rahitnāmā*, and *ardās*.[169] The Namdharis in their own precepts accept the compositions of the *DG* for use in their *nitnem* as well. They focus more on the Chaṇḍī bāṇīs, namely *Chaṇḍī dī Vār* and *Chaṇḍī Charitras* but also the *Akāl Ustati*. One departure from mainstream Sikhism is that they take part in a ritualistic *havan* where compositions from *AG* and *DG* are recited. At this time, 'Five persons at the worship read the scriptures, *Choupae, Jup, Jāp, Chaṇḍī Charitar, Akāl Ustati*'. To these compositions *Chaṇḍī dī Vār* and *Ugradantī* were added at this recital.[170] Therefore, the recitation of *Ugradantī* is also a part of their liturgy, and this is not a new innovation for them. In their collision with the British it was *DG* compositions that gave them their strength and inspiration. One source tells us:

> Lastly, every Kuka who can read has a book printed by Diwan Buta Singh of Lahore, a well-known seditious character. This book contains all the parts of the Granth inciting war, i.e., the 'Ugurdanti' and 'Chandi Path' from Guru Govind Singh's Granth [*DG*].[171]

According to Kapur Singh (see his introduction to Harkrishan Singh [1960]), the composition became a favourite mantra of the Kukā Sikhs after the deportation of their leader, Baba Ram Singh to Burma, in 1872. The Kukās fervently believed that by the concerted repetitions of the *Ugradantī* they would succeed in evoking the spirit of universal destruction, so as to divert its potent wrath against the foreign oppressors, the British.[172] There are also other groups who recite the apocryphal compositions, namely Nankasar Samprādayā, Baba Nand Singh (Jagroan), and the Samprādayā equated with Baba Harnam Singh, Rampurkhera *wale*. This is not an exhaustive list but it shows how the apocrypha continue to be recited by various groups despite there being a standard *DG*.

The Apocrypha and the *Tisārā Panth*

One of the common leitmotivs in the apocrypha seems to be the appearance of the term 'tisārā panth'. We need to examine this term within the apocrypha. It is likely that the vārs of Bhai Gurdas were written in the court of Guru Arjan Dev, and so their status is akin to court poetry and the contents are an exegesis to some extent of the *AG*. In a similar vein the vār of Bhai Gurdas II is likely to have been added to it at the time of Guru Gobind Singh, as there is some evidence that it may have been written in the court of the Tenth Guru. The *Gur Pratāp Suraj Granth* mentions Gurdas as a court poet of the Tenth Master.[173] The contents of this vār are heavily laden with content linked to the *DG*. In style and content, some portions also sound much like the apocryphal composition the *Ugradantī*. The references in the vār about the *khaṇḍe kī pāhul* ceremony would suggest that it was written after it (verse 41-1-5). The name Gurdas is also mentioned. The theme repeated throughout is how the Tenth Guru is both the Guru and the Sikh as he received initiation from the Pañj Piāre.[174] This echoes a distinct line from the *Ugradantī*, along with the duty of the Panth to destroy the wicked.[175] In this vār of Bhai Gurdas II, we can clearly see that up to verse 41-15-18 is along the same lines as the *Ugradantī*. This is the same as the verse 41-6-7 about the destruction of ritualistic religion, and the third path.[176] The end of the vār sounds exactly like the end of the *Ugradantī*.[177] This would suggest that Bhai Gurdas Singh had read the *Ugradantī* and had based his own writing on it. Its importance is also supplemented by the fact that this vār is employed in *kathā* and kirtan in Sikh gurdwaras.

This shows that there is a link with the concept of the tisārā panth which not only appears in the *Ugradantī* and is also mirrored by Bhai Gurdas II. It was also noted that another composition in the apocrypha shared a common theme with the *Ugradantī*, notably the Rāg Asā. Again this composition stresses that the Khalsa would represent the third way. It is important to note that whilst the notion of the Sikhs as a distinct community was present from Guru Nanak, it was to be reiterated with the formation of the Khalsa as is clear in compositions like Rāg Asā. We also see that an old manuscript of *Sau Sākhī* also contains the *Ugradantī*, and this also would fit into the apocalyptical future predictions contained within the sākhīs. In an anecdote, Guru Tegh Bahadur predicts that in his tenth form, a new religion will be formed: 'He will found a third sect, he will fight great battles.'[178] The British had made the connection between these compositions and the *Sau Sākhī* in the nineteenth century.[179] In the apocrypha and the vār of Bhai Gurdas II, the Hindus and Turaks now have a new formidable opponent, the Khalsa. The previous ways are criticized and are said to have abandoned the righteous ways of Akal, and as a result, the tisārā panth is positioned as the only way for salvation.

* * *

In the corrective committee report of the *DG*, they excluded some of the compositions that we have termed as apocrypha. We have looked at these compositions to see their history and their appearance in the Sikh manuscript tradition. The corrective committee rejected the *Ugradantī* as they believed it to be written by a Devi worshipper. They also stated that the composition did not merit inclusion into the new recension as it did not appear in enough manuscripts of the *DG*. They stated that some important manuscripts contained some of these apocryphal compositions; however, they still omitted them for reasons which were not scholarly. They considered the *Asphotak Kabbits* to have been written by the Guru, but they were not included in the standard recension of the *DG* either. The *Sukhmanā Sāhib* and *Mālkauns kī Vār* were rejected because they did not appear in many manuscripts. Another reason why some of the smaller compositions have been written out of history is due to their length being very short, because of which they may have been missed by the scribes and copyists.

The committee only looked at manuscripts in their vicinity, that is, Amritsar, and this meant that they did not have access to other manuscripts like the 'Takht Patna' bīṛh which contains many of the apocryphal compositions. Our discussion shows that the *DG* recensions contained not only apocrypha, but also many guṭkās and pothīs. It is important to note that the AD 1698 date of the 'Patna Sahib' bīṛh would mean that the compositions were written at the time of the Guru. The similarities between the *Ugradantī*, Rāg Asā, and the vār of Bhai Gurdas II also show that the apocrypha were popular with the court poets of the Guru. The various sampradāyā, including the Akali Nihangs, continue the recital of the apocrypha even today. This is highly significant as the apocrypha are still considered to be written by the Guru, and as a result they are a part of Sikh liturgy. If the apocrypha were forged by Sikh sects aligned with the Mughals, they would not contain all the references to warfare, and themes like giving away one's head, and so on. In fact, due to the strong link with the tradition, it is more likely that they were actually composed by the Guru as a record of the Khalsa inauguration.

Notes

1. K.S. Nabha, *Mahān Kosh* (Patiala: Bhasha Vibhag, 1999); Harbans Singh, ed., *Encyclopaedia of Sikhism* (Patiala: Punjabi University, 1992).

2. See Robert Bly and Jane Hirshfield, *Mirabai: Ecstatic Poems* (Boston: Beacon Press, 2004), 71, and D.S. Usahan, *Prem Aṅbodh* (Patiala: Punjabi University, 1989).

3. For example, The Deuterocanonical Books or 'Books of the Secondary Canon' have been included in some versions of the Bible, but which have been excluded at one time or another, for textual or doctrinal reasons.

4. R.S. Jaggi and G.K. Jaggi, *Srī Dasam Granth Sāhib Pāṭh—Sampādan ate Viākhiā*, 5 vols (New Delhi: Govind Sadan, 2000).

5. Jodhi Singh and Dharam Singh, *Sri Dasam Granth Sahib, Text and Translation*, 2 vols (Patiala: Heritage Publications, 1999).

6. Pritpal Bindra, trans., *Chitro Pakhyaan: Tales of Male–Female Tricky Deceptions from Sri Dasam Granth* (Amritsar: B. Chatter Singh Jiwan Singh, 2002); Pritpal Bindra, *Tales in Persian (Hikayaat) from Dasam Granth* (Ontario: Sikh Social and Educational Society, 2002).

7. S.S. Kohli, trans., *Sri Dasam Granth Sahib*, 3 vols (Birmingham: Sikh National Heritage Trust Publishing, 2003).

8. P.S. Sandhu, *Selections from Sri Dasam Granth Sahib*, 2 vols (Amritsar: Singh Brothers, 2004).

9. See Teja Singh Bhasauria, *Khālsā Rahit Prakāsh* (Khalsa Diwan, Bhasaur: Pustak Bhandar, Panch Khand, 1917).

10. See Ran Singh, *Dasam Granth Niraṇe* (Patiala: Panch Khalsa Diwan, 1919).

11. Kirpal Singh, research scholar at the Santokh Singh Library (Shiromani Gurdwara Parbandhak Committee, Amritsar), and Akali Baba Santa Singh, the late head of the Buddha Dal, aided in deciphering the early archaic forms of Gurmukhi. In the photographs of the manuscripts in this book, the continuous writing can be seen.

12. *Anekāth Kosh* is specifically just a Braj Bhāshā dictionary. This is the prominent guide in Gurmukhi on the language of Braj Bhāshā. Kanh Singh Nabha, *Anekāth Kosh* (Amritsar: Sudarshan Press, 1928).

13. C. Shackle, *An Introduction to the Sacred Language of the Sikhs* (London: School of Oriental and African Studies [SOAS], University of London, 1983); R. Snell, *The Hindi Classical Tradition: A Braj Bhāṣā Reader* (London: SOAS, 1991).

14. In the times of the Afghans this jungle of Panjab was in Deepalpur, from the river Satluj near Beas to Sabo ki Talwandi. See Pandit Narain Singh, trans., *DG* (Lahore: Bhai Chattar Singh, 1940), 5:683. A manuscript of the *DG* (London: Royal Asiatic Library, AD 1827), Tod MS, *f.* 708 records this composition without the first two lines by Narain Singh. This seems to be the case with the majority of manuscripts, including the 1698 'Takht Patna Sahib' *DG, f.* 239. This could suggest the Guru composed it earlier than the Jungle episode taking place with the Khalsa and repeated it again there; hence the addition.

15. Pandit Narain Singh, *DG*, 5:683. Within the modern printed edition there is an extra line at the commencement: *Lakhī jaṅgle khālsā aī dīdār kito ne.*

16. Literally, 'a thousand prayers'. This is the metre that the verse is written in. It is sung mostly by Sufis and Qawwali singers.

17. *DG*, 712–6.

18. The word 'Khalsa' appears in various *hukamnāmās* by Guru Tegh Bahadaur. These letters of command were issued many years before the formation of the Khalsa. The term 'Khalsa' here is used to refer to the sangat.

19. The Sikh hagiographic tradition states that Guru Nanak recited 100,000 *Japu jī Sāhib* at this location. It was also visited by Guru Tegh Bahadur.

20. P.S. Bindra, *Guru Kian Saakhian—Tales of the Sikh Gurus* (Amritsar: Singh Brothers, 2005), 205–6.

21. This is the view of Piara Singh Padam, *Gurū Gobiṅd Siṅgh jī de Darbārī Rattan* (Patiala: Kalam Mandir, 1994).

22. Pandit Narain Singh Ji Giani, *Sri Dasam Granth Sahib Ji Saṭīk*, 8 vols (Amritsar: Jawahar Singh and Kripal Singh and Co., [1932] 1992).

23. Daljeet Singh and Kharak Singh, eds, *Sikhism: Its Philosophy and History* (Chandigarh: Institute of Sikh Studies [IOSS], 1997), 315.

24. *Sikh Rehat Marayada*, Article XXIV.

25. Literally, 'the five friends of the hands'. W.H. McLeod, J.S. Grewel, and Pashaura Singh are of this school of thought.

26. *Srī Sarabaloh Graṅth Sāhib jī Saṭīk* (Anandpur: Shiromani Panth Akali Buddha Dal, n.d.), 2:495.

27. Kuir Singh, *Gurbilās Pātishāhī 10* (Patiala: Punjabi University, 2000), 110.

28. An obscure work attributed to Bhai Jaita Singh said to be from the Guru's period lists five *K*s. See Gurmukh Singh, *Bhai Jaita Ji: Jiwan te Rachna* (Amritsar: Literature House, 2003). There are other European accounts but it is beyond the scope of this study to present them.

29. *Bhagautī* is the Braj Bhāshā from the Sanskrit *bhagavatī*, meaning by the Divine or God. In this context it would mean the power

(*shaktī*) of Akal Purakh. It is often symbolized by the *Srī Sāhib* or Divine Sword.

30. According to the version in *Mahān Kosh*, this would translate as: 'The devotee [of God] Bhagautī assists the being [*jan*] who remains composed. You are with, [you are] side by side, that [being] who never gives in.' Whether this has been deliberately altered is unknown, no extant manuscripts reads the version given by Kanh Singh Nabha. This is due to the original *ran* [battle] being replaced by *jan* [being]. This couplet also appears at the end of *Chhakkā Bhagautī jī kā*, aka *Ugradantī*. Also see Harjinder Singh Kanwal, *Dasmesh Bani Darpan: Translation of the Unique Banis of Sri Guru Gobind Singh ji Maharaj in Punjabi and English* (Delhi: Wellwish Publishers, 2002), 60.

31. This is the Braj Bhāshā for *bhagavat* and *bhagavatī*. The play of two opposites, also see *Chaṇḍī dī Vār* first pauṛī. It could also be interpreted to mean *mīrī–pīrī*, the temporal and spiritual.

32. Nārada of the Indian pantheon is known for creating mischief and fights, he is also a chief musician of *rāg*.

33. *Ṭhuṁṭhura*—corpse without heads and arms/legs.

34. The author alludes to the body being the armour and once broken, the soul is released/subdued.

35. The *jamdhar* is a Sanskrit name for the slightly curved punch-daggar, broad at the base, like the *kaṭār*. Lit.—'death bearer'. See W. Egerton, *Indian Oriental Arms and Armour* (London: Arms and Armour Press, [1880] 1968), 23. This is used to 'flank render'—literally, 'to cut and render between the rib and hip'. Also see H.S. Cowper, *The Art of Attack: Being a Study in the Development of Weapons and Appliances of Offence, From the Earliest Times to the Age of Gunpowder* (Ulverston, Lancashire: W. Holmes Printer Ltd, 1906), 93.

36. Dharam-Rāj is the Indian equivalent of the Abrahamic angel Gabriel. In manuscripts this line appears as: *barahara kaṁpai dharamarāi ghāna ghanāi hai*.

37. In this context Hindu and Turak could mean geographical divisions rather than religious ones. See T.P. Hughes, *A Dictionary of Islam* (London: W.H. Allen & Co., 1885), 648.

38. In manuscripts this line reads as: *doharā. āsā na karu brahamanā nā parase para jāi. mama tiāgi dūjai lage kūbha naraka mahi pāi.7.1.* In some traditional hagiographies, the Guru was said to have composed compositions while the Brahmins performed the *havan* at Naina Devi. This would explain the context of the final couplet, as in this episode the fearful Brahmins are said to have tried to escape. It may also translate as a warning to Sikhs not to rely on Brahmins.

39. An alternative name for this composition is *Bhagautī jū kā Chhaṅd*. The *Vār Srī Bhagautī jī kī* appears in older manuscripts as *Vār Durgā kī*

and is commonly known as *Chaṇḍī dī Vār*. It is in the standard *DG* recension and is a different composition.

40. Piara Singh Padam, ed., *Puṅjabī Vārāṅ* (Patiala: Kalam Mandir, 1980).

41. Indian rāg of *Bhairav Taṭh*: *sa, -ga, ma, -da, -ni, sa*, it is sung at midnight and is in both *Sarabaloh Granth* and *DG*. It is known to have a heroic feel when played at a fast tempo.

42. This is written in future tense and is almost identical to the *Kalkī Avatār* from the *DG*. See Nabha, *Mahān Kosh*, 426. Harimandir can mean in the self, in the body, in the heart, or God's temple.

43. *Nīlā* can also mean turquoise, grey.

44. This is a prophecy in Shi'a Islam. This has an interrelationship to a prophecy of Hazrat Ali.

45. Nabha, *Mahān Kosh*, 646. This has an interrelationship to a prophecy of Hazrat Ali as it is the name of his mule.

46. This is from a Puranic prophecy of the coming avatār, from the Hindu scripture *Kalkī Purāṇ*. This features in the *DG*, at the end of the *Chaubīs Avatār* as well as other late seventeenth- and eighteenth-century Sikh scriptures.

47. In some manuscripts this appears as *ja(bh) pile; jap* or *bhaj*. It appears as *jāp* in the 'Takht Patna Sahib' manuscript, bhaj in the Aurangabad 'Daya Singh' manuscript and Giani Hardeep Singh's printed version. In the other two Patna manuscripts it also appears as bhaj.

48. This line is not present in all manuscripts.

49. Some words are the other way round in some manuscripts.

50. The words *Niraṅkār* and *udār* are opposite in some manuscripts.

51. There is also a variation of *do-dodhaṛ*. *Dodhaṛ* can also mean slicing the head of the body, making two pieces, head and body.

52. This line is not in the 'Bhai Daya Singh' Aurangabad *DG*.

53. There is also a variation of the addition of *jamai*.

54. There is a variation of the word *haki* to *hāki*.

55. There is a variation of this line as *kān Krisan*.

56. Literally, 'my head is in front of the Guru'. There are obvious connotations to the asking of a head by the Guru at Vaisakhi.

57. Bhagwant Singh, *Dasam Granth dā Bāṇī Biorā*, R.S. Jaggi, ed. (Patiala: Punjabi University, 2001) records that a longer version of this composition was in a *DG* manuscript in Rawalpindi.

58. There are numerous mentions of such prophecies in eighteenth-century Sikh literature, and this is a topic which certainly requires more examination.

59. The *sarohī* was a favourite blade in Rajasthan. See Egerton, *Indian Oriental Arms*, 105.

60. A Gurmukhi manuscript from AD 1736, which is an anthology of Sikh prayers, has some variations in its passages compared to the modern version presented here, which is from the Buddha Dal. It reads, *Namo loh kī putrikā jhal jhalantī*. See MS. 44469 (SOAS), *f.* 330.

61. A different version of this line has been given by Kanh Singh Nabha, *Gurumat Mārtaṇḍ* (Amritsar: SGPC, [1962] 1978), 735.

62. Some passages of this composition resemble those found in *Shastra Nām Mālā*. For more information on the types of swords, see Egerton, *Indian Oriental Arms*.

63. Giani Gian Singh writes in his *Srī Gurū Panth Prakāsh* that this panegyric by Guru Gobind Singh was recorded in a manuscript at Takht Hazur Sahib, which he copied in 1852.

64. SOAS, MS. 44469.

65. The pothī has compositions from Guru Nanak, Guru Ramdas, Guru Arjan, as well as the *saloks* of Guru Tegh Bahadur as well as *Jāp Sāhib*, *Akāl Ustati*, and *Chaupaī Sāhib*. We thank Harminder Singh Mann (Canada) for bringing this to our attention.

66. Trilochan Singh Bedi, ed., *Sikhān dī Bhagatmālā* (Patiala: Punjabi University, 1986), 151.

67. The most famous of whom is Ragi Balbir Singh who is famous for singing *DG* compositions.

68. This composition is in six verses or chhand. See Nabha, *Mahān Kosh* entry of *chhakkā* and *chhakke*. Kanh Singh Nabha is of the opinion that this composition was written by a devotee of Durga under the name of the Tenth Guru.

69. It must be noted that this composition is dedicated to the Divine feminine aspects of God, as the gender of most of the nouns is female. This is a clear continuation with the symbolism in the previous translation describing the sword.

70. Harkrishan Singh, trans., 'Ugradanti: Guru Gobind Singh's Adoration of Divine Mother', *Sikh Review* 8, no. 8 (1960) translates this line as: 'Master of *yogā* of *yogās*, O Mother, God-Union's Yoker.'

71. *Kāl* can also be time.

72. The three worlds are this world, the celestial world, and the nether world. This could also be the physical world, the astral/mental world, and the celestial world.

73. The *kharag*, often spelt as *khadag* or *kharagh*, is often depicted to represent the discrimination of knowledge over ignorance in Sanskrit

texts. See the illustration in *Bhagautī Asatotra*. The 'Sword of Knowledge' also appears in the *AG*, 966, 983, 1022, 1072, 1087, 1324, and 1414.

74. This demon appears in many of the episodes of the Goddess in the *DG*. He was destroyed when Kali appears from the head of the Goddess. This line also alludes to the drying up of his blood as Kali drinks it.

75. The ancient divisions of the Earth.

76. Harkrishan Singh in 'Ugradanti' translates this line as: 'Waken, upsurge the warriors, the heroes invincible, lion-like.' Ami Shah translates it as: 'Guide the unbeatable valiant Singhs in battle.' Unfortunately, both translators miss the prophetic style of the last few metres of this first *chhakkā*. Ami P. Shah, 'Ugradanti and the Rise of the Tisar Panth', *Journal of Punjab Studies* 15, nos 1–2 (2008): 181–97.

77. *Hinduk* is most likely to mean a geographical area. The term 'Turak' is explained by Kuir Singh (1751), as a person originating from Turkmenistan, a Timurid, usually a Mughal Official.

78. 'The sacrificial havan': Ami Shah translates this as the universal form; Shah 'Ugradanti', 181–97.

79. Eyes lined with *surma*.

80. *Agaṁmaṇa*—One who does not journey, for example, take birth or die.

81. The *hūr* or *hūris* from the Islamic tradition are virgin Angels said to be seen by warriors who fall fearlessly in battle. See *AG*, 1083. The Tenth Guru refers to them several times in *Rām Avatār*; see *DG*, 234–7.

82. It is interesting to note that 'bāṇī' is a feminine noun.

83. An alternative is to translate the names; the line would read: 'Obeisances to the effulgent with heroic spirit, the blissful holy Mother of existence.'

84. Ami Shah has translated this as: 'You, emerging from the pillar, a lion amongst men'. Her translations of the next verses, 36–8, are inaccurate. See Shah, 'Ugradanti', 181–97.

85. Madhu and Kītabh were born out of the wax from Brahma's right ear. All of the characters mentioned in this composition also feature in the *Bachitra Nāṭak Granth*. In fact, it is necessary to explain the *Ugradantī*. A verse by Guru Nanak in Rāg Gauṛī, *AG*, 224 narrates some mythology and of particular note are these verses: *sahasabāhu madhu kīṭa mahikhāsā. haraṇākhasu le nakhahu bidhāsā. daita saṁghāre binu bhagati abhiāsā.6. jarāsaṁdhi kālajamuna saṁghāre. rakatabīju kālunemu bidāre. daita saṁghāri saṁta nisatāre.7.* [The Lord killed the thousand-armed Kartavirya Arjun, and the demons Madhu, Kīt, and Mahikhāsā. He seized Harnākhash and tore him apart with his nails. The demons were slain; they did not practice devotional worship.6. The demons Jarāsandh and

Kāljamun were destroyed. Rakat-bīj and Kālunemu were annihilated. Slaying the demons, the Lord saved His Saints.7.]

86. The warrior clan of the Indian caste system.

87. Krishna's playmate, Krishna's Queen, and Rama's mother.

88. Hanuman's mother, Parasram's mother, and Gautam's wife.

89. This composition is written in saloks. The end of the *Jāpjī* of Guru Nanak is in the same metre.

90. Both the tree and cow fulfil all wishes.

91. The wife of Shiva.

92. The wife of Vishnu.

93. Literally, 'I rub my head on the floor of your doorway.'

94. The *ḍākaṇī* are like witches, the *sākaṇī* accompany the Goddess in her battles and have yogic powers and drink the blood of the demons.

95. The demon who stole the Vedas.

96. Kans was killed by Krishna dragging his hair (kesh), but reference here is made to taking this line to mean Kans and Keshī as two demons killed by Krishna. See *Krishnā Avatār*, verse 733.

97. See *Krishnā Avatār*, verse 849.

98. The *ashtbujā dhujā* is said to be Guru Gobind Singh's surviving weapon from a battle standard at Takht Hazur Sahib; it has eight prongs. In the oral tradition of the Nihang Singh Khalsa (Buddha Dal), this battle standard was presented to Guru Gobind Singh from the *shaktī* of Akal Purukh at the time of the havan episode at Naina Devi, near Anandpur Sahib. This composition is said to have been recited at the same time. Manuscript evidence in the form of the *DG* at Takht Patna Sahib confirms that this composition was written before AD 1698. For more information about the ashtbujā dhujā, see Jathedar Joginder Singh (1967) and Akali Nihang Kaur Singh (1934). The ashtbujā dhujā is shown to the congregation at Takht Hazur Sahib on a daily basis.

99. The four types of creation mentioned previously.

100. We find mention of the slaying of Mahisasur in *AG*, 224.

101. The chief tantric goddess.

102. As stated previously by the Guru, in his view the two religious paths have been polluted by those propagating them. This is a theme throughout the *AG* also and the Guru's *Apaṅī Kathā* in the *DG*.

103. Distinct from the Hindu and Muslim.

104. Kanwal, in *Dasmesh Bani Darpan*, writes, 'In "*Assa-di-Vaar*", the Muslims are the wearers of blue clothes e.g. "Neel bastar ley kapre pehrey turk pathani amal kiya." Meaning: all the people started wearing blue, the attire of the Muslims and also followed their way of life.' He therefore translates this line to mean that the Singhs will make the Turaks

who wear blue flee, which is the Namdhari translation of this line. In Panjabi the word *neel* means green–blue, the same colour of a bruise, a turquoise colour or just blue. Guru Nanak is said to have worn this colour on his trip to the Middle East, as narrated by Bhai Gurdas. If we take into account the *rahitnāme* written around this time, it is clear that this line is clearly talking about the colour blue. This is also reiterated by the contemporary court work *Vār Bhagautī jī kī*, by Bhai Gurdas II, *uṭhe singh bhujaṅgī nīlambar dharā*. This is appended to the famous work or *vārs* of Bhai Gurdas. An original sect of Namdharis still wears the colour blue; they are known as the Neeldharis.

105. The cow could signify the humble people.

106. See the end of *Vār Bhagautī jū kī*.

107. The end portion is known as the *phalashruti* and appears at the end of the other Chaṇḍī compositions in the *DG*.

108. MS 1455 (Amritsar: Khalsa College).

109. Kanwal, *Dasmesh Bani Darpan*.

110. Harkishan Singh, 'Ugradantī'. This article has a foreword by National Professor of Sikhism, Professor Kapur Singh.

111. Shah, 'Ugradantī'.

112. See *DG* recension, British Library, MSS. Panj. D6. There are other anthologies of this composition including one of 26 folios, circa 1750s, Panjab Archives, Patiala, No. 400. Printed versions of this composition also appeared in 1904 by Gulab Singh and Sons and there were also other lithographed copies prior to this.

113. Kuir Singh, *Gurbilās Pātishāhī 10*, 91. Kesar Singh Chhibbar, *Bansavlināmā*, who quotes the beginning of *Ugradantī*, verses 406–16, 418–28, 437–447, 460–70.

114. Kanh Singh Nabha, *Hum Hindū Nahiṅ* (Amritsar: Singh Brothers, 2000), 40–1. Also see the *chhakkā* entry in Nabha, *Mahān Kosh*; Tara Singh Narotam, *Srī Gurmat Niraṇe Sāgar*, Stone print, 1877.

115. This manuscript was examined and photographed on 24 October 2003.

116. Nabha, *Hum Hindū Nahiṅ*, 102, verse 390. This dialogue takes place in *Bansavalīnāmā* and both *Gurbilās* books of the Tenth Guru.

117. Kuir Singh, *Gurbilās Pātishāhī 10*, 91.

118. Kanh Singh Nabha, *Hum Hindū Nahiṅ*, 40–1.

119. Narotam, *Srī Gurmat*.

120. The Mir Mehdi in the *DG* is an example of this also. The Tenth Guru refers to himself as 'Gobind Das'. See *Rām Avatār*, 254.

121. ©*The British Library Board*, London, British Library, Mss. Panj. D6., f. 500 recto, dated AD 1847 and written in Devnagri script. This

manuscript has a note written within it, the 'Grunth Sahib published by Gooroo Gobind Singh', and was presented to the Paris Exhibition Society by Pundit Radha Kishun who is a councellor of Maharaja Ranjit Singh. It is highly decorated with gold, black, and red writing, showing the intricate work undertaken. See C. Shackle, *Catalogue of the Panjabi and Sindhi Manuscripts in the India Office Library* (London: India Office Library and Records, 1977), 8.

122. It is unclear what the first word in the name of the composition actually means—'sukh' means peace or happiness, but this also may refer to a psychic meridian in the brain cited by Yogis. With regard to manuscripts, the British Library version—MS. Panj. B39—has too many errors to be taken as an early copy. Therefore, reference has been made to two manuscripts at Patna Sahib, including the early AD 1698 manuscript, the 'Aurangabad' *DG*, as well as manuscript MS. 771. at Guru Nanak Dev University, Amritsar.

123. Indian musical mode, consisting of the *aroh: sa re ga re ma pa ni sa; avroh: sa ni dha ma pa, dha pa ma ga, ga re sa ni sa, vadi: re, samvadi: pa.*

124. This metre usually has five or more stanzas; this composition has eight. It is also usually connected with the salok. Each line is usually separated by a short pause, caesura. See E. Trumpp, *The Adi Granth or The Holy Scriptures of the Sikhs* (London: W.H. Allen and Company, 1877), 135.

125. The word 'You' has not been used in the poetry but it is clearly in reference to Akal Purakh, so it will be used throughout the translations.

126. A verse normally consisting of one distich, with a caesura normally towards the middle of the line. See Trumpp, *Adi Granth*, 135.

127. Trumpp, *Adi Granth*, 138. This metre is the reverse of a couplet or *dohirā*, with the smaller half preceding the longer half.

128. The three worlds are the physical, mental, and spiritual realms of the Indian cosmology.

129. Similar lines appear in the *AG*, 442: *gura goviṁdu goviṁdu gurū hai nānaka bhedu na bhāī.4.1.8.*

130. A similar composition narrating the devotees is in *AG*, 1106.

131. 'Kalī' could also mean death/darkness/time.

132. A similar criticism is found of this practice by Guru Nanak in *Āsā dī Vār*.

133. What seems to be expensive and inexpensive are the same, as well as the way they smell.

134. The Sikh mantra known as *Gurmantra*.

135. Do not shout bāṇī as the stressful sound of shouting does not match its beauty.

136. *Simran* is a practice of being in constant awareness of the Divine, and according to the tradition, it is achieved by the constant repetition of a mantra. This has been translated here as remembrance.

137. Abu Bakr, Ali, Umar, and Uthman.

138. This is again referring to a passage by Guru Nanak in *Āsā dī Vār* about the *Kuṭhā bakarā*—the *halal* meat of a goat consumed by the Brahmin priests of the time.

139. There are twenty-four avatārs of Vishnu in the *DG*, but the cosmology of the *AG*, and Bhai Gurdas *vārs* recognize only ten avatārs of Vishnu. The others are seen as minor incarnations. See *Vār Malār, AG*, p. 1279; Bhai Gurdas: *Vār* 12, *Pauṛī*. 8, and *DG, Chaubīs Avatār*, p. 156.

140. There are similar passages in the *Sukhmanī Sāhib* of Guru Arjan Dev, and other passages in the *AG*.

141. Four days of birth, youth, middle age, and being elderly.

142. The author draws on some Persian themes here.

143. See *DG, Bachitra Nāṭak, Apanī Kathā, Narāj Chhand.*

144. Various interchangeable names include *Sukhmanā* and *Sangre Sukhmanā*.

145. A nineteenth-century anthology which contains compositions of Guru Tegh Bahadur and Guru Gobind Singh (British Library: MS. Panj. B39). There also appears to be a translation by Sant Sampuran Singh.

146. There are slight variations of this line in extant manuscripts.

147. See the final verses of the *Das Gur Kathā*, MS. 1797A., Khalsa College, Amritsar, *f.* 32.

148. There is an extra line in some manuscripts about destroying the roots of the Turaks.

149. Kavi Kankan, a poet in the Guru's court, had written in his *Das Gur Kathā* written around AD 1700 that the Khalsa Panth became strong like Hanuman. See MS. 1797A, *f.* 32, in Khalsa College, Amritsar. Sikh history also narrates that Guru Gobind Singh kept a copy of the book *Hanūmān Nāṭak* in his *Kamarkasā*. According to another anecdote, he was offered a copy by Bahadur Shah. There is an extant copy of this work at Hazur Sahib, but it is not known whether this is the same copy. For more information, see the article and Gurmukhi text by Kamalroop Singh at www.scribd.com/doc/205998072 (last accessed in July 2015).

150. Another anecdote tells us that when the Guru was stationed with Bhai Dulla, he made the following pronouncement:

> I shall make sparrows destroy hawks. Whoever is my Sikh, shall not be without hair and sword. Without hair and arms, man is incomplete, only half a man. Man is complete only with hair and arms. At the Guru's command, the Sikhs adopted unshorn hair as well as

arms. At the same time the Guru decided to train his Sikhs in the art of war (*Sākhī* 18, Kharak Singh and Gurtej Singh [1708] 1995).

151. It is a known fact that the Guru was fond of his horses. At Takht Hazur Sahib there is a horse named Anmol which is said to be the off-spring of one of the Guru's horses named Dilbag.

152. The text we have used is a printed version copied from a text from AD 1744 from the Dharamsal of Hira, Geela Ram, *Gobind Gita* (Multan: Bharatiya Bhander, n.d.).

153. Ram, *Gobind Gita*, 314.

154. Ram, *Gobind Gita*, 325–6.

155. Ram, *Gobind Gita*, 327.

156. Ram, *Gobind Gita*, 332.

157. Ram, *Gobind Gita*, 420.

158. For more information about the history of standardization, see Chapter 3 of this book. See Sardul Singh, *Rīpoṭ Sodhak Kommittī Dasam Patāshāhī Srī Gurū Graṅth Sāhib jī dī* (Amritsar: Vazirchand Printers, 1897), 1–30. No reason was given in the standardization report. Hereinafter, *Sodhak Committee Report*.

159. *Sodhak Committee Report*.

160. *Sodhak Committee Report*, point 7.

161. This is noted by Rattan Singh Jaggi in *Dasam Granth Bāṇī Biorā*. This manuscript is now in the possession of the Nāmdhārī Samprādayā at Bhaini Sahib. It was originally in the precincts of the Harimandir Sahib complex.

162. *Sodhak Committee Report*, point 21.

163. *Sodhak Committee Report*, 10, 3rd section. The recension said to be compiled by Bhai Mani Singh does not contain the apocrypha, while the Sangrur recension does. Therefore, this may have also been another recension by Bhai Mani Singh.

164. Ami Shah in her write-up states that the *Ugradantī* does not appear in the *Mahān Kosh*. Shah, 'Ugradantī', 181–97; Nabha, *Mahān Kosh*.

165. Kanh Singh Nabha, *Hum Hindū Nāhiṅ*, 40–1.

166. See Giani Hardeep Singh, *Das Graṅthī* (Hazur Sahib, 2009).

167. The importance of this was mentioned to Kamalroop Singh by them.

168. Baba Sahib Singh Kaladhari was the last bastion of the Akalis who had sway over the Akal Takht. In 1920 the Singh Sabha reformers removed his authority together with the importance of the *DG*. This was demonstrated in the removal of the *DG* from many gurdwaras, as many of these places of worship were under the guardianship of the Akali Nihangs.

169. W.H. McLeod, *Sikhism* (London: Penguin Books, 1997), 190–1. Also see Beant Kaur, *The Namdhari Sikhs* (London: Sikhs Historical Museum, 1999). The movement was started by one Balak Singh in the nineteenth century. Their centre of activities was Bhaini, near Ludhiana. They advocated a boycott of British goods which would have inspired Mahatma Gandhi to follow a similar policy.

170. Baba Ram Singh *rahitnāma* quoted in *Rebels against the British Rule (Guru Ram Singh and the Kuka Sikhs)*, eds Bhai Nahar Singh and Bhai Kirpal Singh (New Delhi: Atlantic Publishers and Distributors, 1995), 28.

171. Singh and Singh, *Rebels against the British*, 148. *Memo on Ram Singh and the Kukas by J. W. Macnabb, Esq., late Officiating Commissioner, Ambala Division*, dated 4 November, 1871.

172. Harkishan Singh, 'Ugradantī'.

173. See Padam, *Gurū Gobiṅd Siṅgh jī*, 189.

174. Verse 41-1-8. *Vāhu vāhu Gobiṅd Siṅgh ape gur chelā.*

175. Verse 41-15-9. 'Singhs in blue, the rise of *Bhujangs*.'

176. Verse 41-16-4 to 20 copies the verses *Ugradantī* about the end of false rituals, the worship of idols, demi gods, and the end of all empty religious rituals.

177. Verse 41-20-12 is the *phalshurti* and reads like the end of the *Ugradantī*.

178. Attar Singh, trans., *The Travels of Guru Tegh Bahadar and Guru Gobind Singh* (Lahore: Indian Public Press, 1876), 21.

179. After the annexation of Panjab, reports were surfacing that according to the *Sau Sakhī*, the next person to lead the Sikhs and depose the British would be Maharajah Duleep Singh. His property was confiscated and he was taken by the British and became a personal favourite of Queen Victoria. This prophecy became a major factor in many Sikhs rebelling against the British rule. The prophecy was believed by Duleep Singh who felt it was his duty to return to Panjab and restore Sikh rule.

3

The Throne, Warriors, and the *Granth* of Akal

In the Sikh tradition a Takht Sahib is the highest authority, and is a place where a *gurmattā* or synod can be called.[1] Each Takht Sahib has a leader, sometimes known as a *pūjārī* or *jathedar*. This individual is selected by the previous leader to arrange and perform both *pāṭh* (liturgical ceremony) and *pūjā* (devotional rituals) in the inner sanctorum of the *takhts*.[2] As the leader mobilizes the various *jathās* (sects or units) of the Sikhs, this has led to the term 'General' (jathedar) commonly being employed.

In this chapter we shall examine the importance of the primary seat of authority, 'Sri Akal Takht' or the 'Throne of the Timeless', by considering its history and purpose. We will examine two chief components, namely the ceremonial role played by *shastras* and the *DG* within the takht. We will also consider the various *hukamnāmās* which have been issued from the takhts in relation to the *DG*, and how the history of the takht is connected to the militarization of the Sikh tradition.

The Origins of the *Takht*

Mīrī–pīrī represents the merger of both the saintly (spiritual side) and the soldiery (temporal side). The balance of the spiritual and the temporal is an aim which many religions strive to achieve. Modern historians of Sikhism have failed to recognize the transmission of the temporal aspects like *vīr ras* from the earlier gurus to the Tenth Guru who created the Khalsa. The temporal aspects of the religion came into fruition under the spiritual rule of Guru Arjan Dev. One relatively unknown development was that he recruited a number of soldiers. This was due to the ever worsening relations between the Sikhs and the Mughal rulers. Some notable warriors who sought the Guru and were eventually employed by him included Bhai Kalyan Sood, Bhai Bidhi Chand, Bhai Adit Soni, Bhai Pratap, Bhai Jaita, Bhai Piraga, Bhai Bhanu, and Bhai Ganga Sehgal.[3] The traditional account states that as a result of his growing popularity the Guru was brought before the Mughal authorities where he was tortured and attained martyrdom. This persecution would usher in the notion of martyrdom as being a noble act in the Sikh faith.

The soldiers from the Mughal army needed to be retrained to meet the spiritual and temporal needs of the Sikhs.[4] Their training was completed in the time of the Sixth Master, Guru Hargobind. Warriors like Bhai Sigaru and Bhai Jaita received training in weapons. This would help in obtaining rule (mīrī), but this needed to be balanced with an understanding of the *shabad* so that they could also attain spiritual wisdom.[5]

Then, how did the complete militarization of the religion take place? The architect of the new martial policy was actually Baba Buddha, whose role has seen little scholarly attention but is significant to our discussion. He began as a student of Guru Nanak and was fortunate enough to serve six gurus. A story about his longevity can be traced back to an encounter with Guru Nanak, who predicted Baba Buddha's long life, and explains why he would later participate in defending the new community:

> As a small boy, he [Baba Buddha] was one day grazing cattle outside the village when Guru Nanak happened to pass by. Bhai Bura [Buddha] approached him and bowing with a bowl of milk as his offering,

> spoke to him in this manner: 'O sustainer of the poor! I am fortunate to have had a sight of you today. Absolve me now from the circuit of birth and death.' The Guru said, 'You are only a child yet, but you talk so wisely.' 'Moghal soldiers set up camp in our village,' replied Bura, 'and they mowed down all our crops—ripe as well as unripe. Then it occurred to me that, when no one could check these indiscriminating soldiers, who would restrain death from laying his hand upon us, young or old.' At this Guru Nanak pronounced the words: 'You are not a child; you are wise like an old man.'[6]

Baba Buddha saw the atrocities committed by the Mughal armies and sought guidance from the Guru by asking how their continual attacks could be stopped or challenged. There is also a school of thought and oral tradition which stresses that the martial art originated from Guru Nanak.[7] The training in weapons for the young Hargobind was a turning point that would change the direction of the Sikh *panth*. On his inauguration as Guru by Baba Buddha, the *selī topī* was replaced with a turban, and the Guru also wore two swords denoting the swords of mīrī and pīrī.

For some Sikhs, this was a radical change and not to their liking, as is testified by the contemporary Sikh saint, Bhai Gurdas. He refers to the Guru's martial qualities in his *vārs*: 'This Guru, the vanquisher of armies, is very brave and benevolent.'[8] He states that the Sikh faith required protection, which he describes as 'an orchard requiring the defence of thorny and hedgy Kikar trees'.[9] The present location of Akali Phula Singh Burj and Gurdwara Mal Akhara (Amritsar) is said to be where Guru Hargobind and Baba Buddha gave instruction on *Shastravidiā*, and bouts of wrestling took place.[10]

The first authoritative account that gives details about the creation of Sri Akal Takht and the Harimandir Sahib is *Gurbilās Pātishāhī Chhevīṅ*. The *Gurbilās*, attributed to Kavi Sohan Singh, is the only book with intricate details on the *marayādā* of Sri Akal Takht, which, remarkably, is still followed to this day. The text states that *gurbāṇī* was central to the Sikh faith's development. This account, which is mainly about the Sixth Guru, was based on narrations given by Bhai Mani Singh to the *sangat*, and is likely to have been penned around AD 1718.[11] This book contains an interesting account of how the saints were inspired to become warriors:

He [Guru Hargobind] made the Takht for the [Sikh] Raj, the stone was laid by the Guru, and laboured on by Bhai Gurdas and Bhai Buddha. It was made in a beautiful way. The Guru made it with his own hands. Horses and *Shastras* were donated to the Takht.[12]

Kavi Sohan Singh further states:

A canopy, *nishān* [flag] and bards were brought to Baba Buddha. The Guru had a *Kalgī* [plume] on his *Dastar* [turban]. He looked like a King of kings and Saint of saints. The Guru was adorned in *Shastras* and sat on the throne in great peace.[13]

The Guru's attire symbolized what was to come and shastras were to play an important part in this development.[14] We also learn more about the martial aspects of the throne:

The Takht was called Akal Takht. The Timeless Being commanded [Guru Hargobind to] be seated on this throne and destroy the enemy. The Guru said that after me know the *Shastras* to be my form and keep them in this place in my honour. The Guru sat in *vīr asan* [heroic posture]. The poets sang the praises of the Guru.[15]

The Sikh tradition narrates that Akal Purakh manifested to aid the Fifth Guru in completing the *sarovar* (holy tank). The Divine Being assisted the Guru by collecting mud and depositing it; the place where the mud was collected is known as Hari kī Pauṛī (Steps of Hari), and became the foundations of Sri Akal Takht.[16] Then, in the tradition, the creation of the throne was based on a direct commandment from Akal Purakh. The serenity of the Sikhs, or *shanti ras*, was achieved by the recital of the *AG* in the form of the *Pothī Sāhib*. The poets and bards (*ḍhaḍhīs*) would infuse martial spirit into the populace by reciting poetry expressing vīr ras, with the shastras centrally positioned in the takht.[17] There were two notable ḍhaḍhīs in the court of the Guru, namely Abdul and Natha, who recited vārs (heroic odes or ballads) in praise of the Guru,

Ḍhaḍhī Abdullah sang the praises of the Guru in his *vārs*.
People were donating horses and clothes and came to do *pujā* [worship] of the weapons.[18]

The veneration and worship of weapons is a ritual that modern Sikhs have little understanding of. The offering of incense and other rituals all began during the time of Guru Hargobind. This ethos would also be instilled in the *DG* where numerous passages show the inextricable link between God and shastras. After visiting the takht, the Sikh warriors were said to be reinvigorated: '[T]he warriors came out reborn after visiting the Takht.'[19]

> The *pūjā* at the Takht was undertaken by Bhai Gurdas with flowers and incense. Everyday a recitation of *vārs* was undertaken. The Guru ordered that at first offerings and *pūjā* should be undertaken at Akal Takht and then to Harimandir Sahib. Baba Buddha said Guru ji you are wise and you know what suits the times.[20]

This routine of first offering prayers at the takht is still undertaken by the contemporary warriors named after Baba Buddha, the Akali Nihang Singhs. The Guru knew that Sri Akal Takht would have a separate purpose to the Harimandir Sahib and hence he commanded, 'For peace of mind go to the Harimandir Sahib and for *Rajogunī* [kingship] go to the Akal Takht Sahib.'[21] Whilst *Pothī Sāhib* symbolized pīrī, the mīrī was represented in the form of shastras. Its further representation by the gurus will now be considered in more detail.

Traditional Accounts of the *Graṅth* of Akal

Once again, we turn to the *Gurbilās* to shed light on the formation of the *DG*. In this work, Guru Hargobind prophesies to his brave warrior, Baba Bidhi Chand, how the Sikh scriptures would come into being in his tenth form, but unfortunately, this has not been noted by scholars.[22] According to the account, the warrior Guru wanted his martial tradition to be institutionalized for the Sikhs in his tenth form, and as a result, the fighting force known as Akāl Purakh kī Fauj (Warriors of Akal) was born.[23] Due to the key role played by Baba Buddha, the Khalsa army would carry his name; hence the name Buddha Dal. Interestingly, the official title of the organization is Shiromanī Paṅth Khālsā Akālī Buddha Dal Panjvāṅ Takht Chaldā Vahīr Chakravartī—'The Supreme Tradition of the Khalsa, the Immortal Army of the Wise, the Fifth Throne of the Sikhs, the Circumambulating Formation, and Sovereign in the four directions'. The title references the Akali Nihangs as the Fifth Throne of the Khalsa, who carry out the same traditional ceremonies of a takht on the move, the central focus being the worship of weapons and recitation of the graṅths.

The *khaṇḍe kī pāhul* ceremony institutionalized the consecration of *amrit* by the stirring of a sword in 1699, which was seen as the embodiment of God. According to the tradition, Guru Hargobind states:

> I will recite the *bāṇī* [Guru Granth Sahib] by assuming the form of the nine other Gurus and then the *dutī* [other] Granth [Dasam] which is in *Chhaṅds* I will write in my Tenth form for my pleasure.[24]

Sikh theology states that the gurus shared the same *jot* or light, and, as the body changed, the same aura was transmitted from Guru to Guru. This concept is noted in the *AG*, Bhai Gurdas *vār*s, *DG*, and Bhai Nand Lal's works.[25] This clearly shows the *bāṇī* of the *AG* was to be completed by the nine gurus, and in the tenth form, another graṅth was to be created. This other graṅth was titled the 'Granth of the Tenth King'. As noted in Chapter 1, the *DG* manuscripts dated 1695/1696, the 'Anandpurī' *biṛh* and the 1698 'Takht Patna' *biṛh*, which is entitled *Pātishāhī Dasvīṅ jū kā Graṅth*, testifies to this ongoing sovereignty. This prophetic statement also tells us that this graṅth was to be written in *chhaṅds* (metres), and a close examination of the *DG* shows that the majority of verses are indeed written in chhaṅds. Several early accounts also recorded in the court of the Tenth Guru that both the *AG* and *DG* were ceremonially enthroned.[26] Another account also refers to the Ninth Guru predicting the *Granth of Guru Gobind Singh* at Damdama Sahib. Guru Tegh Bahadur was seen bowing to an empty mound and the Sikhs questioned this action. He replied that he would appear in his tenth manifestation at this location and a grand temple would be built here. He would find a third path (*tisārā* panth) and write a new graṅth.[27] These prophetic statements demonstrate to us that the works of the other nine previous gurus or other poets were not considered by the chroniclers to have been inserted into the *DG*. Therefore, in the tradition, the creation and completion of the *DG* was the preserve of the Tenth King only.

The *Granth* of Guru Gobind Singh at Sri Akal Takht

Bhai Mani Singh was sent to manage the affairs of the Akal Takht by Guru Gobind Singh. Like other early descriptions of the Khalsa, Bhai Mani Singh is described as being dressed in blue with a high turban, reading his *nitnem*, and being armed at all times.[28] As he recompiled the *DG*, there is a good probability that he also enthroned it at Sri Akal Takht while performing his duties. Manuscript evidence points to this, as the report of AD 1897 by Sardul Singh states that a very old volume of the *DG* was present at Sri Akal Takht.[29] An earlier account by Seva Singh (1800) also verifies this description in the report. He narrates that in Vaisākh 1755 VS/AD 1698, Guru Gobind Singh sent Bhai Mani Singh with five Singhs to Amritsar to undertake the care of the Harimandir Sahib complex, and they left Anandpur Sahib with one granth and a *Nishān Sāhib*.[30] At Sri Akal Takht they formally opened the granth (*prakāsh*; open reverence) and did the *ardās*, and raised the standard.[31] This was the same year as completion of the *Rām Avatār*, and in this year, two important *DG* recensions were completed, one is partly extant with a date of AD 1698 and used to be in Amritsar but is now in Panjab University in Chandigarh.[32] It is highly significant that the index of this early recension does not contain *Zafarnāmah* (see Figure 3.1). The manuscript records clearly that it contains the 'bāṇī of the Tenth Sovereign'.[33]

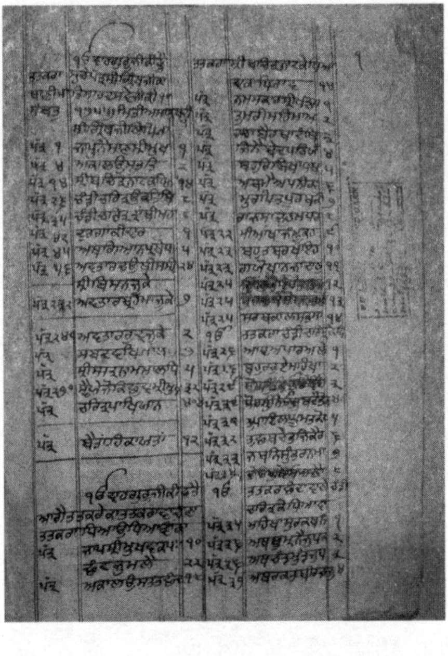

FIGURE 3.1 A *DG* Manuscript Contents Folio from AD 1698 Previously Kept at Sri Akal Takht

Another recension, the Patna *Misal DG*, was kept in prakāsh at Sri Akal Takht around AD 1765. After the reformers took possession of the takht, this recension was no longer placed on enthronement (see Figure 3.2). Occasionally, due to the demand of the sangat, wanting to see its beautiful decorations, it would be enthroned, which is recorded by Kanh Singh Nabha.[34] In *Shahīd Bilās*[35] and *Gur Panth Parkāsh* by Rattan Singh, the authors record Bhai Mani Singh as the custodian of Sri Akal Takht. Significantly, the chapter order in the Patna *Misal DG* is identical to the recompiled *DG* of Bhai Mani Singh. The Patna *Misal* has an identical copy in the *toshekhānā* at Takht Patna Sahib, where another very early extant manuscript of AD 1698 is present. The original *AG–DG* recension was at Hazur Sahib for some time—this is recorded by Akali Nihang Kaur Singh.[36] Manuscripts were readily moved around to different takhts and some prominent Sikhs produced copies.[37]

The tradition of writing manuscripts started in the time of the Fifth Guru, and in the time of Guru Gobind Singh at Adi Singhāsan Damdama Sahib (Bhora Sahib) in Anandpur Sahib. The name would suggest the enthronement of the *AG* at this place also.

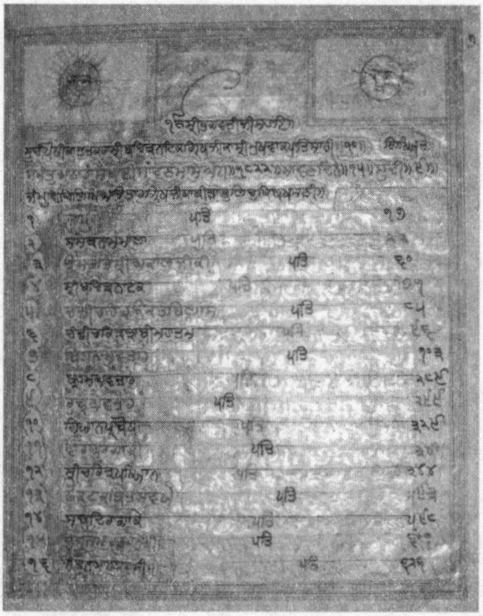

FIGURE 3.2 Patna *Misal DG* Manuscript
Source: Kamalroop Singh.

It was at this location that the Guru started compiling scriptures including *AG*, *DG*, and *Sarabaloh Granth*. Bawa Sumer Singh,[38] the jathedar of Takht Patna Sahib, states that the Guru wrote a copy of *AG* at this time, after asking Dhirmal for the original *AG*.[39] In modern-day Sikhism, or what one could call neo-Sikhism, there is an over-emphasis on *AG* as the only scripture in the Sikh panth. This was possibly one of the reasons to solidify the position of the second Damdama Sahib in Bhatinda as a takht, due to the story of the dictation of *AG* at this place.

The *Marayādā* of the *Dasam Granth* at the *Takhts*

In traditional practices we find the *DG*, and sometimes a third granth, the *Sarabaloh Granth*, alongside the *AG*. This is found at two takhts, Hazur Sahib and Patna Sahib. Some European linguists came across the third scripture; for example, Grierson, who gives an account of the *Sarabaloh Granth* in his work on language.[40] The dual enthronement of the two scriptures was also present in Panjab before and during colonial times. However, in the 1940s, the *DG* was unceremoniously removed and labelled as 'graphic' and 'Hindu' in nature. There is no contention about the *AG* receiving the Guruship, but the real issue is what the Sikh canon consists of.

We can be certain that by the turn of the nineteenth century the *DG* was being venerated together with the *AG* under the orders of Akali Phula Singh at Sri Akal Takht. All important decisions, or gurmattās, were made with both *Granth*s present.[41] The Akali warriors guarded the takht where the tradition of taking khaṅḍe kī pāhul with both scriptures took place and still takes place within the Nihang Dals.[42] The importance of the *DG* was also witnessed in the court of Maharaja Ranjit Singh, who ensured that both *Granth*s were carried in procession when his armies went to battle.[43]

In the eighteenth and nineteenth centuries, we also see other takhts having the *DG* present with the *AG* notably at Takht Patna Sahib, the birthplace of Guru Gobind Singh.[44] The Tenth Guru was born in Patna, Bihar, and spent his early childhood there (see Figure 2.10). His weapons, early writing, bed, clothes, and other relics are still preserved there.[45] Patna developed as a centre of Sikhism during the time of Guru Tegh Bahadur. When the Tenth Guru commenced his scriptural works he communicated with Patna Sahib by sending many encyclical edicts and scriptures there, which are still extant today.[46] In the previous chapter we discussed several *DG* manuscripts bearing a relationship with Patna Sahib. One of the earliest Western references to the marayādā in a takht was by Charles Wilkins. His description of the 'College' at Patna which presumably refers to the takht gives an eyewitness testimony of both scriptures being kept together.[47]

It is quite clear that the *AG* and *DG* being ceremoniously placed together was no anomaly and a part of the tradition. During the British period there are numerous instances of the *DG* being cited in literature alongside the *AG*.[48] After the Anglo-Sikh wars, the British were to become the masters of Panjab, and the Khalsa armies laid down their shastras, an event which was one of the most humiliating scenes that the Sikhs have had to face in their entire history. With the establishment of the British Raj, the Christian missionaries made inroads into Panjab. They were able to define the Sikh religion in their own language, and hence influence generations to come.[49] This also led to Hindus being viewed antagonistically by the Sikhs, due to the differences of the two religions, particularly idol worship. The British saw the veneration of many gods and goddesses as a more primitive form of religion. The monotheistic view of the Sikhs as seen in the *AG* was more in tune with Christian beliefs. As the *DG* contained the description of Hindu *avatārs*, the *DG* began to be seen in the same light as the Hindu scriptures.

While Lt. Col. Malcolm[50] described the marayādā of the *DG*, later accounts, written after the Anglo-Sikh wars, looked at the *DG* suspiciously. The first writer who described the compositions of the *DG* in major detail was J.D. Cunningham in his *History of the Sikhs*.[51] His understanding of the Sikh scriptures was limited and the descriptions of the compositions contradictory. This is surprising as he witnessed the Khalsa Raj of Maharaja Ranjit Singh and was a visitor to his court.

During colonial rule there were still some pockets of resistance in Panjab, with the Kukā Movement and individuals like Bhai

Maharaj Singh who still continued to fight against the British after annexation.[52] The Akali Nihangs tried to maintain the traditions and marayāda of the Khalsa. With the British military in control of Panjab, the influence of the Akali Nihangs at Sri Akal Takht was weakening. This forced the Nihang Singhs to go to the other takht, namely Hazur Sahib. The idea was to consolidate their power far from Panjab.

We also know that Sri Akal Takht made many rulings on the *DG* and we need to consider this in more detail. One of the early edicts issued by Sri Akal Takht in 1934 VS/AD 1878 details the authorized method of preparing amrit.[53] It states what compositions should be read when preparing amrit and the injunctions that the Sikhs should follow.[54] The hukamnāmā mentions compositions from the *AG* and the *DG* and the rules the Pañj Piāre should follow. This edict shows the consistency of Sikh thought throughout the late nineteenth century; it also informs us of the fact that the Sikh martial art was still being sanctioned. It states, 'To practice *Shastravidiā* and keep a *Shastra* in a *gatrā*.' The hukamnāmā was in defiance of the Indian Arms Act introduced by the British in the same year. Nowadays, the Akali Nihangs are one of the only religious groups who have the authority (by licence) to bear arms in India.

The Standardization of the *Dasam Granth*

With the appearance of different recensions of the *DG*, the standardization of the *Granth* was undertaken. The Sodhak Committee was set up under the guidance of Gurmat Granth Parcharak Sabha Amritsar which examined thirty-two different recensions of the *DG*. There were twenty-four members in this team including experts in Gurmukhi and Persian. One scholar had knowledge of *pingal* (metrics) and *rāg* (modes of music), and there was also a *giānī* of Harimandir Sahib and the grandson of Giani Gian Singh.[55] The *akhand pāṭh* of the *DG* was undertaken before the commencement of this important task.

After five years of deliberations and detailed examination of the manuscripts on the second floor of Sri Akal Takht, the eminent scholars clarified the differences in the recensions and published their report in 1897, titled the 'Report of Verification & Standardisation of *DG*' by Khalsa Diwan. With regard to authenticity, they stated that the whole of the *DG* was the work of Guru Gobind Singh and they based this conclusion on many parameters including manuscript evidence. They gave all the internal dates of when the compositions were written in the *DG*, and gave commentaries on all the compositions and reasons why they were written. For instance, with regard to the *Srī Charitropakhyān*, the report states:

> The *Charitropakhyān* 404 is a treasure house of *Rāj-nītī* [statecraft] and worldly arts. With this knowledge we can live in comfort and in these teachings we can stay safe in this world, by worshipping one Akal Purakh and save ourselves from lust, anger, gambling, vices, etc.[56]

They also linked the *Zafarnāmah* with the *Hikāitāṅ* of the *DG*.[57] The pen names of the Guru, Ram and Shyam, were explained. The report writers were aware that both *Graṅths* were ceremonially placed together in the tradition, and as a result, they stated, 'On the seat of Guruship is the *AG* and next to it is placed the Tenth Guru's Granth Sahib hence it can be ascertained that it is orated by the Guru.'[58] They also gave some interesting anecdotes as to the praxis of the *DG*. The recital of certain compositions on auspicious occasions at the Harimandir Sahib and Sri Akal Takht was made apparent:

> If this *bāṇī* was not orated by Sri Gobind Singh [*SrīMukhvāk*] why are all the *bāṇīs* of the Guru, like the *Ten Svaiyes* and *Chaupaī* employed at the time of the *Amrit Saṅchār*, and why is the *pāṭh* of *Rām Avatār* undertaken at Dusshera and *Chaṇḍī Charitrā paṭh* at Navarati at the Takhts, and the *Krishnāvatār Svaiyes* which are read at the time of Holla Mahalla. In the Darbar Sahib all of them are original traditions, and this proves that they are the words of the Guru.[59]

At Hazur Sahib the recitations of the above compositions still take place at these festivals, and the Akali Nihangs' display of warlike fervour is exhibited on these occasions, especially at Holla Mohalla at Anandpur Sahib. Interestingly, to this day, the *kirtānīs* at the Harimandir Sahib recite verses from the *DG* in kirtan. The report also referred to the many manuscripts of the *Graṅth of Guru Gobind Singh*. They gave details about the akhaṅd pāṭhs of the *DG* taking place at Sri Akal Takht and other gurdwaras. The Buddha Dal had been responsible for the upkeep, the restoration, and creation of new gurdwaras and *dharamsālās*, and therefore so many gurdwaras had the *AG* installed together with the *DG*.[60] As the Shiromani Gurdwara Parbandhak Committee (SGPC) took control over many of gurdwaras, they had the *DG* removed from them. Some of the *DG sarūps* that the committee considered were taken from Sri Akal Takht itself.[61] Another sarūp the committee considered was used for prakāsh outside Jhandā Bunga: the space outside the Darshan Deori (gates) where the *jhandās* (flags of mīrī and pīrī) are standing (see Figure 3.3).[62] All the *DG* recensions were placed outside the Darshan Deori presumably to let the sangat have darshan of the many sarūps.[63] It was also seen that the *granthīs* of Harimandir Sahib kept personal copies of the *DG* as well.[64]

FIGURE 3.3 Akali Nihang with a *Nagāṛā* in Front of the Darshan Deori in 1899
Source: Gurinder Singh Mann. Stereoscopic view photographed and published by B.W. Kilburn-Littleton N.H.

After the publication of this report a *DG* recension was published in 1902 by Wazir Hind Press, Amritsar.[65] They printed the *DG* with some compositions being deleted, and this included compositions like *Ugradantī*, *Mālkaunskī Vār*, and *Sanshār Sukhmanā* being excised. They did not give many reasons for these compositions to be taken out (as mentioned in the previous chapter). Although not all sarūps of the *DG* contained the aforementioned compositions, there was enough historical information behind them to be considered as *Srī Mukhvāk*. However, the compositions continued to be recited by the Akali Nihangs and other *samprādāya* like the Namdharis.

The Sikh Reformist Movement and Sri Akal Takht

With the advent of the Singh Sabha Movement, attempts were made to remove the *DG* from Sri Akal Takht. The reform movements were opposed to the increasing mismanagement of gurdwaras. As a result, Hindu idols in the precincts of the Darbar Sahib were removed and the pujārīs who were in charge of the Harimandir Sahib and Sri Akal Takht were also forcibly replaced. In Sikh history, the reform movement was seen as a great development and an attempt for the religion to shed the connotations of Hinduism and other rituals, which the reformers felt were not in unison with Sikh thought. However, the reform went too far with the Bhasauria group and the SGPC attempting to influence the marayādā of the Sikhs. The political movement associated with the reforms cleverly used the name Akali to give themselves legitimacy, and thus displaced the Nihangs from their traditional role as the guardians of gurdwaras.

As a part of the new religious structure in Panjab, the land and gurdwaras associated with the Buddha Dal were brought into SGPC control. One of their targets was the Akali Phula Singh Burj located in the vicinity of the Harimandir Sahib. There were several court cases undertaken by the SGPC to take the Burj into their control. This attempt at bringing the Burj under their control failed, and the Akali Nihangs have kept the marayādā of the *DG* intact at the Burj since that time.[66] Another example of undermining the *Granth of Guru Gobind Singh* by the reformers can be seen in the following description. A copy of the *DG* was desecrated at the historic Gurdwara Ramsar, where *Guru Granth Sahib* was originally compiled. According to the document, *Missī Jatt de Kartūt* (The Deeds of a Hybrid Caste), the prakāsh of the *DG* was taking place at the gurdwara in the 1920s.[67] The author refers to the SGPC as 'Ingrez' Sikhs (English Sikhs) who, in his opinion, were influenced by the British mindset. As the prakāsh was taking place, the granthī undertaking the recital was replaced by an Ingrez granthī. The witness then states the following,

> The *Ingrez* [SGPC] *Granthī* deliberately started tearing out pages of Dasam Guru Granth with a knife. This act was then blamed on a person from Damdama, then a Nirmalā, and then a Namdhari, when the Sangat found out about this desecration there was outrage.[68]

It was quite clear that the desecration of the *DG* was against Sikh sentiments. When this offence took place the prakāsh of the *DG* at Gurdwara Ramsar had been a consistent practice since the last century (see Figure 3.4).[69]

It was only a matter of time until there would be an attempt to remove the *DG*. This was undertaken without any consultation

FIGURE 3.4 Fresco on the Walls of Gurdwara Ramsar Showing the *Prakāsh* of Both *Granths*
Source: Kamalroop Singh.

and without the approval of the sangats. Baba Sahib Singh 'Kaladhari' was seen as the last Akali Nihang jathedar of Sri Akal Takht. Some scholars contend that the Akalis were completely removed from the affairs of Sri Akal Takht after the Anglo-Sikh wars, but our assessment concerns the Nihang Singhs being physically removed in 1920 (see Figure 3.5).[70] The reformer Sikhs not only delivered a major blow to the Akali Nihangs in terms of their traditional authority, but also removed the *DG* from Sri Akal Takht.

Kartar Singh Jhabbar was the senior leader in the gurdwara reform movement and in 1920 he set upon taking control of Sri Akal Takht from the Akali Nihangs. Oral tradition states that he and his group were careful not to send any mobs of men into the takht; instead, they sent a large group of women to attack the Akali Nihangs.[71] Baba Sahib Singh would not retaliate against the women. He stated, '[Y]ou are like my daughters, but if it pleases you, take your anger out on me.' In the process, the Baba's bones were broken and he was heavily wounded.[72]

According to eyewitness accounts, the damage to the 'Amritsar AD 1698' manuscript was due to it being thrown out of Sri Akal Takht during the 'reform', with a spear from the second floor.[73] This is why the volume in question has a large hole through the

FIGURE 3.5 Akali Nihang Singh, Amritsar, 1920
Source: Valentine Chirol, 'India and Its Myriad Races, Beliefs and Customs', in *Peoples of All Nations: Their Life To-day and the Story of Their Past*, ed. John Alexander Hammerton (London: The Fleetway House, 1922), 2823.

underside of the folios where the spear had pierced through half the volume. This later became mouldy, but thankfully, it was digitized before that point. This story has received little or no attention in print or has been intentionally removed from Sikh history, but it continues to be told in the oral accounts of the Akali Nihangs. The SGPC account differs in several respects, alleging that the Akali Nihangs were chased away.[74] The jathedar paid a heavy price for attempting to keep the original marayādā intact and also went to prison for protesting against the size restrictions of the *kirpān* by the British.[75] After the contest at Sri Akal Takht, the reformers wanted to displace the Nihang Singhs, and one way to ensure this was to take the name Akali and create their own political party called the Shiromani Akali Dal.[76]

Principal Harkrishan Singh who was also an eyewitness to the events at Sri Akal Takht describes how the reform movement wanted to eradicate the power of the Akali Nihangs,

> It occurred to us that since they called themselves Akalis and claimed the Akal Bunga or Akal Takht on the ground of their being Akalis, we should also have the appearance of Akalis....
>
> We asked our men and women volunteers to plunge their clothes in blue colour and wear blue dress like the *Nihangs* and call themselves Akalis. *I want to emphasize that this was the beginning of the Akali movement* [emphasis by authors]. The word Akalis and the blue Akali dress were only a boyish prank to silence the Nihang Singhs. 'You call yourself Akalis; we are also Akalis. We wear blue dress. You say Akal Takht belongs to you. It belongs to us as we are also Akalis'. The word Akali and the Akali insignia the blue dress, weighed at that time. This gave the movement a name and gave the party a name. [77]

Accordingly, the Nihangs were displaced from Sri Akal Takht. Harkrishan Singh, after many years of reflection, contends that the Singh Sabha reformers had gone too far and they should have used other tactics to introduce change in gurdwaras. As the number of casualties mounted during the reform movement, individual jathas had a race as to who could control the most gurdwaras, and he states that 'the Akalis [reformers] behaved as very arrogant, proud and indisciplined people'.[78]

This coup d'état on the mīrī institutions of the Sikhs has had a catastrophic effect. For example, the Sikh martial art, *Shastravidiā*, has declined as there are only a handful of practitioners remaining.[79] After its removal, even though the *DG* no longer held an equal position in Sri Akal Takht, it was still brought out on auspicious occasions. One example includes the birthday celebrations of Guru Gobind Singh in 1944. Dr Dharam Pal Ashta states in his work, *The Poetry of the Dasam Granth*:

> In 1944, from December 21 to December 25, on the occasion of the birthday celebrations of Guru Gobind Singh, there was held an Akhaṅd Path of the *DG* at the Akal Takhat by Jathedar Mohan Singh who was then the Jathedar of the Akal Takhat Sahib as well as president of the Shiromani Gurdwara Prabandhak Committee.[80]

We also learn that Randhir Singh, a scholar who was employed by the SGPC, was one of the granthīs who undertook the akhaṅḍ pāṭh.[81] Randhir Singh was no stranger to the *DG* as he had also authored a monumental work on the *DG* entitled *Shabad Mūrati*, as well as a lengthy commentary on the scripture.

The Change in *Marayādā*

The first open call to take away the authority of the moving takht (Buddha Dal) from the Guru Khalsa Panth was by Teja Singh Bhasauria (1867–1933), a civil servant employed by the British administration of Panjab.[82] He wished to make his village into the Fifth Takht, the so-called 'Khalsa Parliament'. He christened his organization the Panch Khalsa Divan, with bold English letters adjoining it as the 'Khalsa Parliament'. His books contain 'resolutions' and the poor use of Western hermeneutics. Generally, his views were and still are considered heretical by most Sikh scholars, and this led to him being declared an apostate (*tankhāiyā*) for altering gurbāṇī.[83] In his *Khālsā Rahit Prakāsh* he calls for the removal of the *DG* from ceremonial placement alongside *AG*, and for *DG* to be edited to include only what he considers to be 'Srī Mukhvāk bāṇī'.[84] He also attempted to move the location of traditional ceremonies.[85] In total, he called for a number of changes, including the editing of *Chaupaī Sāhib* and *Rahirās Sāhib*. This change crept into the Panth due to his loyal supporters, like Giani Kartar Singh Kalaswalia.[86] We learn how this change took place,

> When Kartar Singh Kalaswalia became a *Granthī* at Harimandir Sahib, he along with others made the decision to shorten the length of the *Rahirās*. This new one that was created by Panch Khand Bhasauria should only be read. Twenty-five stanzas of the *Chaupaī Sāhib* should be read. They did this and began to read the *Anaṅd Sāhib*, then *Mundavaṇī*, and started to read the *Ardās* without the three closing compositions of the *Rahirās*. In this way half the *Rahirās* is still recited at the Harimandir Sahib.[87]

Teja Singh was warned by the Maharaja of Patiala not to take the *Rāgmālā* out of *AG*, to stop his plan of printing and distributing his edited version of *AG*, and desist from calling his organization the Khalsa Parliament. This led to him being excommunicated from the Khalsa Panth on 9 August 1928. He had preached and printed books for decades up to this point.[88] The legacy and impact by the Bhasauria group still needs to be fully understood. However, his shortened version of the bāṇīs was initially resisted by Sri Akal Takht, but by the time of the formation of the Sikh Rahit Marayādā in 1945, the changes were irreversible with the shortened bāṇīs now considered to be the norm and a standard practice.[89]

Rulings of the *Takhts*

Sri Akal Takht has deliberated many times on the status, importance, and authorship of the *DG*. In 1977 Giani Bhag Singh wrote a book entitled *Dasam Granth Niraṇai* which again questioned the *DG*. He apologized for his failings at the takht in the same year. On 5 April 2003, another hukamnāmā from Sri Akal Takht was issued, this time to Gurbakhsh Singh Kala Afghana, after his publication of ten volumes titled *Bipran kī Rīt toṅ Sach dā Mārag* or 'From Emulation of the Brahmins to the True Path'. At the tri-centenary celebrations of the Khalsa at Hazur Sahib, the hukamnāmā mentioned—dated 16 September 1998—was issued, stating that all gurdwaras should undertake the prakāsh of the *DG* together with the *AG*:

> It must be also noted that in all the historical Gurdwaras, the places of the Guru, and Takhts, the Sri Dasam Guru Granth Sahib should be *prakāsh* (present with the *AG*) (to celebrate the 300 years of Khalsa fully). As the Amrit Sanchar *bāṇī, Sri Jāpu Sāhib, Sri Amrit Svaiye Sāhib,* and *Chaupaī Sāhib,* recitations are from the Sri Dasam Guru Granth Sahib, and this is the traditional way in all the Takhts, the Sri Dasam Guru Granth Sahib was *prakāsh* up to 1932 until it was stopped.
>
> However at the Takht Hazur Sahib and Takht Harimandir Sahib (Patna Sahib) today this respected tradition is still continuing that the Sri Dasam Guru Granth Sahib is *prakāsh.* For this the whole India Sikh Sangat are requested that at any Gurdwara and historical places the Sri Dasam Guru Granth Sahib should be *prakāsh,* then the 300 years of the Khalsa Panth can be celebrated, and the blessings of the Tenth Guru obtained.[90]

Sri Akal Takht was also asked to intervene again with regard to the directives on the *DG* in the year 2000, when the authenticity of the *Granth* was questioned. The jathedar at the time, Joginder Singh Vedanti, instructed that there should not be any debate on the *DG.* Whilst this was intended to bring some respite, it in fact pushed some groups into publishing numerous write-ups and publications. In sharp contrast to this directive of 2000, he reversed his decision in November 2006. He stated, 'Panthic scholars should refute the baseless claims of these mischievous miscreants using examples from Sikh history and the Divine light of *Gurmat.*' The jathedar quite rightly had taken the middle ground with his first edict, but the number of publications denouncing the *DG* had reached fever pitch, and as a result, the nitnem bāṇīs were under attack.

The takht had spoken again to ensure that the *DG* was protected once more. In the same year, on 11 November, the celebrations known as *Zafarnamāh* Fateh Divas commemorated the importance of the *DG* and the despatching of the *Zafarnāmah* by Guru Gobind Singh.[91] All the jathedars of the takhts attended the event and speeches were made by numerous samprādayās including the Buddha Dal, Damdami Taksal, Nanaksar, Nirmalas, and Udasis. In connection with this event, a council took place among renowned Sikh scholars, religious heads, and gianīs.

In 2008 the Sikh panth celebrated 300 years of the bestowal of 'Living Guru' on the *AG*, and hence in reaction to further criticism of the *DG*, another edict was pronounced.[92] This time, under Jathedar Joginder Singh Vedanti, the edict gave further instructions on the *DG*:

> Debates presented in relation to DG are totally needless. No one has the right to present a questionable debate on the writings from DG, as the Panth has accepted them and employs them for the Sikh Rehat *Marayādā, nitnem* and *Amrit Saṅchār*. The whole Panth should be reminded that DG is an inseparable part of Sikh history, but Guru Gobind Singh did not give it equal status to Sri Guru Granth Sahib, and for this reason no other Granth can be *prakāsh* equal to Sri Guru Granth Sahib.

This hukamnāmā seemed a little confusing as the prakāsh of *DG* is/was prevalent throughout numerous gurdwaras and takhts. Moreover, it was an attempt to make people understand that the *AG* and *DG* were not equal in status 'as the Guru'. Another factor which needs clarification is that the *DG* is not in prakāsh as an equal to the *AG*, and this can be witnessed when viewing the *palkīs* of the *DG* at the takhts which are lower in height.

As the celebrations for *Gur-Gaddī* or bestowing of the *AG* at Takht Hazur Sahib, Nanded, gathered pace in October 2008, several more important proclamations were made from the takht and other samprādayās. The '*DG* Pāṭh-bodh Samagam' or 'Recitation and Understanding Conference of the *DG*' was undertaken by the Damdami Taksal at Hazur Sahib.[93] The next Sri Akal Takht jathedar, Giani Gurbachan Singh, commented on the relationship of the *AG* and the *DG*, '*Purātan rahitnāmās* state that the Dasam Granth and the Guru Granth Sahib should be read together.' The jathedar of Takht Sri Patna Sahib, Giani Iqbal Singh, stated, 'Those against Dasam Granth are trying to tarnish the name of the Dasam Granth.' He continued, 'Takht Patna Sahib is the flag bearer of *DG*, ensuring it is respected and protected.' Jathedar of Hazur Sahib, Giani Kulwant Singh, stated, '[V]arious Panthic groups who teach the *saṅthiā* of Guru Granth Sahib should also undertake the *saṅthiā* of *DG*.'[94]

At the conclusion of the celebrations in November 2008, Jathedar Giani Kulwant Singh stated that no objections regarding the *DG* should be raised, and it was the moral duty of all Sikhs to give the *DG* due honour and respect.[95] It was interesting to note that as the *AG* celebrations were being commemorated, the *DG* was being discussed, presumably to show the unity of the Sikh scriptures. This was in tune with the marayādā and the tradition of mīrī–pīrī and *Sant Sipāhī*. Even more recently, it was noteworthy that a former Sri Akal Takht jathedar, Ragi Darshan Singh, was declared tankhāiyā by the current leader, Giani Gurbachan Singh, for failing to explain comments made by him in a discourse at Rochester Gurdwara, New York.[96] His discourse explained *Charitras* (21–3) very poorly, and was centred on the tale of a Raja visiting a prostitute. It was argued that Darshan Singh appears to have misquoted the *Charitras* from the *DG* and ascribed a situation which was not directly related to Guru Gobind Singh.[97] As a result, the jathedars of the seats of polity summoned Ragi Darshan Singh and decided to punish him. Further, they also gave him a month to clarify his position regarding the discourse on *Charitra* (21–3) by 7 January 2010. He failed to appear, and in an unprecedented move, he was given an extension until 29 January 2010. As a result, this led Sikhs to look more closely at the *DG*; the jathedars explained the issue was Ragi's incorrect narration of the *Charitras* and not the *DG* per se. Jathedar Giani Gurbachan Singh stated that the marayādā of the *AG* and *DG* at the Akal Takht, Patna Sahib, and Hazur Sahib were traditional practices or a *purātan marayādā*.

The *DG* is still ceremonially placed in a central position with *AG* in two of the five sacred takhts of the Sikhs. Furthermore, if the Buddha Dal is seen to be the fifth throne of the Guru Khalsa, and having a legitimate tradition, then the *DG* still occupies a key position. This is in stark contrast to the neo-Sikhism that had modified the Sikh praxis and Rahit Marayādā of the Tenth Guru.[98] Two other traditional Sikh theological works support this view, the first being Sant Giani Gurbachan Singh in *Gurbāṇī Pāṭh Darpaṇ*.[99] In this work, one chapter is dedicated to the *DG*, and is similar to the material written by Nihang Teja Singh in *Adi Dasam Srī Gurū Granth Sāhib jī*,[100] an internal publication of the Buddha Dal. This work provides us with a model of the praxis in the traditional schools of Sikhism. It is brief but gives an accurate account of the rituals of the *DG* in tradition. As Takht Hazur Sahib has both the

AG and *DG* in the main takht, the Hazuri Sikhs claim it is a direct praxis from the Tenth Guru.[101] In *Hazurī Sāthī* by Akali Nihang Kaur Singh[102] we find the same description by Jathedar Joginder Singh in his work on the tradition at Hazur Sahib.

Prakāsh of Both *Granths*

Now we need to turn to some of the architectural aspects of Sri Akal Takht which shed light on the prakāsh of the *AG* and *DG*. Some aspects related to the marayādā of the *DG* and how it was to be placed at the takht have not been considered. The presence of the *DG* at Takhts Hazur Sahib and Patna Sahib does give us some answers on this. A closer examination of how the *AG* is presently kept at Sri Akal Takht suggests there is something missing. Looking at the frontal view of how the *AG* and the shastras are arranged, we see that the arrangement at the throne differs from that at gurdwaras. In a gurdwara, the *AG* is placed on a *palikī* (ceremonial canopy) and on some occasions, shastras are placed in front of it and the sangat approaches the *Granth* and bows before it. The granthī sits behind the *AG*. At Sri Akal Takht the shastras are placed within a palikī, and the *AG* is in prakāsh to the left of them. The *AG* is placed on its side and as a result the sangat would *mathā tekh* (bow) to either the shastras, which would face them, or to the left, where the *AG* is in prakāsh (see Figure 3.6).

Anyone facing the palikīs and the shastras will notice that there is a void to the right of the shastras making the whole arrangement appear strange. Why is there a space on the right of the shastras and why is the *AG* placed on its side? It is our position, after examining the history and photographic evidence, that this space would have been reserved for the 'Granth of the Tenth King'.

We also need to consider the arrangements of the *Granth* at the other takhts. At Takht Hazur Sahib, there are two palikīs in the main *divan* area; the one on the left is larger and is where the *AG* is placed. In the space between the palikīs at the back is the area known as Angithā Sahib where the numerous historical weapons of the Tenth Guru and the Khalsa are kept. On the left hand side, there are smaller palikīs where the *DG* is housed. The large size and shape of the dome makes it clear that the *AG* is the prominent

FIGURE 3.6 *Prakāsh* of *AG* at Sri Akal Takht
Source: Ripudaman Singh.

Granth (see Figure 3.7). All the major gurdwaras around the takht which are served by the Akali Nihangs house granths, including Shikar Ghat, Nagina Ghat, and Mata Sahib Deva Gurdwara. Currently, the daily routine at Takht Abachal Hazur Sahib includes

FIGURE 3.7 *Palikīs* of *AG* and *DG* at Takht Hazur Sahib
Source: Gurinder Singh Mann.

taking hukamnāmās and reciting shabads and kathā from both *Granths*.

In the evening there is the recitation of the *āratī* that contains substantial portions of the *DG* and *AG*. This is performed standing up, with lamps (*dīvā*), and was a ritual associated with honouring the ancient kings of India, saints, and elders. The Singh Sabha reformers banned this in Panjab, labelling it 'Hindu'. Nonetheless, it is still found amongst the Buddha Dal, Nirmala, Nanaksar, and Namdhari Sikhs.[103] One of the previous jathedars of Hazur Sahib, Baba Joginder Singh, wrote the aforementioned book in defence of this practice as well as the enthronement of the *DG* in *Srī Hazurī Marayādā Prabodh*. At Takht Harimandir Sahib, Patna, we again see that there are two palikīs housed at this location (see Figure 3.8).

The way both *Granths* are laid out at the takhts shows that the placement of the *Granths* should follow a similar pattern; therefore, in reference to Sri Akal Takht, the missing space was for the *DG*. This is probably due to the takht being formed earlier than Hazur Sahib and Patna Sahib. This symbology follows the lines of mīrī–pīrī whereby the bāṇī of shanti ras and the bāṇī of vīr ras are kept side by side. Also in line with past tradition, shastra darshan takes place at all the takhts where all the historic weapons of the gurus and Sikh warriors are shown to the sangat, and their respective histories told.

FIGURE 3.8 *Palikīs* of *AG* and *DG*, with the Jathedar of Takht Patna Sahib
Source: Gurinder Singh Mann.

Material Heritage of the *Takht*

The final area which deserves our attention is the frescoes within Sri Akal Takht. This material heritage is important not only from an aesthetic point of view but also in terms of what significance it holds within the takht. It is unfortunate that many of the frescoes were removed and destroyed in the aftermath of Operation Bluestar in 1984, and also in the rebuilding of the takht. After Baba Santa Singh restored Sri Akal Takht, it was knocked down after the Sikh sangat were not happy, due to the political situation.[104] After it was rebuilt, no attempt was made to restore the frescoes which had previously been there; in fact, many of them were completely erased or white-washed. This style of fresco is known as *Naqqashi*.[105] The originals were commissioned by Maharaja Ranjit Singh and blended traditional Sikh and mythological themes from Sikh scripture.

In the *Srī Charitropakhyān* composition of the *DG*, there is a story which spreads across three *Charitras*, namely 21–3, which we discussed earlier in relation to Ragi Darshan Singh's excommunication. According to reports, the closing verses of this *Charitra* were inscribed on the walls of Sri Akal Takht,

> In the Akal Takht of the Amritsar, on the stairs of the left hand side there were passages on the marble from a long time from the wisdom of the Anup Kaur *Sākhī*.
>
> Why would all the *Giānīs* and participants of Akal Takht allow anything immoral if the passages were not from Guru Gobind Singh?[106]

This is highly significant as it shows not only the importance of this *Charitra* but also that it was important enough to be included on the walls of the takht itself. The other Indian themes that were also erased were those pertaining to *yudh* (battle/war), hence depicting the overall standing of the takht as a military throne.

* * *

Guru Hargobind brought the mīrī–pīrī concept to the forefront at the time of his accession to Guruship. On that day he wore two swords declaring one to be the symbol of the spiritual (pīrī) and the other that of his temporal investiture (mīrī). As a result, the symbology of shastras within the takhts and gurdwaras represents this mīrī side of the Sikhs. The *DG* represents the same symbology and hence the warrior spirit (vīr ras) is enshrined within this *Granth*. There are various aspects which show the importance and significance of the *DG* at Sri Akal Takht and other takhts as well. The ushering in of a new martial policy by Baba Buddha and his army, the Akal Purakh kī Fauj, would ensure that Sri Akal Takht would have new guardians.

The Akali Nihangs, the vanguard of the Sikhs, have ensured that the *Granth of Guru Gobind Singh*, which contains the martial policy of the Khalsa, would remain their preserve. Hence, to this day, the *DG* is synonymous with this group. The ḍhaḍhīs were the martial orators, and the Tenth Guru preserved this tradition and gave the Sikhs a martial scripture. The *DG* was written as a complementary or a secondary scripture to the *AG*. With the advent of the British and Sikh reformist movements, the power of the Akali Nihangs weakened and attempts were made to dislodge the scripture from Sri Akal Takht. This also led to the removal of the *Granth* from many gurdwaras which were in the care of the Akali Nihangs, and ultimately the *DG* compositions were also shortened in the daily liturgy. The importance given by Sri Akal Takht to the *Granth of Guru Gobind Singh* has been reinforced with the hukamnāmās it has issued. The veneration of the *DG* has also been a key feature at the takht, a significant part of marayādā, which no longer takes place. However, a careful analysis and comparison of the other takhts shows that both *Granth*s being placed together is a historical fact. This vacuum at Sri Akal Takht is noticeable and according to the saying of the Akali Nihangs, 'The Sikhs will only have real power when the *DG* makes its return to the Sri Akal Takht.'

Notes

1. This chapter is based on Gurinder Singh Mann's research showing the relationship of the Sikh martial tradition of Sri Akal Takht with the *DG*. This chapter also includes contributions from Kamalroop Singh.

2. This tradition started from the times of the Guru, but the Shiromani Gurdwara Parbandhak Committee (SGPC) broke away from this tradition

on its formation in the 1920s. Under the SGPC the method of selection of the jathedar has become less clear, and some argue that the Akali Dal political party has the biggest influence on this.

3. For descriptions of the Sikhs under Guru Arjan Dev, see Trilochan Singh Bedi, ed., *Sikhāṅ dī Bhagatmālā* (Patiala: Punjabi University, 1994). One must bear in mind that this was written at a much later date.

4. Bedi, *Bhagatmālā*, 124. Bhai Ganga Sehgal was employed by the Mughal army but was asked by Guru Arjan to fight battles for the Sikhs and, as a result, he attained salvation.

5. Bedi, *Bhagatmālā*, 126.

6. Bedi, *Bhagatmālā*, 126.

7. Guru Nanak has traditionally known to have kept a *barchā* (spear) with him on his travels.

8. Bhai Gurdas, *Vār* 1, *pauṛī* 48.

9. Bhai Gurdas, *Vār* 26, *pauṛī* 25.

10. This gurdwara should not have been confused with Gurdwara Mal Akhara, Khadoor Sahib, which was the family home of Guru Angad.

11. Recently, this text has seen some debate regarding date and authorship. Jathedar Joginder Singh Vedanti (together with Amarjeet Singh), who released a recent edition, has heavily footnoted his version and given expansions on themes within the text. See Sohan Singh, *Gurbilās Pātishāhī Chhevīn* (Amritsar: SGPC, 1999).

12. Sohan Singh, *Gurbilās*, 210.

13. Sohan Singh, *Gurbilās*, 211.

14. In the times of the Tenth Guru all three takhts had weapons ceremonially placed next to the scriptures, the worship of which is recorded in the court works like *Prem Sumārag Granth*, the *rahitnāmā* of Bhai Daya Singh, and the *Tankhānāmāh* of Bhai Nand Lal. This worship is known as 'shastra pūjā', which involves worshipping the sword by cleaning it daily, sharpening it, offering incense to it, and repeating specific compositions. The Bhai Daya Singh *rahitnāmā* records a conversation between himself and the Guru, 'keep the *Sri Sahib* unsheathed'. This shows that martial traditions were taken very seriously at the time. Piara Singh Padam, *Rahitnāme* (Amritsar: Singh Brothers, 2002), 69, 75. There in an injunction in the *Prem Sumārag Granth* to keep five weapons (Padam, *Rahitnāme*, 124). Also note that the 'Khalsa is the one who wears weapons' (*Tankhānāmāh*, verse 31). In the code recorded by Chaupa Singh, he writes, *Gurū kā sikh sirī sāhib dā adab kare pujā karai. Āpi sāhib pūjā kitī hai. Gurū kā sikh karad bhet kie binā prasādi nā chhakke.*

15. Padam, *Rahitnāme*, 212. We also hear of an anecdote when Guru Gobind Singh was parting company with Mata Sundari from Panjab to

Hazur Sahib. The Guru gave her his shastras and stated that when she wanted to see a glimpse of the Guru, he would be seen within the weapons themselves.

16. Avatar Singh, *Khālsā Dharam Shāstar* (Amritsar: Gurmat Press, 1919), 203.

17. Even more interestingly, the *Granth* of Guru Gobind Singh records the origins of the ḍhaḍhīs. In the composition *Chaṇḍī Charitra*, we see that Mahākāl fights the demons. However, due to all the fighting, he starts sweating and from this sweat is created Bhattacarya, the founder of the Bhaṭṭs, and from this character's sweat the character Dhadsen was born who was the first ḍhaḍhī singer. It was Dhadsen who recited heroic vārs in the battle which aided in winning the battle against the forces of evil. Modern-day ḍhaḍhīs quote extensively from the verses of the *AG* and *DG*. See Michael Nijhawan, *Dhadi Darbar: Religion, Violence, and the Performance of Sikh History* (New Delhi: Oxford University Press, 2006).

18. Nijhawan, *Dhadi Darbar*.

19. Sohan Singh, *Gurbilās*, 214.

20. Sohan Singh, *Gurbilās*, 216.

21. This established the tradition of Sri Akal Takht being a political and religious throne that commands Sikhs to incorporate the edicts issued from it into their lives. The attack on the Harimandir Sahib and Sri Akal Takht in 1984 had a profoundly negative impact on Sikhs and continues to do so to this day.

22. A battalion of the Nihang Singhs is named after the Sikh warrior and known as the Baba Biddhi Chand Dal.

23. Another description given to the warriors from the time of Guru Arjan Dev and Guru Hargobind is *Akal Purkhīs*, that is, believers in Akal Purakh.

24. Sohan Singh, *Gurbilās*, 245. Translated by us.

25. In the Sikh tradition, the exegesis of Bhai Gurdas's *Vār* 1, *pauṛī* 48 is that when Guru Hargobind is asked about the number of the Sikh gurus in the future, he responds with the following, '[T]he Sikhs prayed and asked that they have seen the six Gurus (how many more are to come),' and the Guru replied, 'Four more Gurus will come to earth (yuga 2, yuga 2 i.e. 2 + 2 = 4).' *Vār* 3, *pauṛī* 12 also shows the unity of the Gurus. Also see *DG*, *Bachitra Nāṭak* and *Chaṅḍī dī Vār*.

26. Rai Jasbir Singh, ed., *Bhāī Kesar Singh Chhibbar krit Bansāvalināmā Dasi Pātashāh kā* (Amritsar: Guru Nanak Dev University, 2001), 164, verses 264–8. There are small number of manuscript copies that are extant that have colophons that are from this period.

27. See S. Attar Singh, trans., *The Travels of Guru Tegh Bahadar and Guru Gobind Singh* (Lahore: Indian Public Press, 1876), *sakhīs* 18, 21.

28. Seva Singh, *Shahīd Bilās* (Ludhiana: Panjab Sahit Academy, 1961), verse 185.

29. Sardul Singh, *Rīpoṭ Sodhak Kommittī Dasam Patāshāhī Srī Gurū Granth Sāhib jī dī* (Amritsar: Vazirchand Printers, 1897), 13. Hereinafter *Sodhak Committee Report.*

30. Seva Singh explicitly mentions the recension/biṛh, not *Guru Granth Sahib.*

31. This episode is also mentioned by Kaushish (1797), and Seva Singh, *Shahīd Bilās*, 65.

32. Panjab University, Chandigarh, *DG*, MS. 1190. This recension was originally from Lokh Sahit Parkashan, Amritsar. It contains 528 folios; folios 401–528 are badly damaged, as noted in the report of the *DG* committee at Sri Akal Takht by Sardul Singh. On enquiry it was also confirmed that the manuscript came from Sri Akal Takht.

33. It also contains no *Zafarnāmah*. This was added later to the volume with the *Hikāitāṅ*, around AD 1704.

34. Kanh Singh Nabha, *Mahān Kosh* (Patiala: Bhasha Vibhag [1930] 1999).

35. Seva Singh, *Shahīd Bilās.*

36. Akali Nihang Kaur Singh, *Hazūrī Sāthī* (Lahore: Akali Patrika Press, 1934).

37. An extant manuscript of the *Safarī* recension of *DG* of Baba Dip Singh is at Damdama Sahib; another good example is the manuscript at John Rylands Library, Manchester, MS. 44–10. The reason for manuscripts moving around is the *chakkarvārtī* status of the Khalsa, and in times of war, the Khalsa would relocate or fight a pitched battle.

38. Bawa Sumar Singh, *Gurpad Prem Prakāsh* (Patiala: Punjabi University, 2000).

39. Bawa Sumar Singh, *Gurpad Prem Prakāsh*, 281–2.

40. G.A. Grierson, *The Modern Vernacular Literature of Hindustan* (Calcutta: Asiatic Society, 1889), 128. He lists the *Prem Sumārag Granth, Sarabaloh Parkash (Sarabloh Granth)* and others. He seems to be ill-informed about the scriptures.

41. Lt. Col. J. Malcolm, *The Sketch of the Sikhs: A Singular Nation Who Inhabit the Provinces of the Punjab Situated Between the Rivers Jamna and Indus* (London: John Murray, 1812).

42. 'A Sikh wishing to become a Singh finds no difficulty in accomplishing his proselytization. He goes to the Akalees, or priest of the sect, at Amritsur ... after the performance of certain ceremonies he is given to drink a sherbet made of sugar and water, from the hand of an Akalee.' See Tour to Lahore, *The Asiatic Annual Register*, vol. xi—for the Year 1809

(London: printed for T. Cadelland, W. Davies, etc., 1811), 421–40. And J.C. Murray-Aynsley, *Our Visit to Hindostan, Kashmir, and Ladakh* (London: W.H. Allen, 1879), 252.

43. He was always attended on his tours by a priest with a volume of each of the two chief scriptures (*AG* and *DG*). They were wrapped up in rich pieces of silk, placed in a cot under a big canopy, and thus borne from one place to another. A special military escort was provided; each member of which carried a Sikh banner. The procession was often followed by a number of priests on elephants. Besides this, every regiment had its own volumes of the *Granths* and religious insignia. Even the ministers of state carried separate copies of the *Granths* on their journeys. Mufti 'Ali ud-Din, *Ibratnama*, quoted in Gulshan Lall Chopra, *The Punjab as a Sovereign State (1799–1839)* (Lahore: Uttar Chand Kapur & Sons, 1928), 204.

44. Monier Williams refers to the Sikh scriptures at Takht Patna Sahib in the nineteenth century. He states, 'On the other side was a kind of low altar on which were lying under a canopy a beautifully embroidered copy of the Adi-Granth and of the Granth of Govind [*DG*]. In the centre, on a raised platform, were a number of sacred swords, which appeared to be as much objects of worship as the sacred books.' See *Religious Thought and Life in India. An Account of the Religions of the Indian Peoples, Based on a Life's Study of their Literature and on Personal Investigations in Their Own Country* (London: John Murray, 1883), 174–5.

45. Tara Singh Narotam, *Srī Gurū Tīrath Saṅgrahi* (Kankhal: Nirmal Akhara, 1883), 127.

46. Bawa Sumar Singh, *Gurpad Prem Prakāsh*, 281.

47. Charles Wilkins, 'The Sicks and Their College at Patna, 1 March 1781', *Transactions of the Asiatick Society* (Calcutta, 1788), 1: 288–94.

48. 'The Sikhs have no idols; but in their shrines are copies of the Adi Granth or Old Testament compiled by the fifth Guru, Arjan ... and the New Testament or Book of the Tenth and last Guru, Gobind Singh.' Walter Del Mar, *India of To-day* (London: Adam and Charles Black, 1905), 234.

49. The UK parliament initiated the Charter Act of 1813 giving the green light for Christian Missionaries to preach in India. Prior to this, their activities were restricted and they faced opposition by the East India Company who felt they would get in the way of their commercial activities.

50. Malcolm, *The Sketch*.

51. J.D. Cunningham, *History of the Sikhs* (Delhi: Low Price Publications, [1849] 1990).

52. There is a *guṭkā* attributed to Bhai Maharaj Singh at the British Library which combines compositions from the *AG* and *DG*. See MSS. Panj. A4. a and b.

53. The document is dated 1934 VS (AD 1878) and bears an official *mohur* (stamp) from the 'Srī Takht Sāhib Akāl Bungā'.

54. This hukamnāmā is kept in a private collection of Navjot and Preeti Randhawa of Delhi.

55. See the section 'The Standardization of the *Dasam Granth*' in Chapter 2 of this book. Manna Singh, Secretary of the Sabha, who had knowledge of English, Persian, and Gurmukhi grammar; Bhai Narain Singh who was proficient in Persian; Bhai Thakar Singh; Bhai Hazura Singh; and Secretary of Sangat Lakar Mandi, Bhai Darbara Singh. See *Sodhak Committee Report*, 16, point 2.

56. *Sodhak Committee Report*, 4.

57. This is also supported by manuscript evidence with pothīs of the Persian works of *DG* only. See manuscript SHR: 2218 at Khalsa College, Amritsar.

58. *Sodhak Committee Report*, 9, point 21.

59. According to *Gurbilās Pātishāhī 10*, the reading of *Rām Avatār* was undertaken at the time of Dussherā by Guru Gobind Singh. To this day, the Nihangs have a granth named *Dussherā Mahātam Granth* written by Baba Mitt Singh, considered by the Nihangs to be one of the greatest Sikh scholars, mystic, warrior, and freedom fighter of the last century. After reform of SGPC the tradition of Dussherā nearly ended, and therefore the Buddha Dal wrote a whole composition to ensure this was not lost. Kesar Singh Chhibbar in his *Bansāvalīnāmā* also states the importance of worshipping one's weapons and reciting the *Chaṇḍī* compositions at the time of *Dussherā* (*Sodhak Committee Report*, 9, point 20).

60. *Sodhak Committee Report*, 14, point 12. This is an important point and illustrates that the decline of the Akalis is related to the decline of the *DG*.

61. *Sodhak Committee Report*, 13, point 3.

62. *Sodhak Committee Report*, point 4.

63. *Sodhak Committee Report*, 16f.

64. *Sodhak Committee Report*, 13, points 10, 11, and 14.

65. This recension was numbered with the similar number of pages (*angs*) of the *AG*, which is 1428.

66. Recently the Gurdwara Mal Akhara has been created by the Akali Nihangs. This gurdwara has prakāsh of *AG*, *DG*, and *Sarabloh Granth* as in many other Nihang gurdwaras.

67. Sardar Bhagat Singh, *Missī Jatt de Kartūt* (Amritsar: Sri Chandar Press, 1923); Panjab D. 898, British Library.

68. Bhagat Singh, *Missī*, 14–15.

69. *Sodhak Committee Report*, 13, point 5.

70. Madanjit Kaur, *Golden Temple, Past and Present* (Amritsar: Nanak Dev University, 1983), 104.

71. Akali Baba Anup Singh Nihang from Gravesend, UK, was interviewed by Kamalroop Singh in 2004. Baba Anup Singh served with Baba Sahib Singh Kaladhari at Sri Akal Takht and was present when the SGPC came in with the army of women. This interview also features in Francisco Jose Luis, 'Sex in Sikhi: The Erotic in the Sikh Tradition and the Politics of De-Eroticisation', unpublished paper.

72. Baba Ram Singh Nihang, *Akāl Purakh kī Fauj* (Gurdaspur, n.d.), 104.

73. In addition to Akali Baba Anup Singh making this account, this is categorically recalled by all the Nihang Dals to this day, as well as being stated by some senior members of the SGPC. A forthcoming work from the authors goes into more detail regarding the Akali Nihang history.

74. The account given by Narayan Singh states that the pūjārīs at the takht called the Nihangs to take control of it. A fight broke out and a woman single-handedly removed the Nihang Singhs from the takht. The Nihang Singhs allegedly fled the scene through the back doors. See Bhai Narayan Singh, *Illustrious Hero of the Akali Movement: Jathedar Bhai Kartar Singh Jhabbar—The Life and Times*, trans. Karnail Singh (Amritsar: SGPC, 2001).

75. Baba Ram Singh, *Akāl*, 104. Another description of when the *DG* was removed is given by the granthīs at Hazur Sahib. In their hukamnāmā of 16 September 1998, they state that the prakāsh of the *DG* was removed in 1932, but it continued at the other takhts.

76. George Batley Scott writing not soon after states, '[T]hey formed a self-constituted committee under the name of the *Shrimani Gurudwara Parbhandak*, or committee of Gurudwara management, and decided to take forcible possession of all gurdwaras. They assumed the title, style, tenets, black turbans and other symbols of the *Akhali*, who had formed the bodyguard and were the most truculant of the followers of Guru Govind.' See *Religion and Short History of the Sikhs—1469 to 1930* (London: The Mitre Press, 1930), 89–90.

77. Kirpal Singh and Prithipal Singh Kapur, *The Makers of Modern Punjab: What They Had to Say* (Amritsar: Singh Brothers, 2010), 54. The colour black was then adopted by the Akali reformers for their turbans.

78. Singh and Kapur, *Modern Punjab*, 60.

79. *Shastravidiā* should not be confused with *Gatkā* which is a drill and decorative art only. See Manjit Singh, *Shastarnāmā* (Amritsar: Chattar Singh Jivan Singh, 2005). See Kamalroop Singh, 'Gatka', in *The Oxford Handbook of Sikh Studies*, eds Pashaura Singh and Louis E. Fenech (New York: Oxford University Press, 2014).

80. D.P. Ashta, *The Poetry of the Dasam Granth* (Delhi: Arun Prakashan, 1959), 5.

81. Ashta, *Poetry of the Dasam Granth*.

82. This type of decision was based primarily on the puritanical arguments found in earlier Nirmala works like *Gur Niraṇai Sāgar* by Pandit Tara Singh Narotam, who argues that the Khalsa can never equate with the Guru. This type of thought was based on renunciation and pacifism, while the Khalsa had always been a sovereign body, as granted by the Guru. The court poet of the Tenth Guru, Bhai Gurdas II, records that Guru Gobind Singh and his student are one, due to the ontotheological notion of non-duality in *AG*.

83. Sahib Singh in his autobiography recalls how in the girls' school, the girls had ink over their hands. When he asked them what they were doing, they told him, 'We are writing the *Hazūrī* recension.' On checking, it appeared that this manuscript was an edited mixture of both *AG* and *DG*. Sahib Singh was told that it would be buried to make people think it was the authentic recension that received Guruship. See Sahib Singh, *Merī Jīvan Kahāṇī* (Amritsar: Singh Bros, 2001), 166–8.

84. Amritsar, Guru Ram Das Library, no. 609 and also British Library, Panj d. 549; Teja Singh Bhasauria, *Khālsā Rahit Prakāsh* (Khalsa Diwan, Bhasaur, Pustak Bhandar, Panch Khand, 1917), 53–9. A manual of Sikh social and religious rites, nine editions were printed up to 1924. He also called for all Sikh women to wear turbans.

85. Bhasauria, *Khālsā Rahit Prakāsh*, 43.

86. See Sant Gurbachan Singh Bhinderwale, *Gurbāṇī Pāṭh Darpaṇ* (Amritsar: Print Well, [1973] 1996), 181–7. Kalaswalia became the new head granthī at Darbar Sahib. Over a number of years he managed to force the sangat to read the edited version of evening liturgy.

87. Bhinderwale, *Gurbāṇī*, 188–90.

88. For more information, see Harbans Singh, 'The Bakapur Diwan and Baba Teja Singh of Bhasaur', *The Panjab Past and Present* (Patiala: Punjabi University Patiala, Publication Bureau, October 1973). Teja Singh's influence can still be seen today.

89. *Sikh Rehat Marayada*, 9–10.

90. Hukamnāmā issued by Takht Hazur Sahib on 5 September 1998. See Gurinder Singh Mann and Kamalroop Singh, *Sri Dasam Granth Sahib: Questions and Answers* (London: Archimedes Press, 2011), 76.

91. This was celebrated at Gurdwara Zafarnamah Sahib, Bhatinda, between the dates 11 and 13 November 2006.

92. The debate on the *DG* at this time was being propagated by the former jathedar of Sri Akal Takht, Ragi Darshan Singh. The jathedar has

been undertaking the kirtan of the *DG* for the most part of his life. In 1984, he clearly stated in one of his discourses that Guru Gobind Singh's bāṇī makes one 'Sant Sipāhī' and prepares him for 'dharam yudh'. However, he later changed his mind and decided to speak out against the scripture, although it is not known why this was the case.

93. The Samagam took place in September and October 2008. *Dasam Granth path-bodh* Samagam ends in Hazur Sahib, 27 October 2008, http://www.sridasamgranth.com/#/dasam-granth-blog/4526703344 (accessed 10 April 2013).

94. Originally written in Panjabi by Harvinder Singh and published in *Ajit* newspaper. Translated into English on the *Dasam Granth* website at http://www.sridasamgranth.com/#/dasam-granth-blog/4526703344 (accessed 10 February 2014).

95. Varinder Walia, 'Jathedar Dispels Doubts about Dasam Granth', *Tribune India* (online edition), 4 November 2008, http://www.tribunein-dia.com/2008/20081104/punjab1.htm (accessed 10 April 2011).

96. The discourse took place at Rochester Gurdwara, New York. Ragi Darshan Singh was declared tankhāiya on 5 December 2009 by Sri Akal Takht.

97. The whole episode was brought into the open by Gurcharanjit Singh Lamba, ed., *Sant Sipāhī*, on a New York TV show, *Jus Punjabi*. Gurcharanjit Singh Lamba and Ragi Darshan Singh debated the *Charitras* in question on 24 October 2009, when it became clear that Ragi Darshan Singh was unable to clarify his remarks. The *Charitra* revolves around a Raja being put in an awkward situation when he was nearly caught in the web of a seamstress. The lady by the name of Nūp (Anūp) Kaur tried to seduce the Raja but her plan failed; the moral being that men should avoid the company of other people's wives and that chastity should be maintained. The concluding lines are purported to be of Guru Tegh Bahadur giving advice to Guru Gobind Singh.

98. See Jathedar Joginder Singh, *Srī Hazurī Mriyādā Prabodh* (Nanderh: Takht Hazur Sahib, 1967).

99. Bhinderwale, *Gurbāṇī Pāṭh Darpaṇ*.

100. Nihang Teja Singh, *Adi Dasam Srī Gurū Granth Sāhib jī* (Buddha Dal, 1980).

101. The *Sarabaloh Granth* is also present in the Bunga of Mai Bhago in the complex.

102. Akali Nihang Kaur Singh, *Hazūrī Sāthī* (Lahore: Akali Patrika Press, 1934).

103. Giani Ditt Singh was a prominent member of the Singh Sabha reform; he was against ritualism and managed to stop the traditional

ritual of *āratī* (literally, before night/remover of darkness), using lamps and incense to make a devoted supplication before Akal Purakh in Sikh temples. It is no surprise that before becoming a Sikh he was a Gulābdāsī, a sect that is known to be fiercely against any form of ritualism. He wrote the *Āratī Prabodh* on the subject. See the article and translation of the āratī by Kamalroop Singh at www.scribd.com/doc/183005595 (accessed December 2013).

104. Baba Santa Singh, leader of the Buddha Dal, was asked by the Congress government to rebuild Sri Akal Takht, due to the traditional role of the Nihang Singhs being the guardians of the takht, and he undertook the task because of the fact that the Damdami Taksal insisted that they would leave the takht damaged as a reminder to Sikhs of the government actions. The idea was not to the liking of many, and as a result, this restored Sri Akal Takht was knocked down and rebuilt completely. He was declared a tankhāiyā and readmitted into the Sikh fold in 2001. At this time he stated that he was trying to create harmony at this difficult time and his position as a jathedar of the Buddha Dal was created in line with the marayādā of Sri Akal Takht. See *Tribune India*, 'Nihangs Recognise Santa Singh as Jathedar', http://www.tribuneindia.com/2001/20010326/punjab1.htm (accessed 10 April 2011).

105. Further information on the type of artwork employed in the main Sikh shrines can be read in the paper 'Art Work in Historic Sikh Shrines: Need for Documentation and Conservation' delivered at XXI International CIPA Symposium, 1–6 October 2007, Athens, Greece, by Dr Balvinder Singh, Guru Ramdas School of Planning, Guru Nanak Dev University, Amritsar.

106. See article by Gurcharan Singh Veda in Giani Harbans Singh, ed., *Dasam Granth Darpaṇ* (Patiala: Gurmat Narain Prakashan, 1980), 43. This is also corroborated by Sardar Kapur Singh in his essay, 'Qissā Raṇī Rūp Kaur dā', *Gurmat Prakāsh* (Amritsar: SGPC, 1959).

4

The Seed of the Khalsa Raj

As we have seen, Sri Akal Takht was a powerful symbol of Sikh sovereignty where the Khalsa armies came to make their plans. Many historians have noted that the *DG* was an integral part of the *gurmattā* and contained the Sikh warrior ethos that came into fruition in the eighteenth and nineteenth centuries.[1] As we have seen, early accounts and traditions demonstrate that the *DG* was enthroned next to the *AG*, and its compositions were/are recited in the Khalsa initiation. In Chapter 1 of this book, the compositions of the *DG* were described, including their position in liturgy. The Khalsa initiation or *khaṅḍe kī pāhul* also employs the same devotional compositions from the *DG*.[2]

In the first part of this chapter, we will examine the scripture of the *DG* and this initiation from early sources of Sikh history. The *DG* verses are also readily sung in Sikh musicology (*Gurmat Sangīt*) in Darbar Sahib, and are employed as slogans in the Sikh martial arts. As we shall see later in this chapter, the slogans of *rajnītī* taken from the *DG* were readily inscribed on coins and became part of battle cries. We will address the term *degh–tegh–fateh* in detail. The major leitmotiv in the scripture is the *chhatrī* tradition where the Divine Sword and *dharam yudh* are praised by the Guru in the *vīr ras* genre. Clearly the *DG* was a major source of inspiration for Sikh warriors, especially the Akalis, but are there any explicit examples of this connection? In the final part of this chapter, we give one example of a Sikh weapon of choice, the *chakkar*. It is discussed in reference to its use in the Sikh kingdom and its relationship to its source, the *Shastra Nām Mālā Purāṇ* from the *DG*.

The *Khaṅḍe Kī Pāhul* Ceremony

In the traditional praxis and modern-day ceremony, the five *nitnem* compositions are recited by the Paṅj Piāre in the khaṅḍe kī pāhul ceremony.[3] Svarup Singh Kaushish narrates that the five nitnem compositions were recited in the first Khalsa initiation ceremony.[4] The traditional view of Kaushish is supported by an early *rahitnāmā*, which is a discourse between Guru Gobind Singh and Bhai Daya Singh. The code describes the procedure for the khaṅḍe kī pāhul and lists the scripture to be read:

> First the complete *Japu jī Sāhib* [1] from beginning to end, as well as a complete *Jāp* [2] should be recited from beginning to end, the *Chaupaī* [3], the five five *svaiye*:[5] *Srāvag, Dīnan kī pratipāl, Pāp saṅbūh bināsan, Sati sadaiv sadā brat* (five stanzas) [4], the *Pauṛī* of *Anaṅd Sāhib* [5]. The *amrit* should be stirred with a sword by them.[6]

It also serves as a military code and contains an injunction for the worship of weapons—*shastra kari pūjo*. We find the following: 'I myself (*srī mukh*) communicated the *Chaupaī* and *Svaiye* for focusing the minds [of my followers and to prepare them for] battle.'[7] Later it follows with the 'True Guru Speaks' (*Sri Satigurū Vāch*) that describes the Akalis thus:

> An Akali is one whose form is covered in blue dress, repeating *Gurbar Akāl* and wearing Iron weapons. With a white Kach and blue clothes, repeating *Jap jī* and *Jāp*, contemplating *Akāl Ustati* and *Chaṇḍī dī Vār*, and committing them perfectly to memory. Meditating with each hair on the body and renouncing all actions of the body. Who is devoted to the Guru Granth and one who runs away from the five thieves.[8]

From the above injunctions we can see that the initiation of the Khalsa was via the double-edged sword, and that the *DG* compositions were intended to boost the morale of the Khalsa, by recital of its liturgical compositions. The previous translation, from the code of conduct attributed to Bhai Daya Singh, formulates a chhatrī ideal for the vanguard. McLeod dates this document to be from the late eighteenth century or early nineteenth century, while Padam is silent on this issue. There also seems to be little or no manuscripts of this rahitnāmā, and McLeod mentions none. Kanh Singh Nabha mentions in passing that a rahitnāmā of Bhai Daya Singh is seen.[9] This detailed prescription about the first *amrit sañchār* (Khalsa initiation) is similar to the modern-day practice of initiation, while Takht Hazur Sahib and the Buddha Dal follow this procedure exactly, as they recite the extra *svaiye*.[10]

The Liturgy of the Khalsa

Another rahitnāmā called the *Tankhāhnāmā* by Bhai Nand Lal, who was the poet laureate in the court of the Guru, is very significant.[11] Padam argues that this document was written after the Guru, in the times of the up-and-coming Khalsa, due to the use of the word *tankhāh*, which means penalty due to violation of Khalsa *dharam*.[12] Very early extant manuscripts exist of the *Tankhāhnāmā*, and the text itself records a colophon of AD 1695.[13] All the scriptures of the mystic poet Nand Lal 'Goya' is considered *bāṇī* and is readily sung in kirtan.[14] In the rahitnāmā of 'Goya', we find two references to the *Jāp Sāhib*: 'Bath (then) read *Jap* and *Jāp*.1. Read the *Jap jī* and *Jāp* with concentration.13.'[15] Previous to this the Guru states, '[K]now my form to be bāṇī, and the Granth'—he instructs the Sikhs to read *gurbāṇī*. Then, again, we have references to bāṇī from the *AG* and *DG*, the *Japu* and *Jāpu*.[16]

The rahitnāmā of Bhai Prahlad Singh is well known; he was a court scribe of the Tenth Guru, and within this rahitnāmā is the famous *tukh* (verse) said by the Guru: 'The Sikh of mine that lives with the correct conduct is the master, and I am their slave' (verse 36). Before the Tenth Guru established the Guruship of the *Granth* and Panth, there is the injunction in this rahitnāmā that the Khalsa Panth and *Granth* is the Guru (verse 24). We find a similar reference to the *Jāp* as in the previous two codes, 'He who eats food without first reciting *Japu jī* and *Jāp* is [worth as much as] a worm's excrement, and has wasted [the opportunity afforded by his human] birth.13.'[17]

Another rahitnāmā, written by Bhai Desa Singh, is an early eighteenth-century document. Padam states that the document is from the late eighteenth century. Kanh Singh Nabha states that Desa Singh has a rahitnāmā to his name but goes no further. McLeod concedes that this may also be the case, but believes the document to be an amalgamation of two other compositions. He also believes that taking into account the fact that Bhai Desa Singh claims to have a vision of the Tenth Guru, who narrates to him the bāṇī that he wrote, adds little merit to the validity of this document. McLeod states, 'In this vision Guru Gobind Singh assured Desa Singh that he had written the whole of the Dasam Granth ... Similarly the vision of Desa Singh must be rejected, as only a small portion at most of the Dasam Granth can claim to be the work of the Guru.'[18] McLeod's opinion is unusual considering that he was an expert on the rahitnāmās, and must have been aware that nearly every composition of the *DG* gets mentioned throughout the earliest codes, like in Chaupa Singh's which he translated into English.[19] In the Desa Singh code, like the previous rahitnāmās, we find mention of a similar praxis:

> Get up early and bath. Keep reciting on the lips the *Japu* and *Jāpu*.[20] Couplets.
>
> 'Arise at dawn and having bathed recite both *Jāpu* and *Japujī* [At the end of the day] recite the four portions of *So Dar*. Do not be lazy about this.37.
>
> 'When the first watch of the night has passed recite the *Sohilā* order *(Kīrtan Sohilā)*. Each day select some portion from the text of Granth, [the *AG* or the *DG*], and commit it to memory.38.
>
> 'Celebrate as festivals the birthdays of all the Gurus, from the tenth back to the first. Prepare on these occasions some food and cooking it in an iron bowl *(kaṛāh)* feed it to the Khalsa Sikhs.39.'[21]

Another late seventeenth- or early eighteenth-century rahitnāmā is the *Prem Sumārag Granth*. In this text we find references to the *DG* compositions to be recited early in the morning (*amrit velā*). McLeod translates this passage as: 'Recite the *Japu* [ji] and *Jāp* five times each and likewise *Anand*.'[22] The word *verī* can also mean 'time', another translation is possible: '[A]t this time recite the five *Japu*, *Jāp*, and as a part of the five read *Anand* at this time.' The *Prem*

Sumārag then also states when two watches of the day has gone, read again the *Japu* and *Jāpu* once. Then follows an injunction to read the first portion of the *Mūl Mantra*, and *mangal* (invocatory verses) of the *Jāp* seven times. In the evening the *So Dar Rahirās* should be read, and following this the *bhog* should be performed with the *Japu* and *Jāpu* (verse).[23] Then follows an injunction to read bāṇī from the First Guru to the Tenth: 'The *bāṇī* from the First Emperor (Guru Nanak) to the Tenth's *Bachitra Nāṭak* and any other Emperor's (Gurus) *bāṇī* from the Granth should be read.'[24]

A much later account, by Rattan Singh, of the first *amrit sanchār* narrates that the *pauṛī* of *Pritam Bhagautī* was read at the time.[25] The recitation of the *ardās*, then the ritual of the Khalsa initiation took place, with the additional narration of the *Thirty-Three Svaiye* stating what the Khalsa is. The *bhagautī* is the double-edged sword in the ritual.[26] Rattan Singh states that the invocation of *Bachitra Nāṭak* was said. Once again, another famous writer is narrating the symbolism of the saintly knighthood via the power of the double-edged sword, where the compositions of the *DG* feature. Rattan Singh also narrates that the Guru gave injunctions to read gurbāṇī, from the *Jap* and *Jāp Sāhib*, *Anand Sāhib*, and *Rahirās Sāhib*.[27]

The Warrior Tradition and the *Dasam Granth*

From this brief but repetitive analysis it is clear that the compositions of the *DG* are a part of the liturgy of the Sikhs. The compositions are in praise of the Divine Sword, the Srī Bhagautī. This leitmotiv is found throughout the *DG* and is related to warfare, clearly invoked for protection in war, and found in compositions like the *Shastra Nām Mālā* and the *Avatār* narrations of the *Bachitra Nāṭak*. As we have seen, this theme is also common in the apocryphal compositions; this vīr ras or warrior spirit was to inspire the Khalsa to be chivalrous. The military manual for the Khalsa is the *DG* which deals with the world and 'is the fortress, while the *AG* is the temple' which deals with the spirit.[28] Both scriptures clearly represent *mīrī–pīrī*. See Table 4.1.

An important component of the *DG* is *shastra pūjā* and a remnant of this is the ceremonial display of weapons in front of the

AG. This can also be seen in a folio of an early *DG* manuscript with a tiger-knife beautifully arranged within the writing (see Figure 4.1).

TABLE 4.1 The Temporality and Spirituality of Sikhism

degh	*Tegh*
sant	*sipāhī*
pīrī	*mīrī*
bhaktī	*shaktī*
shāstra	*shastra*
shanti ras	*vīr ras*
AG	*DG*
yoga	*rāj*
bāṇī	*bānā*

Source: Authors.

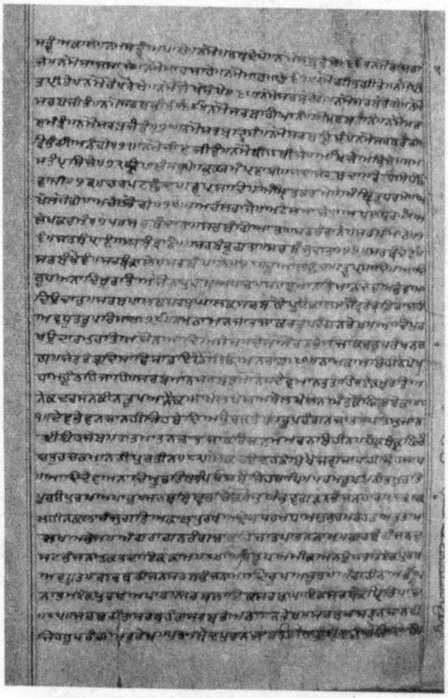

FIGURE 4.1 A *DG* Folio from the Late Seventeenth Century Showing a Tiger-knife Depicted within the Sacred Text Itself
Source: Kamalroop Singh.

The ceremonial enthronement of weapons in front of the *AG* is traditionally believed to be due to the original *marayādā* left by Guru Hargobind and Guru Gobind Singh, that is still practised at the Akal Takht, Takht Keshgarh Sahib, Takht Hazur Sahib, Takht Patna Sahib, and the traditional Fifth Takht—the Akali Nihang Singh Khalsa.[29] The historical context of the *DG* is clearly the one related to the court and the regal way of life associated with Guru Gobind Singh. His court boasted Braj poetry, music, weaponry, falconry, and horsemanship. The Guru is known as the Tenth Sovereign, and according to history, his way of life reflected this. Pandit Sharda Ram, a Panjabi historian of the last century, explains the Guru's purpose in 'A Narration of How the Sikhs Gained Their Kingdom'. He writes:

> The Guru wished to compose a scripture, by which the Sikhs could learn politics, martial skills, and by such intelligence be able for war. On that day a large scripture was commenced which was completed in the month of Sunday 1753 VS/September 14, 1696 AD, it was called the scripture of the tenth Sovereign.[30]

The Guru himself may have had this purpose in mind, when he wrote in his typical heroic style in the *Chaṇḍī Charitra*:

> Oh Lord grant me this boon that I may never be afraid to perform righteous acts. That I may never be afraid, when I go to battle, assure my victory. May I instruct my mind to have the desire to sing your praises, when the last moment comes, may I die fighting courageously on the battle field.231.[31]

M.A. Macauliffe states there were three reasons for the Guru's translations of 'Hindu' mythology and epics:[32]

1. To dispel cowardice and incite bravery by filling the minds of his followers with heroic examples.
2. To show what a brave woman (the goddess Chandi) could achieve in battle so as to spur brave men on to surpass her achievements.
3. To have his Sikhs see the inferiority of the Hindu sacred writings and so appreciate those of their own gurus more.

The third point seems unlikely, as the bulk of the translation in the court of the Guru were of Sanskrit texts.[33] The main reason for the translations, based on the internal parameters of the compositions, was to educate and incite bravery in all, not just the Sikhs. The other work of the court poets in the *Vidiāsāgar Granth*, a larger volume separate from the *Granth of Guru Gobind Singh*, was probably to educate members of the *sangat*, but it should be noted that the works of the Guru are more than translations, and were written to inspire dharam yudh. A counter argument to the theory that the *DG* is a Hindu scripture is that idol worship and Brahmanism is criticized, and many Zoroastrian, Persian, Islamic, and Sufi narratives are found. Firstly, in the *Hikāyats* which are a part of the *Zafarnāmah*, there is an example of Sufi poetry, and there are also references to the *Shahnāmah* in the *Zafarnāmah*. Throughout the *DG*, there are literally hundreds of Persian loanwords. In some of the myths there are clearly Zoroastrian and other ancient motifs employed. The bulk or framework of the *DG* is largely a Puranic translation of the various episodes of mythic words of the gods and demons, but they are intertwined with many other minor metanarratives that are clearly not Puranic. For instance, in the episode of *Kalkī Avatār*, also known as *Nihkalaṅk Avatār*, we find the story of Mīr Mehdī from Shi'a Islam. Significantly, it follows the closing section of the *Kalkī* episode, forming a critique of both stories. The Hindu Kalkī is killed by the Islamic Mīr Mehdī, who is later killed by an insect crawling into his ear and infecting his brain. Therefore, it is questionable if this scripture was written by a Hindu or a Muslim.

In the account by Giani Gian Singh, who wrote his work in the years of the Singh-Sabha, the *Navīn Paṅth Prakāsh* and the *Tvārīkh Gur Khalsā* describe the style of poetry in the *DG* as consisting of '*chamak, damak, ras, rīt, alaṅkār, lachhan, dhunī, avarev,* and *bayanjnadik* or—embellishment, rhythm, aesthic quality, traditional forms, literary forms, behaviours, sound, riddles, and conversation'.[34] He also records that as the Pandits would not teach Sanskrit to low-caste Sikhs, the Guru started a scriptural project by writing himself and with the court poets, and by sending Sikhs to Benaras to increase the scholarship of the Panth.[35] He states that in 1742 VS/AD 1675 the Guru commenced composing poetry.[36] He describes the material written into *Bhakhā* (vernacular language) in the court: *Devī Bhagat, Bishan Bhagat,* Mahābharat, *Vishnūpurāṇ, Hitopdesh,* Upanishads, *Bhoj Prabandh, Shukra Nītī, Manudil Graṅth.* He further states that while the Mahābharat,

Upanishads, *Vashist Purāṇ*, *Hitopdesh*, *Chaṇakyā*, *Jaimane*, and *Ashmedh* are still extant, it may be possible that some works were lost when the Guru left Anandpur Sahib.[37] Gian Singh also writes that the Guru gave orders in his edicts that the sangat should come to him armed, and learn the art of weapons.[38] Here we can see a general trend in all the texts mentioned. He also mentions the five nitnem prayers within the *Tvārīkh Gur Khalsā*.

In the courts of India learned poets would sing metrical pieces in time to dance. We find some remnants of this in the *DG* but 'dance' is now changed to 'paintrā'. The martial arts were often discussed as dance in India like Kathak-Kālī.[39] The metres in the *DG* reflect this on close analysis and practice. For instance, the rhythm of the *Sangīt Bhujaṅg Prayāt Chhaṅd* in *Chaṇḍī Charitra* can have a corresponding motion calculated from it. This can also be sung and played on the Pakhawaj, an ancient Indian drum. There are other compositions in the *DG* that are meant to be sung like in the *Parasnāth Avātar*, in *Shabad Hazāre*, and the apocryphal compositions such as *Mālkauns*.

There is a clear theme of bhagautī in the *DG*, the purpose of which was to inspire righteous war, which is stated by the author again and again (see Table 4.2). Giani Teja Singh Nirmala presents this view in his book *Dashmesh Udesh* (*Mission of the Tenth Guru*).[40] He quotes heavily from the *DG* with regard to the contents being

TABLE 4.2 Invocations to the Divine Sword in the *Dasam Graṅth*

Jāp Sāhib	*Bhagavātī Chhaṅd*
Srī Akāl Ustati	*Sarabaloh dī rachhā*
Bachitra Nāṭak	*Namaskār Srī Khaṛag*
Chaṇḍī Charitra	*Srī Bhagautī jī Sahāī*
Chaṇḍī Charitra Ukati Bilās	*Srī Bhagautī jī Sahāī*
Chaṇḍī dī Vār	*Srī Bhagautī jī Sahāī*
Giān Prabodh	*Srī Bhagautī jī Sahāī*
Chaubīs Avatār	*Srī Bhagautī jī Sahāī*
Shastra Nām Mālā	*Srī Bhagautī jī Sahāī*
Srī Charitropakhyān	*Srī Bhagautī e Nam*

Source: Kamalroop Singh (2013).

solely related to war. He is correct, as the bulk of it is either battle narratives or events related to the battlefield. In the Sikh tradition, the value of the scriptures is the ras it conveys, and some scholars argue that the *DG* and *AG* are opposed. This is correct as the essence of each scripture is different, but this is for good reason, as they are for different purposes. The selection of the goddess of war, Durga, by the Guru was to arouse the heroic spirit of the Indian populace against the Turaks. The Guru was not a worshipper of the goddess, and time and time again he invokes God as the feminine Divine Sword, and then narrates the tales of the goddess, as the power of God (*shaktī*) in action. The same sword is related to the Khalsa initiation, which gives the initiate spiritual and warrior ideals. The first twenty-seven verses of the *Rosary of the Names of Weapons* is to the sword.[41] This is found in other traditions, for example, the Dhul'fiqar of Imam Ali, the myths of the Excalibur of King Arthur, and the sword in the Knighthood, as well as in veneration by the Knights Templar.

Degh–Tegh–Fateh: The Establishment of Sikh Sovereignty

Guru Gobind Singh's legacy can be described in a multitude of ways. He can be seen as the Guru who solidified the mission of the previous gurus by creating the order of the pure, or the Khalsa. He has also been described as the master warrior who was valiant in battle and tried to uphold righteousness. The canonization of the Guru's works in the form of the *Shabad Guru*—the *AG*—is another one of his lasting achievements. In the tradition, he is seen as a literary genius and a poet who brought about a literary revolution by penning numerous compositions of the *DG*. Whatever the description, Guru Gobind Singh was a spirited figure who changed the history of India. His contribution has reached beyond the borders of Hindustan, but unfortunately, the social and philosophical connotations of his mission are still misunderstood and at times just reduced to a few paragraphs of discussion.

One concept that merits discussion is that of degh–tegh–fateh, which has been popularly represented in Sikh thought and through material heritage. The term appears in the ardās, which is recited after most Sikh rituals and ceremonies.[42] This prayer is important for the Sikhs as it reminds them of the sacrifices that the gurus and other *shahīds* made. The following couplet appears at the end of the ardās,

Degh Tegh Fateh
Panth kī jīt
Jo Bole So Nihāl Sat Srī Akāl

May the Free Kitchen and Arms
remain always victorious!
May the Panth be victorious!
Whosoever shall say this will be
Blessed: True is Timeless Being[43]

This slogan is derived from three words and deserves a closer look in terms of its origins and impact on the Sikh psyche. The words have Persian origins and were not a new inclusion in Sikh thought. Previously, Persian words were incorporated and adopted in the *AG*, largely due to the impact of Islamic rule, and particularly because of the fact that Persian was the state language. The *Zafarnāmah* and the other *Hikāyats* are all written in Persian verse. The first word 'degh' refers to a kettle or cooking pot. This is a direct reference to the nourishment of the sangat that is seen in the institution of the *langar* which had been flourishing since the time of the early gurus. This important institution was set up to eradicate the caste difference prevalent in Hindu society. Degh also refers to the *karah prashād*, the sanctified food in the form of a pudding, which is served in the gurdwara. We also see that within the langar the prashād is only sanctified after the *kirpān* has stirred the food, symbolically showing degh and tegh coming together.

In the time of Guru Gobind Singh, the langar was a prominent feature of his reign and certain anecdotes tell us that the Guru was keen to ensure that this was not abused. One example tells us that the Guru disguised himself as a pilgrim and visited numerous places in search of food but it was only Bhai Nand Lal who was praised for keeping his langar plentiful. We also see in Takht Hazur Sahib, Nanded, that there is a gurdwara dedicated to the tradition of sanctified food, called 'Guru ka Langar'.

The term 'tegh' refers to a type of sword which is used in warfare. The tegh differs from other swords and can be described as quite short, single-edged and curved. The employment of weapons in Sikh theology was revised by Guru Gobind Singh, with the aim of elevating these weapons to the status of God. It was through the employment of these weapons that the Sikhs could achieve their Raj and hence receive their boons. It is a mistaken view that the weapons of the Sikhs are mere instruments of violence; moreover, the kirpān is defined as the 'instrument of mercy'. The whole ritual of 'shastra pūjā', or 'the worship of weapons', is a study in itself and involves giving incense and treating the weapons as the embodiment of Akal Purakh. The Guru himself was instrumental in ensuring that the Sikhs had a fighting spirit which could uproot the tyranny that was present in his time. Whilst the tradition of the sword was started by Guru Hargobind with his installation as Guru, it is Baba Buddha who is credited with the original idea of carrying arms. The combining of the spiritual and temporal was started by Guru Nanak himself who initiated the idea of mīrī (signifying temporal power) and pīrī (signifying spiritual authority). The combination of both became the cornerstone of early Sikh thought. This concept was further employed in the moulding of the Khalsa in 1699 by Guru Gobind Singh, with the initiation ceremony, khaṅḍe kī pāhul, calling on Sikhs to carry arms. The Sikhs became 'saint soldiers' or 'sant sipāhī'. The Tenth Guru employed numerous terms for describing weaponry in his compositions, and the *Shastra Nām Mālā* is a unique composition stringing together the various forms of weapons. The reminder that the call to arms should only be the last resort (*Zafarnāmah*) is a legacy of the sant sipāhī model.

The term 'fateh' is a term that can be heard by Sikhs who greet each other and which refers to victory. The term appears in the Sikh salutation, 'Vahiguru ji ka Khalsa Vahiguru ji ki Fateh', hence denoting that victory comes from God.[44] The last part of the greeting appears in the *manglacharans* (invocations) of *DG* compositions. The use of the word 'fateh' continuously appears in Sikh history, and was employed by Sikhs when facing tremendous odds in battle. This representation is noted on the largest Sikh cannon which was captured by the British during the Anglo-Sikh wars. The cannons of the Sikhs were given individual names and this particular one was named 'Fateh Jang' or 'Victory in Battle'.[45]

The terms when combined together give us a new sense of instruction for the Khalsa. The term has also been used in a modified form from the late seventeenth century in the compositions of Guru Gobind Singh. In the composition *Krishnā Avatār*, the Guru states,

> Sustain me, considering me as Thy own and destroy my enemies, picking them up; O Lord with Thy Grace, let the free kitchen and Sword (for the protection of the lowly) ever flourish through me and none should be able to kill me except you.[46]

This clearly shows that the degh and tegh were prominent features of the Guru's mission and that he had the theological belief that only the Lord of Time could take his life.

In the composition *Chaṇḍī dī Vār* the poet asks for the assistance of the *khaṅḍā* in helping to complete the *Granth*. This is clarified in the following lines, 'God created the *Khaṅḍā* which manifested the world.'[47] Then, in Sikh thought, the khaṅḍa is a functional object of God. Its significance in the khaṅḍe kī pāhul ceremony is based on the power that the Guru has described in the composition. Despite the various names the Guru has given to the sword, the symbolism and importance of the sword to the Guru is the same.

The words 'degh' and 'bhagautī' (in the context of a sword) are mentioned together in the *DG*, this time in the *Srī Charitropakhyān*, where the notion of battle is prominent: 'To give in charity and the use of the sword, both are two honourable acts in the world.'[48] We also see the term 'bhagautī' actually inscribed on swords, including the one attributed to the Tenth Guru.[49] This unity of degh and tegh was not only a feature for the Sikhs but was an ideal everybody could aspire to. The Guru even gave Emperor Aurangzeb credit for achieving this whilst admonishing him for his other traits and characteristics. In the *Zafarnāmah* or 'Epistle of Victory', the Guru states, 'With the help of your intelligence and the sword, you have become the master of degh and tegh.'[50] As the epistle was written in Persian, the terms would have been clearly understood by the Emperor. The degh–tegh–fateh concept was made clear from the early days of Guru Gobind Singh's rule. One anecdote, by Sewa Das,[51] describes the Guru's battle with the Hill Rajas:

> The Guru at once took the bow and arrow in his hands, stood on his cot, touched the earth with his arrow on the four sides, and in a loud voice recited the sloka: 'Degh Tegh Fateh Bedrang Simrite Guru Nanak Fateh Guru Gobind Singh.' ('Victory in battle, and prosperity; Concentrate on Guru Nanak, victory is with Guru Gobind Singh.') Reciting this he pulled the bow string with all his might and shot the arrow into the sky. The sky echoed and the mountain shuddered. All men standing on the hill fell to ground because of shuddering, and repeatedly beseeched the Guru to protect them. The hills shuddered for some time. Soon it was calm again. The Guru sent the horseman back to the Khalsa with the message, 'Go and fight the rajahs without any fear. Victory will be yours.' At this command from the Guru the Khalsa pounced upon the rajahs, and won.[52]

This *sākhī* not only shows the Guru participating in battle, but using the term in the midst of battle, and moreover as a battle cry. After the writings of the *DG* became more prevalent, this slogan would be recited by the Khalsa. It was later recorded as a final verse in manuscripts of the *Sarabaloh Graṅth* with colophons of AD 1698.[53]

This slogan would also be employed in the seals of the Guru's followers, for example, Banda Singh Bahadur's hukamnāmās. Banda Bahadur had been sent on a mission by the Guru to reclaim Panjab from the clutches of the Mughals. His seal in Persian runs as follows:

> *Deg Tegh Fateh O Nusrat Baidarang*
> *Yaft uz Nanak Guru Gobind Singh*
>
> The Kettle, sword and the resultant victory
> Achieved with the help from Guru Nanak to Guru Gobind Singh[54]

The Khalsa was now setting its sights on proclaiming its sovereignty especially after Banda Bahadur's successes in Sirhind and other territories. A number of important hukamnāmās followed, including one delivered to the sangat of Jaunpur, dated 12 December 1710, and one sent to Bhai Dharam Singh.[55] However, the real importance of the degh–tegh–fateh concept was witnessed in the striking of the first Sikh coins. Within two years of the Guru's death, the Khalsa was declaring their sovereignty, as there is no feature of sovereignty more symbolic than the striking of a coin.

Banda Bahadur paid homage to Guru Nanak and Guru Gobind Singh after being victorious in his campaigns. The first coin with this concept was issued in the year 1710. This imprint was not a one-off occurrence and the Khalsa ensured that this feature continued in their expression of sovereignty and victory in the future. Mata Sahib Kaur, the wife of Guru Gobind Singh, also used the same seal in her hukamnāmās. The edicts were sent from Delhi where she was residing and controlling the affairs of the Sikhs together with Mata Sundari.[56] After various battles, the Sikh sardars and the various *misls* came together in 1765. This was the second phase of the striking of Sikh coins which were pressed from two mints, one in Lahore and the other in Amritsar.[57] The Lahore coin contained the words 'degh–tegh–fateh' but the Amritsar coin contained the terms 'tegh' and 'fateh' only. This concept continued with Sikh coins minted during the Ranjit Singh era but the establishment of British rule in Panjab finally meant the demise of this seal in 1850. Interestingly, the rulers of Patiala also used the concept on these coins in their own personal ceremonies which were seen on the occasion of Dussherā. The coins were not used as currency as such, but rather as tokens to be distributed to household staff and state officials. One example of this is what can be described as a garland made of gold, silver, and enamel with a medal featuring a picture of Guru Gobind Singh. The inscription on the medal states 'Deg-Teg-Fateh, Sache-Pātshāh'. This order of distinction was created by the Patiala ruler, Maharaja Bhupinder Singh.[58] The state of Nabha also used the same seal on its Nazrana (presentation) coins up until 1948.

Whilst Sikh coins provided one avenue of this concept, the Nishān Sahibs were another. There has been little research undertaken in the area of how and what the Nishān Sahibs looked at the time of the gurus. However, we can turn to various anecdotes which can help provide further evidence.[59] Firstly, we can turn to a painting which depicts Guru Gobind Singh's journey to the Deccan, and is dated c. 1770–80. It shows Guru Gobind Singh on horseback together with five disciples, who are presumably the Pañj Piāre. Leading the procession is one of the five who is dressed as an Akali Nihang and, more importantly, carrying a battle standard. The yellow battle standard features representations of three things. First, there is a depiction of a *kaṭār* and also a tegh (which is depicted as a curved sword), together with what looks like a *ḍhāl* (shield). The ḍhāl does not have any inscriptions on it, and so the round object could be a pot which represents a degh.[60] It could be argued that if we take the mīrī–pīrī concept into account, the representation is more likely to be that of a pot.

This painting of the Nishān Sahib with similar features also appears in other representations. Inside the gurdwara of Baba Atal Rai in Amritsar, we find that there are again many frescoes of the gurus and the Khalsa.[61] One of the panels on the outside of the gurdwara depicts Guru Gobind Singh together with his Khalsa engaged in battle. Again, a battle standard is represented and a closer inspection of it reveals that it also features a katār, kirpān, and a circular object. Then, this confirms the belief that this battle standard was a feature of the Khalsa. Whilst there have been different styles of Nishān Sahibs in Sikh history, we see the degh–tegh–fateh concept elaborated with great effect on the ones described above.

We also see the concept extended to weapons. The inscription on weapons belonging to the Guru and his followers shows how the transmission of the compositions in the *DG* extended to material heritage (see Chapter 1). We learn of a sword that was in the possession of the Raja of Nabha carrying the phrase, 'Badhe degh te ya tegh te' or 'Great are the degh and the tegh'.[62] There is no doubt that other weapons also bear this inscription. In the Sikh regiments during the World Wars, it became a motto and a battle cry. J.D. Hookway, in writing about the history of the Mazabhi and Ramdasia regiments, gives the meaning as: 'We all wish at all times for our victory in War, which is the victory of our sword, and also our economic prosperity in peace and war—more food, better standard of living and all other riches for our country.'[63]

The concept of degh–tegh–fateh also extends into *mohurs* or stamps used in recensions of the Sikh scriptures. There are several types used on manuscripts that clearly mark the place of compilation. Manuscripts which were created at Damdama Sahib bear the term 'degh–tegh–fateh'. One *DG* manuscript kept at Hazur Sahib in the eighteenth century bears one of these mohurs, which contains the words degh–tegh–fateh in Persian, and it is stamped on a folio of the *Zafarnāmah*. It seems more than coincidence for the stamp to appear on this folio—it appears to be intentional to show the Persian link of the seal and the composition. There are indeed many other instances where this concept appears and we have alluded to some examples to show how the concept continues to remain in the psyche of the Sikhs. What seem like mere cursory statements in the compositions of *Krishnā Avatār*, the *Zafarnāmah*, and *Sri Charitropakhyān* can actually be seen as markers of Sikh sovereignty for the Khalsa. We shall now consider how another symbol of the Khalsa, the chakkar, was utilized in war, and its relationship with the *Shastra Nām Mālā*.

Sikh Martial Tradition: The Quoit, the Akalis, and the Rosary of Weapons

See the Akalees fiercely are raging in fight,
See them bathing in red blood scimitars bright,
See them hurl from their finger the murderous ring,
Surpassing in swiftness the proud eagle's wing.[64]

Henry F. Brooks, eloquently describes the method the Akalis used to deliver the 'murderous ring'; he is referring to the *chakram* or quoit. Brooks's poetry was criticized for being partly 'fictional' and partly based on fact.[65] The purpose of this chapter is to separate fact from fiction and examine the use and effectiveness of the chakkar.[66] In addition, the final part of this chapter discusses the chakkar and its relationship with the *Shastra Nām Mālā*—the *Holy Rosary of the Names of Ancient Weapons*—that is located around halfway through the *DG*.[67]

Before we examine the accounts about the 'murderous ring', it is necessary to re-familiarize ourselves with the Akalis. The 'Immortals' are an institution that can be traced back to the elite corps of the Tenth Guru, and to the earlier militarization of the Sikh Panth by the Sixth Guru. Guru Hargobind ordered the formation of an elite military corporeal body of the Guru Panth, the Akali Dal (Immortal Army).[68] This organization exemplified the saint-warrior ideal of the Guru, by strictly following the Sikh *rahit marayādā*. Historically speaking, the Akalis were the custodians of Sri Akal Takht and would initiate new Sikhs with khaṅḍe kī pāhul. In early accounts of the Akali Sikhs their position in the Panth was clear, as well as their relationship with weapons. J. Malcolm narrates:

> The mode is as follows. The convert is told that he must allow his hair to grow. He must clothe himself from head to foot in blue clothes. He is then presented with the five weapons: a sword, a firelock, a bow and arrow, and a pike*. One of those who initiate him then says, 'The Guru is thy holy teacher, and thou art his Sikh or disciple.'[69] Some sugar and water is put into a cup, and stirred round with a steel knife, or dagger, and some of the first chapters of the *Adi-Grant'h*, and the first chapters of the *Dasama Padshah ka Grant'h*, are read.[70]

The motive behind this ritualistic initiation into the use of arms by the Akalis is brought to light by Malcolm. In the footnotes he records a verse from the *Shastra Nām Mālā*:

> *The goddess of courage, Bhavani Durgá, represented in the *Dasama Pádsháh ka Grant'h*, or book of kings of Gúrú Góvind, as the soul of arms, or tutelary goddess of war, and is thus addressed: 'Thou art the edge of the sword, thou art the arrow, the sword, the knife, and the dagger.'[71]

Malcolm appears to be talking about how the weapons are addressed at the time of initiation. Kuir Singh also mentions five weapons of battle, taken by the Guru and his army into a battle. Alongside this he quotes the warrior dialogue of dharam yudh from the *Granth of Guru Gobind Singh*.[72] He refers to the five handy weapons of the Khalsa warrior as the *panch hathiyār*; one of the five sacred weapons is the quoit, and its usage is found within the *DG*.[73]

From the early European and Sikh accounts it is clear that the Akali Nihangs were the leading force of the Guru Khalsa Panth, between the eighteenth and nineteenth centuries.[74] The great martyr Akali Phula Singh was from the ranks of this organization and was the leader of the Khalsa Panth.[75] There are a number of portraits of Akali Phula Singh drawn by Europeans throughout his life. Several of which depict Akali Phula Singh heavily armed, adorned with a number of quoits and the brooch *Adi Chaṅd* visible on his turban.[76]

This adornment of weapons by the Akalis is seen in other nineteenth-century descriptions, drawings, and paintings. Leopold von Orlich narrates: 'On our return several Akalees jeered at us, at the same time—giving us a specimen of their dexterity in the use of their quoit.'[77] This description is given with a detailed illustration, which depicts two Akalis heavily armed with rifled muskets, swords, and chakkars. They seemed to be on a raised position, and one is whirling the chakkar around his finger to release it on his target (see Figure 4.2).

From the first few accounts, it is clear that the chakkar was a part of the early uniform (*bānā*) of the Khalsa army. This decoration with sacred steel, *Sarabaloh*, in the form of weapons, was and remains a distinct feature of the Akalis:

> The Akalis and the Nihungs have kept themselves more free from Hindúism that [*sic*] the other two classes; they may be distinguished by their blue turbans, and are never without the five K's. The former are looked upon as their priests, are maintained by public charity, and, as a rule, lead a monastic life; they also use peculiar modes of speech, one of which is that they always speak in the masculine gender. They wear in their turbans two or three different styles of ornaments: these are invariably of iron, which they consider possesses very sacred properties. Some have a row of

FIGURE 4.2 Akalees by Leopold von Orlich, 1845
Source: Leopold von Orlich, *Travels in India: Including Sinde and the Punjab*, 1845.

small instruments stuck in the front of their head-dress, much resembling spillikens in form and size; others, again, have iron rings, of the quoit shape, round the head. Some have an iron torque worn in the same manner, or a large round brooch in the centre of the front of the turban.[78]

J.C. Murray-Aynsley[79] describes the appearance of the Akalis as ascetic-warriors having quoits, small sharp weapons, and the *Adi Chand* on their turbans. Her account was written seventy years after Malcolm, but both descriptions of the Akalis are quite similar. The other two classes she is referring to are the Nirmala and Udasi Sikhs, who were the traditional Sikh 'missionaries' in India. She rightly notes that the Akalis clearly distinguished themselves from Hinduism.[80]

Now we have familiarized ourselves with the Akalis and their traditional dress. It is now necessary to discuss various accounts narrating the use of the Sikh quoit. In other accounts we find detailed descriptions about how the chakkar was thrown, and about its accuracy as a weapon. A British General narrates in his memoirs the Sikhs of Nanded in 1817–19:

> The Seik student always appears in public well dressed; and in stature, deportment, and habit, strikes the visitor at once with a prepossession in his favour. They are generally tall, of elegant symmetry, and in their countenances alone carry an expression of superiority and manliness far above any other tribe in India. They generally dress in dark clothes, with lofty blue turbans, and are on all occasions armed with a sword and shield, and many of them with an instrument of war, which they use with the greatest dexterity and effect.
>
> This weapon resembles a common quoit, with this difference, that the plate of the former is perfectly flat on both sides, and not above the eighth of an inch in thickness. These are commonly carried in a dozen or two on the upper ball or crest of the turban, where they sit close together, and quite at hand for service. In using these missile weapons, the fore finger of the right hand is introduced into its cavity in the centre, and the inner edge brought to rest firmly on the ball of the same finger; the thumb is applied outside and over the edge (which is as sharp as a common knife), merely to direct the aim. The right leg is then drawn back, and the Seik, raising his arm above his head, and inclining his body downwards, discharges it in a horizontal direction, just as a boy skims a sheet of water with a slate. These weapons fly through the air faster than the

> eye can follow them, and the Seik makes as sure of hitting an object the size of a man at seventy or eighty yards, as the best marksman could with a rifle. These weapons are used with best effect against bodies of cavalry, where, even at the distance of two hundred yards, one of them coming in contact, with the horse's leg or body will be sure to break the former, or plunge right into the latter. The Seiks use also bows and arrows with great skill, and are elegant horsemen, on these occasions using the spear and matchlock, and on all public ceremonies displaying their beautifully embroidered black banners, with curious devices upon them. This class of people bear the most deadly antipathy to the Mahomedans.[81]

Another military officer, Major Bevan, records before the Anglo-Sikh wars:

> They are a fine athletic race of men; they use a singular weapon, something like a quoit, which they throw with such precision as to cut off the legs of sheep at a distance of fifty or sixty yards. We were gratified by several exhibitions of their skill while we remained in the neighbourhood.[82]

While the previous accounts are generous, generally the European officials, who recorded most of the accounts available, frowned upon the Akali's complete disregard of worldly authority. This disregard often extended to the European officials and Maharaja Ranjit Singh in the form of insults, and sometimes physical attacks:

> In addition to the regular and irregular army the Lahore government has also in its pay a body of irregular cavalry, (to the number of between two and three thousand) called Akalees. They are religious fanatics, who acknowledge no ruler or law but their own; think nothing of robbery, or even murder, should they happen to be in the humour for it, Runjeet Singh himself on more than one occasion narrowly escaped assassination by them. They are without any exception the most insolent and worthless race of people under the sun. They move about constantly armed to the teeth, insulting everybody they meet, particularly Europeans, and it is not an uncommon thing to see them riding about with a drawn sword in each hand, two more in their belt, a matchlock at their back, and three or four quoits fastened round their turbans. The quoit is fastened round their turbans. The quoit is an arm peculiar to this race of people; it is a steel ring, varying from six to nine inches in

> diameter, and about an inch in breadth, very thin, and the edges ground very sharp: they throw it with more force than dexterity, but not so (as alleged) as to be able to lop off a limb at sixty or eighty yards. In general, the bystanders are in great danger than the object aimed at.[83]

Even though Henry Steinbach[84] is quite scathing, he nonetheless provides us with a useful description. He tries to put an end to the fame of the legendary use of the chakkar, by creating doubt about the ability of the Sikh warriors. It might be that the Akali who was witnessed using the quoit was not proficient in its use. In a military magazine after the Anglo-Sikh wars we have a succinct history of the militarization of the Panth and a cynical description about the use of the chakkar:

> According to the advice of their leader, they generally wore arms, or at least carried steel in some form about them. The exhortation to carry arms was obeyed even to fanaticism by some amongst the Sikhs, who always went about heavily armed, carrying a drawn sword in each hand, two additional swords in a belt, and as if these were not sufficient for their defence, these warriors carry a gun slung on their back, and on the turban is fixed a number of iron quoits, with the outer edge sharpened. They are said to be very dexterous in the use of these quoits, cutting off the leg of an elephant at one blow. Such accounts must be taken with some grains of allowance, as it does not appear very easy to understand how a man bearing a sword in each hand finds means of throwing a quoit. Be this as it may, these fanatics, who were called 'Acalis', or immortals, had become, from their lawless habits, very dangerous to the country, and were suppressed by Runjeet Singh.[85]

After the death of Maharaja Ranjit Singh, the British seized their opportunity and the Anglo-Sikh wars took place. The Nihang Singhs took to the vanguard and many fell in the theatre of war. There are a number of Akali turbans called *dastār bungās* (crowned towers) and quoits in British museums, which were taken as spoils of war from the fallen Akalis.[86] The turbans and quoits became fascinating objects for Europeans, and began to feature in exhibitions and books, due to—it could be argued—common knowledge amongst Europeans about the devastating use of the chakkar by Sikhs in battle. This ancient weapon gained a mythical reputation when the British saw it being worn and thrown by the fey-looking Akalis. The contemporary accounts of officers were undecided if any troops were ever injured or killed by the quoit.[87] This need to investigate led to the following incident:

> February fourth,—Not being on duty to-day, have had leisure to stroll round and examine our position. About one mile and a quarter of dusty glacis extends between the two camps. We have many advanced posts; most of which are vacated at sun-set. The Seik troops occupy both sides of the river, having, beside a ford, a well-constructed bridge of boats. The territory of the Punjaub looks quite sterile a waste as our own. We have many captured Seik prisoners in the camp; two fresh ones were brought in just now. They are both Akalis, an independent sect of religious fanatics: tall, hirsute, specimens of humanity, above the ordinary height of Europeans, literally armed *cap a pie*. One musket, three swords, two bows, and a whole *chevaux de frise* of dirks and pistols, formed part of the defensive equipment of each. On their heads they wore high pointed leather caps, on which were strung, graduating up from a large size to small, the sharp quoits, which they know how to use to such deadly effect. They were quickly stripped of all this gear, and were marching off under the guard, When Colonel C____ called them back, and placing in the hands of one of them a quoit, bade him throw it. The fellow at first refused; but upon being twitted by a native Soubidar as to his ability to do so, the desire to vindicate his prowess quickly overcame his determination; seizing the quoit in his right hand, and inserting the forefinger as an axis on which to revolve it, he caused it to rotate rapidly over his head, looking around at the same time for an appropriate mark. Sixty yards off, on a small mound, stood Colonel C ____'s favourite milch goat; another instant, and the quoit had quitted the Akali's finger, and the goat lay quivering in death, nearly decapitated; while, with a grin of malice at the dismayed C_____, the Seik faced to the right-about, and marched off with his captors.[88]

This eyewitness account dispels the doubt about the efficiency of the chakkar, as it clearly was a devastating weapon in the right hands. To kill a goat from 60 yards (approx. 54 metres) away is no easy task, and the Sikh warrior in question undoubtedly had great skill. Amongst Sikhs, the mythical status of the chakkar was such that even after the Anglo-Sikh wars and the Arms Act, many veteran Sikh warriors were seen adorning a chakkar, as testified by

European paintings and travel narratives. For example, in William Simpson's exquisite watercolour of an Akali priest outside Sri Akal Takht, his quoits are clearly visible; he faces the Sri Darbar Sahib, using a *bairagan*, a meditation staff to prop himself up.[89]

After the annexation of Panjab, and the formation of British Sikh regiments, an ornamental or real chakkar formed a part of the turban. It was seen as the national weapon or symbol of the Sikhs. The legend spread that a chakram could 'cut off a man's head in a moment'.[90] The Sikhs at that time still took pride in the skill of throwing it.[91] Unfortunately, many Akali weapons were lost due to the Arms Act of India.[92] Some were sold as scrap metal and melted down, others were sold in auctions, and found their way to museums and private collections in Europe.

The legend of the Akalis became such 'that the quoit was a favourite spoil of war for the British Administration, and were [*sic*] exhibited largely. The Paris exhibition of 1867 showed off a golden pair of Quoits, with *koftgari* work on polished steel, from the collection of H. R. H. the Duke of Edinburgh.'[93] Some examples of its use were faithfully recorded, as the British wished to keep this intimidating weapon alive in the newly formed Sikh regiments.[94] Lieutenant Lewin narrates:

> On the march we met a Sikh regiment, who were going to our late quarters at Futtehpore, and I was most kindly entertained by the officers, after the hospitable custom of the country. The Sikhs are extremely fine bodied and handsome men. Many of them wore polished circlets of steel, sharp edged, around which their many-folded turbans were twisted.[95]

He then narrates how he watched the Sikhs hit trees with quoits, from two hundred yards, followed by a war-dance (paintrā), timed to rhythm, from drums and music, while the Sikhs sang verses and clashed their swords.[96] This is the Sikh martial art called *Gatkā* or *Shastravidiā*. In the Sikh martial arts today, passages are repeated from *DG* compositions like the *Shastra Nām Mālā*. There is a good possibility that the verses they sang were from the *DG*.[97]

As the chakkar reached European exhibitions, the interest grew enough to merit elaborate drawings in books. An illustration by Wood has two quoits around it, with a number of other smaller swords. He writes:

It is made of thin steel and is sharpened to a razor-like edge on the upperside. The mode of casting it is to spin it on the forefinger and then to hurl it. The reader may imagine that such a missile, which not only strikes an object, but revolves rapidly at the time, must be a very formidable one. It is generally aimed at the face of the adversary, and a skilful warrior will hurl four or five in such rapid succession that it is scarcely possible to avoid being struck by one of them and having the face laid open, or the nose or lip absolutely cut off. These quoit-like articles are carried upon a tall, conical head-dress worn by the natives, into the folds of which they also put several small knives, as labourers stick their pipes in their hats. [See Wood's illustration.][98]

Similar spoils of war made it to other establishments. The photograph below is of a turban extant in the Royal Armouries (see Figure 4.3).

It was acquired from the East India Company in 1851, and five steel quoits and various *Adi Chaṅd* are visible. It is also adorned

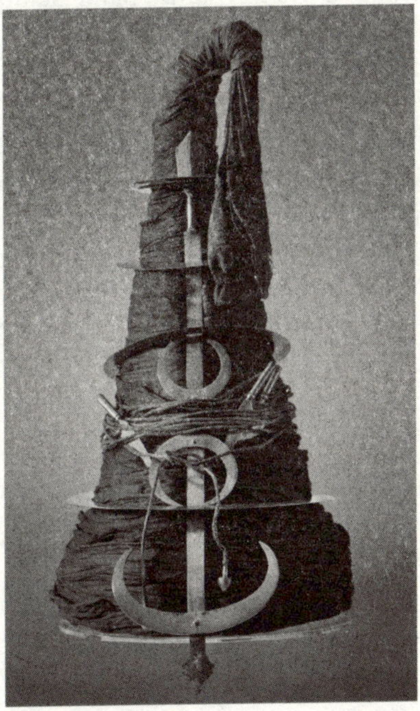

FIGURE 4.3 Royal Armoury Quoit-Turban[99]
Source: Royal Armouries (26A.60).

FIGURE 4.4 An Officer of the 14th Sikhs Infantry, British Indian Troops, Chinese War, China, with the Quoit Adorning His Turban[100]
Source: Kamalroop Singh; image taken from a postcard from the period.

with various spillikins for use as weapons. The plume at the top is known as a *faṛlā*, and is a miniature battle standard, a tradition started by the Tenth Guru.

This traditional turban was then modified by the British for use in the Sikh regiments. Figure 4.4 shows a photograph of a Sikh officer, with the large turban and quoit, with the other novel feature of the British regiments, the neatly tied beard.

Describing the 14th Sikh regiment of the British Army, Craik states that they marched and wore 'white puggarees, each with the war-quoit twisted in its folds'. Later in the text, he describes that when meeting the Council of the Regency in Patiala, the men 'showed their skill with this old Sikh weapon'.[101] The use of the chakkar in the newly formed Anglo-Sikh regiments as a military exercise is described as:

> They are thrown with great accuracy, and, though not now used for war purposes, the Sikh soldier, in his *kusrut* or display with his weapons—a kind of assault at arms—will cut in two a gourd elevated on a stick to the height of a man's head, at a distance of fifty or sixty yards.[102]

It was said to fly like a boomerang, and also made to ricochet off the ground.[103] In war, a number of them were thrown rapidly in succession.[104] The same technique and skill is also narrated by W. Egerton, that the chakrum is whirled around the finger and the head, and when released, is enough to kill at man at 80 paces.[105] Other commentators also report that 'these thin rings of steel were the most deadly and terrible projectiles'.[106] Egerton with a description provides an illustration, with a Sikh whirling the Quoit over his head. He also provides a drawing of an ornately decorated quoit from Lahore, this shows the chakkar was more than just a weapon but was also the jewellery and a symbol of the Khalsa.[107] The chakkars could be used in close quarter fighting, where a volley of them would be released, or from a raised position, like a hill, where larger ones could be thrown. As the steel was thin and aerodynamic, the chakkar, if thrown with adequate spin and force, would maintain its trajectory well even in windy conditions. It was also sometimes dipped into poison, with devastating effect. The diameter would vary between 9 and 12 inches in length, and 1 and 1.5 inches in width. The chakkar was often inscribed or engraved with verses of *gurbāṇī*, or heavily decorated with exquisite *koftgari* or *neilli* work, in silver or gold.[108] In the colonial period, some workmen were still able to make the chakkar with high-quality sword steel that was slightly blue or black in appearance. Workshops were opened in Amritsar, Lahore, and Ferozepur.[109] The chakkars were produced in workshops around Darbar Sahib, and were sanctified by Sri Akal Takht, before being used by Sikhs. The normal target for practice was a plantain tree.[110] At that time the chakkar was a part of village sports of Panjab, along with wrestling, fencing, archery, hunting, and so on. Normally, fist fighting would be taught, followed by wrestling with the arms and legs, stone throwing, then the use of clubs. Later on the student would learn the bow and arrow, the quoit, then how to wield a sword, and finally the gun.[111]

Towards the end of the nineteenth century, an Udasi Sikh who was an attendant at Gurdwara Vadh Tirath found some relics of the Tenth Guru in the *sarovar*.[112] He presented these to the Namdharis, of which one relic was a chakram which has a gold nugget melted into the steel, which is said to be a characteristic of the Tenth Guru's chivalrous code.[113] It is still in the *toshekhānā* of the Namdharis. In the treasury of Maharaja Ranjit Singh was a Sikh quoit turban called a dastār bungā; it is said that he would pay his respects to it every day, as it was the turban of a famous martyr.[114] After annexation this was taken by the British administration. The photograph in Figure 4.5 is of this particular turban.

FIGURE 4.5 Akali Phula Singh's Turban[115]
Source: Museum Number: 3458: 1 to:11/(IS); © Victoria & Albert Museum, London.

This was a rare find for the time; as stated earlier in this chapter, many of the weapons of the Akalis were lost in the Arms Act of India. Many colonial accounts state that martial practices were extinct amongst the Sikhs, although the traditions lived on with the Akalis.[116] This tradition continues today, although it is very rare.[117] Akali Baba Bali Singh, whose photograph is shown in Figure 4.6, is one of the last exponents of this art in Panjab. He narrated the various techniques of its use. He spun the chakkar around his finger, as well as showing the methods to throw it from the side and the front of the body like a frisbee. It requires a great deal of dexterity of the fingers. He demonstrated a similar method to those narrated in this chapter.[118]

Recently, the Discovery Channel aired two documentaries on the chakkar. The first one was called *Weapons Masters* by Mike Loades and aired in 2008 and the other was called the *Deadliest Warrior: Indian Rajput versus Roman Centurion* which was aired in 2010,[119] that featured the use of the chakkar. In the second documentary, the chakkar easily sliced a neck-thick piece of meat into two when thrown from a distance. In the other documentary, Mike Loades came to the conclusion after experimentation that the Sikh quoit was efficiently deadly.

FIGURE 4.6 Akali Baba Bali Singh of *Taranā Dal* Demonstrating with a Sikh Quoit
Source: Kamalroop Singh.

On the other hand, a recent publication by Ian Heath and Michael Perry called *The Sikh Army 1799–1849* expresses doubt about its ability.[120] In conclusion, from the accounts discussed in this chapter it is clear that when used with skill, the chakkar was deadly. The reason the British did not record the fatalities from the Sikh quoit was quite simple, as the myth would have got stronger and the British soldiers would have been terrified and intimidated even before approaching the battlefield. The chakkar and its legend is very powerful; hence its adornment on the turban of the Akalis even today.

In the third and final part of this chapter, we will now address the scriptural relationship of the chakkar. The Akalis, while tying their turbans, read some passages from the *AG*. The composition by the fifth Guru in Sri Rāg describes the tying of the *ūch dumallārā* (high turbans) on winning a wrestling competition.[121] Within this prescriptive liturgy for tying the dastār bungā is a composition known as the *Dumāllānāmā Pātashāhī Dasavīṅ* (*The Epistle of the Conical Turban, by the Tenth Sovereign*).[122] In this composition, there is a reference to the chakkar: *sir par mukaṭ, mukaṭ par chakkar*—on my head is the crown, crowned with the chakkar (here the chakkar seems to represent temporality). A chakkar at the New York Metropolitan Museum has passages of protection inscribed in gold, which is a *mantra* repeated by the Nihang

Singhs when tying their tall turbans. The first line reads, 'The Lord is the protector of our foreheads, hands and body.'[123] This passage is also recorded on the *chāraīnā* of Guru Gobind Singh which we referred to in Chapter 1.

References to the chakkar are also found throughout the many Puranic narrations in the *DG*. The *Shastra Nām Mālā Purāṅ* is a part of the recension of the *DG*.[124] 'Shastra' translates as weaponry, 'nām'–names, 'mālā'–rosary, and 'purāṇ'–ancient; hence this composition is 'The Ancient Rosary of the Names of Weapons'. In the *Shastra Nām Mālā Purāṅ*, a whole chapter is dedicated to the Quoit out of the five important weapons, *paṅja shastra*.[125] The ratio of the verses dedicated to each weapon in the *Shastra Nām Mālā* shows us the practical thinking of the author, Guru Gobind Singh:

Bhagautī (Sword): 1–27
Chakkar (Quoit): 28–74
Bān (Bow): 75–252
Paṅsh (Noose): 253–460
Tupak (Gun): 460–1318

Shastra Nām Mālā Purāṅ appears roughly half-way through the volume of the *DG*. In Sikh praxis, the *madh*, or middle of the constant recitation (*akhaṅḍ pāṭh*) of the *DG*, is the *Shastra Nām Mālā Purāṅ*. At this point either black male goats are decapitated or sugar canes are chopped, depending upon diet. Normally, the martial Akali Nihang Khalsa will use a goat, while the *sattvic* Sikhs, the Nirmale, and the Damdami Taksal will sacrifice vegetarian offerings. We find that in the praxis of the *AG*, karah prashād (degh) is also served at the madh, which is the mid-point of the recital.

The history of the *chakra* is ancient as is proven by its references in the *Rigveda*. In ancient iconography, it is part of the five sacred weapons of war (*panchayudhu*), and Vishnu is depicted as having a chakra, known as the Sudarshan Chakra.[126] The Sikh symbol khaṅḍā also has a chakra within it, and in both cases it represents omnipotence, wisdom, eternity, infinity, grace, and liberation (*mukatī*). The word 'sudarshan' is derived from two words, *su* (auspicious) and *darshan* (presence). The word chakra is derived from *chruhu* (movement) and *kruhu* (doing/spinning). Thus, chakra means that which is revolving and moving.[127] According to the Purāṇas, Vishnu could simply release it and it would chop off a demon's head and return back to his finger. In the *Shastra Nām Mālā Purāṅ*, the Guru refers to the auspicious chakra of Vishnu within the composition. A translation of this section on the chakra from the *Shastra Nām Mālā Purāṅ* is given below:

Ath Srī Chakkar Nām (Now the Description of the Holy Names of the Chakkar)[128]

Doharā (Couplet)

Pronouncing the word 'Vishnu' in the beginning and then say 'weapon', many names of Sudarshan continue to be formed.57.[129]

Saying firstly the word 'Mur' and then pronouncing the word 'Mardan', the name of Sudarshan Chakra is taken internally by the wise.58.

Saying 'Madh' and then pronouncing 'Ha', the name of Sudarshan Chakra is spoken correctly by the poet.59.

First pronounce the word 'Narakāsura' and then the word 'Ripu' is expressed, the names of Sudrashan Chakra are comprehended by the wise.60.

Say the name of the demon 'Bakatra' and then speaking the word 'Shūdan', the names of Sudarshan Chakra are eternally known within.61.

Firstly forming the name 'Chanderinath', and then speaking the word 'Ripu', the names of the Chakra are formed.62.[130]

Saying the name 'Narakāsura' and then speaking the word 'Maradan', the name of Sudarshan Chakra is taken correctly by the poet.63.

Saying the word 'Krishan, Vishnu' and then speaking the words 'Anuj' and 'Āyudh', many infinite names of Sudarshan Chakra continue to evolve.64.

Speaking the words 'Vajra and Anuj' in the beginning and then adding the word 'weapon', the names of Sudarshan Chakra are taken internally by the wise.65.

Pronouncing the word 'Virah' in the beginning and then saying 'weapon' many times, names of Chakra continue to be formed.66.

First pronounce the name of 'Vahai', the support of all powers and perfection, then adding the word 'weapon', the names of Chakra continue to be formed.67.[131]

Pronouncing the word 'Giradhar' in the beginning and then speaking the word 'Āyudh', many infinite names of Sudarshan Chakra continue to evolve.68.

Saying the word 'Kalī nath' in the beginning and then adding the word 'weapon' at the end, innumerable names of Sudarshan Chakra continue to form.69.

First pronounce the name of the killer of 'Kansa–Keshi' and then reflecting on the names of 'weapons', the name of Sudarshan Chakra is taken correctly by the poet.70.[132]

Saying the words 'Bakī' and 'Bakāsura' and then pronouncing the word 'Shatru', the infinite names of Sudarshan Chakra continue to form.71.

Pronouncing 'Aghanāsan Aghahā',[133] and then describing the weapons, all the wise people know the names of Sudarshan Chakra.72.

Speaking various names of 'Upendra' and then adding the word 'weapon', the names of Sudarshan Chakra are all understood, by those with Divine knowledge.73.

Kabiyo Bāch (Speech of the Poet):

Dohara (couplet)

All warriors and all good poets should understand in their minds. Between Vishnu and the names of his Chakra there is not even the slightest difference.74.

This is the auspicious end of the second chapter 'Names of the Chakra' in *Sri Nām-Mālā Purana.*

It is a certainty that this composition serves as an incantation to weapons. We also find a reference to the chakkar in the verses of Bhagat Namdev in the *AG*, 'My father, *Madhu,* you are blessed, with kesh and dark-skinned, my darling.1. Pause. Adorned with the *chakra;* you came down from the Heavens, and saved the life of the elephant.' There are various myths regarding the creation of this chakra before Vishnu obtained it:

1. That it was formed by the combined energy of Brahma, Vishnu, and Shiva.
2. The Guru of the deities, Bruhaspati, presented it to Vishnu.
3. Krishna procured it from the realm of the deities (*devata mandal*).

4. Krishna and Arjun assisted Agani in burning the Khandav forest. In return she presented Krishna with a discus and a mace.
5. That it was made by the architect of demi-gods, Vishvakarma. Vishvakarma's daughter Sanjana was married to Surya, the Sun God. Due to the Sun's blazing power she was unable to go near the Sun. Vishvakarma made him shine less, the leftover Sun dust was collected by Vishvakarma and he made three things out of it, the third was the Sudarshan Chakra of Vishnu.
6. The Chakra was given by Shiva to Vishnu when Vishnu asked Shiva for the all powerful weapon that would destroy the forces of evil.
7. In the *Dhanurveda*, the Sudarshan Chakra was made from the bones of Maharishi Dadhich.

Arjun, the loyal follower of Krishna, was also famed for his skill at using the chakkar and was known to have never missed his target. The original chakkar had crossbars in the middle, and flame-like projections or pointed projections around the periphery. It was with this weapon that Shiva beheaded Parvati's son, and then replaced it with an elephant head to give birth to Ganesh. Many followers of Vishnu are branded with a chakram mark, and this symbol is also found engraved on antique Indian swords.[134]

There are also examples of its use from outside India, for instance, Tiberius ordered an inventor's head to be cut off by a chakkar. There are also some very early accounts, for example, from a Portuguese traveller, Duarte Barbosa, in AD 1516. Jean B. Tavernier records of a party of *fakirs*, when they employed a chakkar that they carried with them, that 'they throw them with force at a man, as we make a plate to fly, they almost cut him in two'.[135] It is clear that the myth of the chakkar started well before the Sikh Panth, and that its effects were known hundreds of years earlier. Military historians like Oppert narrate that 'it is most probably identical with the quoit still in use in some Sikh regiments and also among the troops of Native Indian princes'.[136] There is also an indigenous origin as the Bhuyan, a forest tribe of India, also use a similar weapon.

In ancient scriptures we find explicit details about the chakkar, in *Aganī-Purāṇ*, we find references to its usage:

> The cakra (discus) has the form of a circular disk with a quadrangular hole in its midst. Its colour is like that of indigo water and its circumference amounts to two spans or 10 cubits according to the Śukranīti. Five or seven motions are connected with the discus practice.[137]

The name of the Sikh martial art Gatkā comes from the same root word—*gatayas* or motion. The chakra had a crossbar in the centre and flame-like projections on the periphery. The circle and cross are both ancient symbols of the Sun. In fact, the *Rigveda* records, 'Endowed with augmented vigour he hurled (against the foes) the wheel of the chariot of the sun.'[138] The Tenth Guru was descended from a solar lineage; therefore, the early Khalsa Panth referred to itself as 'Soḍhī *vans*', 'Raghu *vans*', and 'Suraj *vans*'. The chakkar was also a powerful symbol of this.[139]

It is clear that Guru Gobind Singh has drawn on the myths of ancient India to empower the common man of the time, to take up arms against the Turaks, as non-violent philosophies were dominating India. The quoit has legendary origins in India, and the adornment and use by the Khalsa would naturally give status to the Khalsa in the Indian world. Some of the European commentators of weapons have classified the chakkar with the boomerang, also having ancient origins. Its use in ancient India can still be found in frescoes, and references in ancient Indian scriptures that the *Shastra Nām Mālā Purāṅ* refers to. The *DG* is full of references to this ancient weapon and its use. Further work could involve examining the stories related to the chakra. The relationship of the Khalsa to the chakkar was so strong, that even in World War I it was launched by the Sikh regiments on the battlefield. From the earliest accounts—like Malcolm's—to modern Sikh practices, it is clear that ritualistic use of weapons was and still is an important part of the Sikh tradition. The quoit is a spiritual–temporal praxis of the Akalis, but the root of its importance can be found in the *Shastra Nām Mālā Purāṅ*.

There is also a relationship with one of the five *Ks*, that is, the *kaṛā* and the quoit, as a thin kaṛā is often called a chakkar by Sikhs. The symbol of the quoit is associated with Sikhs in the form of the Sikh symbol, the khaṅḍā, which consists of the chakkar, two swords, and a khaṅḍā. This symbol is readily used as a coat of arms by Sikhs (see Figure 4.7). In modern times, the chakkar has been popularized by Xena, the warrior princess, on television. While this book was in the process of being written, an extraordinary documentary was televised on the Discovery Channel presented by Mike Loades. He showed conclusively that the chakkar is a deadly weapon, by his various tests. The narratives in this chapter clearly show the same, and that the use of this weapon was motivated by its praises in the *DG*.

We can see how the powerful notion of degh–tegh–fateh inspired Sikh warriors, and how it was based on the mīrī–pīrī concept developed by Guru Nanak and further developed by Guru Hargobind. This also clearly suggests that there is a continuation from Guru Nanak to Guru Gobind Singh. The slogan was a striking feature of the Khalsa stamping its seal of sovereignty and spirituality. It appears that it was also used as a battle cry by the Guru before war commenced. These representations were also seen in the seals and hukamnāmās of Banda Singh Bahadur. The stamping of sovereignty was solidified with the minting of coins bearing this concept, and has also been seen symbolically on the Nishān Sahibs, the battle standards of the Khalsa. The term plays a part in the Sikh ardās and it is clear that degh–tegh–fateh was a new concept but based on the continuity of earlier precepts of mīrī–pīrī and sant sipāhī. Guru Gobind Singh instructed that his Khalsa would only be victorious if they nourished the sangat and always remained armed. The seeds of the Khalsa Raj are embodied within Sikh symbols and the material heritage preserved. The slogans from the *DG* were to be roared in the battlefields across the world in World War I and World War II, where even the chakkar was employed, and tens of thousands of Sikhs died in battle. The powerful words of degh–tegh–fateh of Guru Gobind Singh echoed on and became a part of the world stage.

FIGURE 4.7 The Sikh Symbol Called the *Khaṇḍā*[140]

Notes

1. See Jeevan Deol, 'Eighteenth Century Khalsa Identity: Discourse, Praxis and Narrative', in *Sikh Religion, Culture and Ethnicity*, eds Christopher Shackle, Gurharpal Singh, and Arvindpal Singh Mandair (London: Curzon, 2001). J. Malcolm, *The Sketch of the Sikhs: A Singular Nation Who Inhabit the Provinces of the Punjab Situated between the Rivers Jamna and Indus* (London: John Murray, 1812).

2. We could say this initiation is like a mystical knighthood. One of the earliest accounts of the ceremony is by Bhai Jaita Singh, the author mentions the five *K*s and the five prayers of the *nitnem*, but there needs to be further research on the manuscript copies of this work before we can draw any conclusions.

3. This chapter is partly based on a presentation given at the Oxford University Sikh Society by Kamalroop Singh on 30 April 2008.

4. Svarup Singh Kaushish, *Gurū Kiāṅ Sākhīā Krit Bhāi Svarūp Siṅgh Kaushish*, 2nd ed., edited by Piara Singh Padam (Amritsar: Singh Brothers, [1797] 1991). It must be noted the Shiromani Gurdwaṛa Parbandhak Committee (SGPC) has changed the liturgy of the original five nitnem to three compositions to be recited in the morning, evening, and once before sleep. On the other hand, in the tradition the *Chaupaī Sāhib* is repeated twice, once in the morning and once in the evening as a part of *Rahirās Sāhib* with the six *pauṛī*s of *Anaṅd Sāhib*.

5. This could be translated to be ten, as ten *svaiye* are read. The words of the opening verses of some of the *svaiyas* are then given. Takht Hazur Sahib recite the above svaiyas with another, the fifth, *jo kich*, at the end, which is known as the 'Praise of the Khalsa' (*Khālsā Mahimā*), from the *DG*.

6. Bhai Daya Singh *Rahitnāmā*: *pratham saṅpūran japujī sāhib ādi aṅt pūran pūran jāpu jīādi aṅt kī pāṭh kare caupī paṅj paṅj savaiye bhiṅna bhiṅna 1 srāvaga 2 dīnan kī pratipāl 3 pāp saṅbūh bināsan 4 sati sadaiv sadā brat paṅj, pauṛī anaṅd jī kī karad aṁrit bīch phere apanī ora ko*. See the translation by W.H. McLeod, *Sikhs of the Khalsa: A History of the Khalsa Rahit* (Oxford University Press: New Delhi, 2003), 311. However, in the original there is no full stop after *brat* and five follows it. This should mean five of the 32/33 svaiyas. Then the pauṛīs of *Aṅand*. The 32/33 svaiye are an early composition of the Tenth Guru, according to Chaupa Singh; W.H. McLeod, *The Chaupa Singh Rahit-nama* (Dunedin: University of Otago Press, 1987).

7. For another translation, see McLeod, *Sikhs of the Khalsa*, 311.

8. Bhai Daya Singh *Rahitnāmā*.

9. McLeod, *Sikhs of the Khalsa*, 71–2; P.S. Padam, ed., *Rahitnāme* (Amritsar: Singh Brothers, 2000), 47–8; K.S. Nabha, *Mahān Kosh* (Patiala: Bhasha Vibhag, 1999), 621.

10. For more information about the Akalis and takhts, see Chapter 3.

11. See Ganda Singh, *Bhai Nańd Lāl Grańthāvalī* (Patiala: Punjabi University Publication Bureau, 2000), 1–14. Also McLeod, *Sikhs of the Khalsa*, 15.

12. Padam, *Rahitnāme*, 47.

13. Jeevan Deol discovered a manuscript document (MS. 770.) in the Library of Guru Nanak Dev University with a date of AD 1718–19. See Deol, 'Eighteenth Century Khalsa Identity'. For a recent English translation, see Karamjit K. Malhotra, 'The Earliest Manual on the Sikh Way of Life', in *Five Centuries of Sikh Tradition: Ideology, Society, Politics and Culture (Essays for Indu Banga)*, eds, Reeta Grewal and Sheena Pall (New Delhi: Manohar, 2005). The name on this document is *Nasīhatnāmā*. This further adds to the high probability that it was indeed written in the court of the Guru. Also see Wellcome Trust, MS. 198. The colophon is 1752 VS or 1695 CE stating, 'Written on the Satluj river edge, at Anandpur Sahib.'

14. It is interesting to note that most middle-class Sikhs who were fluent in Urdu did not reject the *Zafarnāmah* or the works of Bhai Nand Lal, but rejected the Braj Bhāshā parts of *DG*.

15. *Kara isanān paṛathe japu jāpu.1. japujī jāpu paṛathe cita lāi.13.*

16. In terms of traditional exegesis the term *japu jāpu* is interpreted to mean the five compositions of the nitnem.

17. Padam, *Rahitnāme*, 47. Some manuscript copies have the pen-name of *Srī Mukhavāk Pātisāhī 10*. See S.H.R MSS. 1797 B, Khalsa College, Amritsar. Also see Guru Nanak Dev University, MSS. 880 KH; McLeod, *Sikhs of the Khalsa*, 287.

18. See Padam, *Rahitnāme*, 49; K.S. Nabha, *Mahān Kosh*, 648; McLeod, *Sikhs of the Khalsa*, 68, 114.

19. Recent manuscript research by G.S. Mann shows that this composition is from the Guru's court. See *Journal of Punjab Studies*, 15 (Spring–Fall, 2008): 1–2.

20. Bhai Desa Singh, *Rahitnāmā*: *prātahi uṭh iniānahi karai. pun mukh te japu jāpu ucarai.*

21. The translation is from McLeod, *Sikhs of the Khalsa*, 299. Bhai Desa Singh, *Rahitnāmā*; Padam, *Rahitnāme*, 149. An alternative translation of verses 38 and 39: 'Everyday select some *bāṇī* from both Granths, and commit it to memory again and again.38.'

22. W.H. McLeod, *Prem Sumārag—The Testimony of a Sanatan Sikh* (New Delhi: Oxford University Press, 2006), 14. The original passage is in Randhir Singh, *Prem Sumārag* (Jalandhar, 1953), 3: *pańja verī japu te jāpu paṛathai. nāle anańd. pańja verī paṛathai.* John Leyden also translates this portion; he gives seven instead of five. See British Library: Mackenzie collection, Add. 26588.

23. Randhir Singh, ed., *Prem Sumārag* (Amritsar: Sikh History Society, 1965), 4–5.

24. Singh, *Prem Sumārag.*

25. Rattan Singh Bhangu, *Srī Gurū Panth Prakāsh*, ed. Balwant Singh Dhillon, vol. 1 (Amritsar: Singh Brothers, [1841] 2004).

26. Rattan Singh Bhangu, *Srī Gurū Panth Prakāsh*, trans. Akali Baba Santa Singh Nihang (Buddha Dal) (Amritsar: Singh Bros, 2004) 1:76: '*prithama Bhagautī vāra ju pauṛī paṛ prithamaiṅ āp satigura joṛī*'. This text is in prose.

27. Rattan Singh Bhangu, *Panth Prakāsh*, verse: 16, 78. Akali Baba Santa Singh narrates that '*Jap* and *Jāp*', means the nitnem of the five prayers.

28. C.H. Loehlin, *The Granth of Guru Gobind Singh and the Khalsa Brotherhood* (Lucknow: Lucknow Publishing House 1971), 58.

29. Bhasauria called for a Fifth Takht to be local to Panjab, but in the tradition the Fifth Takht is the Guru Khalsa Panth. This is recorded in Avatar Singh Vahiria, *Khalsā Dharam Shāstar* (Lahore: Arorabans Press, 1894), and Kanh Singh Nabha, *Mahān Kosh*, 1932. Later the SGPC made Damdama Sahib into a Fifth Takht.

30. Pandit Sharda Ram, *Sikhā kā Rāj kā Vitihyā*, ed. Pritam Singh (Jalandar Hind Publishing, [1866] 1956), 78. This date is the same as the oldest *DG* recension discussed in Chapter 1.

31. *DG*, *Chaṇḍī Charitra*, 99, verse 231.

32. M.A. Macauliffe, *The Sikh Religion: Its Gurus, Sacred Writings and Authors*, 6 vols (Oxford: Clarendon Press, 1909), 5:84.

33. Islamic literature was also translated.

34. Gian Singh Giani, *Tvārīkh Gurū Khalsā* (Patiala: Bhasha Vibhag, 1993), 819.

35. Gian Singh Giani, *Tvārīkh Gurū* Khalsā, 819.

36. Gian Singh Giani, *Tvārīkh Gurū* Khalsā, 820.

37. Gian Singh Giani, *Tvārīkh Gurū Khalsā*, 863, verse 20.

38. Gian Singh Giani, *Tvārīkh Gurū Khalsā*, 868.

39. Mark Knowles, *Tap Roots: The Early History of Tap* (North Carolina, McFarland & Co. Inc., 2002), 168. Discussing the roots of Kathak, Knowles narrates, 'Many gestures of the kathak were initially based upon the movements of martial arts, and the training of dancers originally grew out of military exercises.'

40. Giani Teja Singh Nirmala, *Dashmesh Udesh* (n.p., 1931).

41. *DG*, *Shastra Nām Mālā*, 717.

42. The modern ardās is recited after every kind of Sikh recitation or ritual whether that is an akhaṇḍ pāṭh, or after the *rahirās pāṭh*, and so on. The inclusion of this concept together with the opening lines from the *DG* composition, *Chaṇḍī dī Vār*, shows the far reaching impact that the *DG* has had on the Sikh religion even today.

43. See *Sikh Rahit Maryada*, SGPC. A modified version of this couplet is recited with the hoisting of a new *Nishān Sahib* and also in the culmination of *nagar kirtans* (ceremonial march) and recited in the displays of *Shastravidiā*.

44. The salutation 'Vahiguru ji ki Fateh' appears at the beginning of some of the compositions in the *DG*. In the Sikh tradition, this shows that the compositions were God-ordained, and their recitation brings victory as well.

45. Ian Heath, *The Sikh Army 1799–1849* (Oxford: Osprey Publishers, 2005), 19.

46. *DG, Krishnā Avatār*, verse 436.

47. *Chaṇḍī dī Vār, DG*, p. 119.

48. *DG, Charitrā* 297, dealing with the story of Sakuch Mati.

49. On a sword which was bestowed to Bhai Trilok Singh at Damdama Sahib, one side of the blade bears the *DG* invocation, 'Srī Bhagautī jī Sahāi Pātishāhī 10'. See Ishar Singh Nara, *Safarnama and Zafarnama: Being an Account of the Travels of Guru Gobind Singh and the Epistle of Moral Victory Written by Him to Emperor Aurangzeb* (Delhi: Nara Publications, 1985), 305.

50. *DG, Zafarnāmah*, verse 90.

51. Kharak Singh and Gurtej Singh, eds, *Episodes from the Lives of the Gurus—Parchian Sewadas—English Translation* (Chandigarh: Institute of Sikh Studies, [1708] 1995).

52. Kharak Singh and Gurtej Singh, *Episodes from the Lives of the Gurus*, Episode no. 30—'The Fighting Prowess of the Guru'.

53. http://www.gurmatveechar.com/books/Puratan.Sarbloh.Granth.Saroop.(GurmatVeechar.com).pdf (accessed September 2013).

54. Surinder Singh, *Sikh Coinage—Symbol of Sikh Sovereignty* (New Delhi: Manohar, 2004), 31–2.

55. The hukamnāmās can be seen in the book, Ganda Singh, *Hukamnāme: Gurū Sāhibān, Mātā Sāhibān, Bandā Singh ate Khālsā jī de* (Patiala: Punjabi University Publication Bureau, 1985). According to Surinder Singh, who visited the dera of the present-day *Bandeis* (descendants of Banda Singh Bahadur), he also saw a seal from the period in question which matched the ones seen in the hukamnāmās. See Surinder Singh, *Sikh Coinage*, 45. Interestingly, after Banda Singh Bahadur split with the Tat Khalsa, he coined a new salutation, 'Fateh Darshan', again relating to victory.

56. Ganda Singh, *Hukamnāme*, 149.

57. Ganda Singh, *Hukamnāme*, 61–2. According to Surinder Singh, it was Jassa Singh Ahluwalia who minted the first Sikh coin, but there is no coin that is available or forthcoming from that time period.

58. This medal is at the Sheesh Mahal Museum, Patiala. See Daljeet, *The Sikh Heritage—A Search for Totality* (London: Mercury Books, 2005), 58–9.

59. We are thankful to Ranjit Singh Chohan, Luton, UK, for providing us with information related to Nishān Sahibs.

60. This painting is part of the collection of S.S. Hitkari, New Delhi.

61. In recent times, some of the frescoes in Baba Atal Rai Sahib have been whitewashed out of history. This is a major loss to Sikh heritage.

62. Macauliffe, *Sikh Religion*, 5:311.

63. J.D. Hookway, *M & R: A Regimental History of the Sikh Light Infantry 1941–1947* (Beckington, Bath, England, 1999), 10.

64. Henry F. Brooks, *The Victories of the Sutlej* (London: Arthur B. Keen, Dublin, and Longman & Co., 1848), 15. This was a controversial poem at the time as it was seen to be sympathetic towards the Sikhs; it won the first prize at Trinity College Dublin. This is one of the many accounts of the Akalis use of the quoit.

65. *The Calcutta Review*, vols 11–12 (Calcutta: University of Calcutta, 1849), 251.

66. In Sanskrit the quoit is known as the *chakra* and is known by Sikhs as the *chakkar*.

67. It is a lexicon of weapons—consisting of riddles and references to weapons in ancient Indian scriptures. It is written in Braj Bhāshā verse, mainly in the *doharā, aṛīl, channd, channd vadhā, chaupaī, channd ruāmal*, and *soraṭha* metres.

68. For more details, see Sohan Singh, *Gurbilās Pātasāhī Chhevīn*, eds Jathedar Joginder Singh Vedanti and Amarjit Singh (Amritsar: SGPC, 1999).

69. This was due to the soteriological enthronement of the Khalsa, as the eleventh Guru, by Guru Gobind Singh. This notion is echoed in the court poetry spoken in the audience of the Tenth Guru. Bhai Gurdas Singh II writes *vāhu vāhu Gobiṅd Siṅgh, āpe Gur chelā*—Hail Hail Gobind Singh, who is both the Guru and the Sikh; *Vārāṅ Bhāī Gurdās, Vār* 41.

70. Malcolm, *Sketch of the Sikhs*, 182.

71. Malcolm, *Sketch of the Sikhs*, 182. This is probably the earliest translation of the popular opening verse of *Shastra Nām Mālā Purāṅ*.

72. Kuir Singh, *Gurbilās Pātishāhī 10* (Patiala: Punjabi University, 2000), 252.

73. Kuir Singh, *Gurbilās Pātishāhī 10*, 252.

74. William Crooke, *North Indian Notes and Queries* (Allahabad: Pioneer Press, 1894), 93, uses the term 'Gobind Singhis' to describe the Nihang Singhs.

75. In the Sikh tradition an ascetic Akali would be the chief custodian of Sri Akal Takht, and SGPC publications on Sri Akal Takht acknowledge the traditional Nihang Singh lineage of leaders. Up to 1920 the Chief of the Guru Khalsa Panth was an Akali Nihang Singh. It is beyond the scope of this chapter to discuss this further; for more information, see Jathedar Kirpal Singh, *Srī Akāl Takht Sāhib ate Jathedār Sāhibāṅ* (Amritsar: Chattar Singh Jivan Singh, 1999) and Harjinder Singh Dilgeer, *Akal Takht* (Jullunder: Punjabi Book Company, 1980).

76. One can be seen in George Carmichael Smyth, *A History of the Reigning Family of Lahore: With Some Account of the Jummoo Rajahs, the Seik Soldiers and Their Sirdars* (Calcutta: W. Thacker and Co., 1847), 184. For an account of this great Sikh leader, see 'Phoola Sing, The Akalee', 185–92.

77. Leopold von Orlich, *Travels in India: Including Sinde and the Punjab*, trans. Hannibal Evans Lloyd (London: Longman, Brown, Green, and Longmans, 1845), 217.

78. J.C. Murray-Aynsley, *Our Visit to Hindostan, Kashmir, and Ladakh* (London: W.H. Allen, 1879), 249–50. She also narrates the Akalis performing the Khalsa initiation at Sri Akal Takht, 252.

79. Aynsley, *Our Visit to Hindostan.*

80. Some of the liturgy of the Nihang Singhs states it to be the third or *tisarā* panth, distinct from Abrahamic and Oriental religions. This is a leitmotiv in early Sikh scriptures of the seventeenth and eighteenth century. This is a feature of the apocrypha, the translations of which feature in this book, and some of which is in Nihang Singh liturgy.

81. 'Summary of the Mahratta and Pindarree campaign, during 1817, 1818, and 1819, under the direction of the Marquis of Hastings: Chiefly embracing the operations of the army of the Deckan, under the command of His Excellency Lieut.-Gen. Sir T. Hislop, Bart. G.C.B. with some particulars and remarks', London, 1820.

82. Major H. Bevan, *Thirty Years in India: or, a Soldier's Reminiscences of Native and European Life in the Presidencies,* 1808–1838 (London: Pelham Richardson, 1839), 2:5–6.

83. Henry Steinbach, *The Punjaub: Being a Brief Account of the Country of the Sikhs, Its Extent, History, Commerce, Productions, Government, Manufactures, Laws, Religion, etc.* (London: Smith, Elder, & Co., 1846), 68–9. Steinbach was a Lieutenant Colonel, and in the Sikh mutiny he narrowly escaped with his life.

84. Steinbach, *The Punjaub*.

85. *Colburn's United Service Magazine and Naval and Military Journal* (London: Hurst And Blackett, Publishers, 1857), 3:565.

86. This word, 'dastār bungā', is an example of the Akalis unique language known as *Khālsā ke bol bale* (the speech and sayings of the Khalsa), or *gargajh bole* (thunderous language). For a good example of a dastār bungā, see Victoria and Albert Museum, London: No. 3462:1 to 8/(IS), and Royal Armouries: No. XXVIA.60. Two quoits are present at Pitts Rivers Museum, Oxford, No. 1906.64.1.

87. Henry Steinbach, *The Punjaub*, 69. Capt. D.H. Mackinnon, *Military Service and Adventures in the Far East—Including Sketches of the Campaigns against the Afghans in 1839, and the Sikhs In 1845–6* (London: John Olliver, 1849), 279: 'nor did I see a man wounded by a Quoit in any of the battles'. He notes that this is 'the favourite weapon of the Akalees'.

88. This is taken from a journal entry at the Battle of Sabroan on 4 February 1846, Macmillan's Magazine, 'Extracts from an Indian Journal', David Masson, George Grove, John Morley, Mowbray Walter Morris, 1858, 611.

89. William Simpson, 'Seated Holy Man with Figures' (Amritsar, Punjab, 1864).

90. Cunningham Geikie, 'Samson and Eli', *Hours with the Bible, or, the Scriptures in the Light of Modern Knowledge* (New York: J. Pott & Co, 1882), 18.

91. 'Indian Arms', *The Eclectic Magazine of Foreign Literature, Science, and Art*, vol. 44 (New York: Leavitt, Trow, & Co., Aug 1886), 168.

92. R. Bosworth Smith, *The Life of Lord Lawrence*, 1849–1852 (London: Smith, Elder & Co., 1883), 252. 'We had thus disbanded the Sikh army. It remained to disarm the population and so to deprive them of the temptation to violent crime and disorder which the possession of arms always gives.' This was a part of the pacification of Panjab, where in the previous battles Sikh warriors had been paid money to hand in their weapons, and return back to farming.

93. *The Archaeological Journal*, British Archaeological Association, Royal Archaeological Institute of Great Britain and Ireland, 1873, 96.

94. After the Mutiny of 1857, there was another general disarmament, but there was one distinctive weapon, the chakra or quoit, which the British administration wished to keep the tradition of ('Indian Arms', 168).

95. *The Badminton Magazine of Sports and Pastimes*, vol. 23 (London: Longmans, Green, and Company, 1906), 330.

96. Thomas Lewin, *A Fly on the Wheel* (London: Constable & Company Ltd, 1885), 46–7. This was on 13 January 1859 according to his entry in his diary. As well as a real quoit, an ornamental quoit was represented on the 45th Rattray Sikh regiment badge.

97. The Sikh martial tradition has been presented in detail in the book by *Gatkā* master Manjit Singh, *Shastarnāmā* (Amritsar: Chattar Singh Jivan Singh, 2005).

98. J.G. Wood, *The Uncivilised Races of Men in All Countries of the World* (London: G. Routledge and Sons, 1883), 2: 1403, 1406. A good illustration of the dastār bungā is Plate XII. See W. Egerton, *Indian Oriental Arms and Armour* (London: Arms and Armour Press), 130. It is reproduced in this chapter.

99. Quoit turban (dastār bungā). Indian, Akali Sikh, Lahore, 18th century (XXVIA.60) ©Royal Armouries (XXVIA.60). For a similar turban, see 'Turban, Worn by Akali Sikhs', Lahore, Pakistan, nineteenth century, Victoria & Albert Museum, London: Inv.: 3458 (IS).

100. Another Sikh regiment, the 36th Sikh infantry, fought in World War 1; their turbans were also adorned with the chakkar.

101. H. Craik, *Impressions of India* (London: Macmillan, 1908), 20, 155.

102. Gustave Doré, 'Indian Arms', in *The Eclectic Magazine of Foreign Literature, Science, and Art* (New York: E.R. Pelton, 1886), 166–77.

103. H.S. Cowper, *The Art of Attack: Being a Study in the Development of Weapons and Appliances of Offence, from the Earliest Times to the Age of Gunpowder* (Ulverston, Lancashire: W. Holmes Ltd, 1906), 171–2.

104. Cowper, *Art of* Attack, 171–2.

105. W. Egerton, *An Illustrated Handbook of Indian Arms* (London: William H. Allen & Co., 1880), 128.

106. *Notices of the Proceedings at the Meetings of the Members of the Royal Institution of Great Britain*, Royal Institution of Great Britain, 1912, 314.

107. Egerton, *Illustrated Handbook*, 128–9. Akali Nihang Baba Bali Singh of Tarana Dal demonstrated a similar method. Another skilled master in Sikh martial arts, Baba Giana Singh, explained the system of training required to throw the chakkar, which has been documented and will be published soon.

108. Egerton, *Indian Oriental Arms*, 174. This is also noted in Egerton, *Illustrated Handbook*, 128.

109. Nowadays the chakkar is still made in Amritsar, but it has no edge, or curvature for flight.

> 110. They are very skilful in throwing the quoit—another of those five mysterious emblems of the Khalsa, which are fashioned in the precincts of the Golden Temple, and solemnly blessed by the High Priest. These circles of burnished steel skim through the air with a marvellous rapidity at an enormous height from the ground. Quoit-throwing is a distinctive feature in any display of 'up-country' sports, and the mark is usually a full-grown plantain-tree, which, at fifty yards' distance, is cut through in a moment (R. Jones, *The Leisure Hour* [London: Religions Tract Society, 1894], 445).

111. This system could have a relationship with the five sacred weapons of the Khalsa, the Panj Shastra: sword, gun, lance, quoit, bow and arrow. Sometimes instead of the lance, the noose is listed.

112. The find was noted in J. Wilson, *Final Report on the Revision of the Settlement of the Sirsa District in the Punjab* (Calcutta: Central Press Company 1884), 142.

113. M.M. Ahluwalia, *Kukas: The Freedom Fighters of the Panjab* (Bombay: Allied Publishers, 1965), 184.

114. The toshekhānā '... contains, also, the sword of Rustrum and a suit of Akali Arms, with an Akali *pagri*, or turban, made of black stuff, with divers steel quoits fastened to it. This is a weapon peculiar to the Akalis. Govind's sword is also here; Runjit Singh was in the habit of performing puja to it every morning' (Mrs Colin Mackenzie, *Life in the Mission, the Camp, and the Zenáná, or, Six Years in India* [London: Richard Bentley, 1853], 162). There are some Akali *pagris* or *dastārs* at the Victoria and Albert Museum. This included what might be the turban of Akali Phula Singh. See, Kamalroop Singh and Gurinder Singh Mann, *Akali Phula Singh and His Turban* (Archimedes Press, forthcoming).

115. Quoit Turban. Cotton over a wicker frame, with quoits and other embellishments of steel overlaid with gold; Lahore, Pakistan, mid-nineteenth century, Museum Number: 3462:1 to 8/(IS), © Victoria and Albert Museum, London. See the illustration of it in Egerton, *Indian Oriental Arms*, Plate XII, 130. This turban is the same style as another turban at the Victoria and Albert Museum and another in the Royal Armouries.

116. Still it must be remembered that the Sikh troops, though disbanded, retain the formidable character inseparable from their habits and education. Under institutions which make every man a soldier, and war the chief duty of a citizen, it is difficult to break effectually the force of a nation. We have seen that it is one of the characteristics of this singular race, that even when beaten by a more powerful enemy, they have ever reappeared on the field with unsubdued and almost undiminished vigour. Nor is the fanatical spirit extinct among them. Though the generality of the Sikhs have for some time disused many of the more rigid observances of their sect, yet the true spawn of the old brood still survives in the Akalees—those desperate enthusiasts, who, formidable by their numbers as well as daring, affect an unchanging attachment for all the harsh peculiarities of the ancient discipline. Even under Runjeet these Ironsides are said to have been so indiscriminately dangerous, that they were always paraded at a review, between two battalions of ordinary troops,—lest they should make a dash at anything upon the field! ('The Punjab', *Edinburgh Review, or Critical Journal* [London: Longmans, Green & Co.] 89 [1849]: 218–19).

117. G.F. MacMunn, *The Martial Races of India* (London: Sampson Low & Co, 1933), 132: 'In many a Sikh town and fair, bodies of this sect dressed in dark blue, wearing the sacred quoit and as many arms as the law will permit.'

118. The use of the chakkar was described to Kamalroop Singh. Photo courtesy of Sodhi Singh.

119. Benjamin Adams Trueheart, *Weapons Masters Episode 5—The Deadly Chakram*, Halfyard Productions for Discovery Channel, 13 September 2008; Kiran Gonsalves and Michael S. Ojeda, *Deadliest Warrior: Season 2 Episode 6: Indian Rajput versus Roman Centurion*, Spike TV, Wednesday, 25 May 2010.

120. Ian Heath and Michael Perry, *The Sikh Army 1799–1849* (Oxford: Osprey Publishers, 2005), 34.

121. *AG*, 74, 258, and 1358–9. This composition was said to have been recited at the *Mal Akhārā*, the wrestling arena, created by the fourth Guru. The fifth Guru celebrates a victory by this composition. The sixth Guru also trained in this area, which later became the headquarters of Akali Phula Singh.

122. This composition also goes by the name *Salok Dumāle dā*.

123. *AG*, 1358–9. For another inscription, see Kerry Brown, ed., *Sikh Art and Literature* (London: Routledge, 1999), 40–1. In relation to the Nihang Singhs, Brown writes, 'They could wield them like latter-day Vishnus, whirling their weapons with deadly and terrifying effect. Even more revealing of their Weltanschauung is the inscription engraved on the disc, which quite vividly reflects the simple and steadfast minds of these warriors.' The closing lines of the inscription on this chakkar read, 'These are times for good deeds. Once dead this time will be out of your grasp' (Brown, *Sikh Art*).

124. The *Shastra Nām Mālā Purāṅ* runs from *DG*, 717–808.

125. *DG, Sri Chakkar*, 718–21. Strictly speaking, the chakkar is an *astra*—a missile. Both types of weapons are recorded in the compositions in the *DG*.

126. *Sankh, Chakram, Khadga, Gada*, and *Saranga* (the Conch, Chakram, Broad Sword, and Mace).

127. The story of the origins of Sri Vishnu's chakra is in Muir's translations of Sanskrit texts, IV, 159.

128. In the 57th couplet, the references to the chakkar begin. The translation is by the author of this essay.

129. The special weapon of Vishnu was the Sudarshan Chakra. It is difficult to translate 'Sudarshan'; it can mean the auspicious sight, glimpse, or presence.

130. Krishna used it to slay Chanderinath Shishupal in the great epic Māhābharat.

131. Ishvara.

132. Krishna.

133. The destroyer of sins.

134. Macauliffe, *Sikh Religion*, 428: 'The quoit is one of the emblems of Vishnu, with which his worshippers are frequently branded.'

135. V. Ball, ed., *Tavernier's Travels in India by Jean B. Tavernier* (London: MacMillan & Co., 1889), 1:82.

136. Gustav Oppert, *On the Weapons, Army Organisation, and Political Maxims of the Ancient Hindus, with Special Reference to Gunpowder and Firearms* (Madras: Messrs. Higginbotham & Co., 1880), 15.

137. Oppert, *On the Weapons*; Oppert translates the *Agnī-purān* II.12; IV, 47–8: *Cakrum tu kundalakaram ante svasrasmanvitam. Nilisalilavarnam tat pradesadvayamandalam. 47. Granthanam bhramanam caiva ksepanam parikartanam. Dalanam ceti pancaiva gatayascakrasamsritah. 48.* Oppert states that similar cantos are in the *Sukrānītī*, Chapter V, al.156; and others in the *Agnī-purāṇ*, 151, 8; the *Sukrānītī* was written by the Guru of the asuras (demons), about political maxims, weapons, and army organization.

138. Rigveda, III, 35, Rajendralal Mitra, *Indo Aryans Indo-Aryans: Contributions towards the Elucidation of Their Ancient and Medieval History* (London: Edward Stanford, 1881).

139. See Akali Nihang Sampuran Singh, *Sūraj Vānisiyā Khālsā Panth. A Survey of Various Sectarian Movements among the Sikhs* (Amritsar: Svami Santoshanand, 1923). Also see *Apanī Kathā, Bachitra Nāṭak*. The chakkar was seen as a symbol of freedom by the Khalsa, so much so that Bhai Maharaj Singh wore two that are now preserved in the British Library.

140. This symbol is also known as *Adi Shaktī*, and a variation with a crescent moon is worn by the Nihang Singhs which is probably an earlier version of the modern 'khaṅḍā'. This symbol is worn on the turbans of the Nihang Singhs, and is known as *Adi Chand*, or simply as *Chand*. For more information, see the *Sikh Review*, 53, 43.

Glossary

Ādi Granth	the first scripture of spirituality compiled by Guru Arjan Dev in 1603–4. The sacred scriptures of the Sikhs are known as *granths*. The *AG* is the paramount Sikh scripture that enshrines the spirit of peace (*shanti ras*). The *AG* is also referred to as *Srī Gurū Granth Sāhib* and *Gurū Granth Sāhib*. To differentiate one from later scriptures, this recension was known as the first *granth*, that is, *Ādi Granth*. When the *AG* received Guruship in the form of the *Damdamī* recension, it was then termed *Ādī Srī Gurū Granth Sāhib*, literally translated as the first Guru *Granth*, in relationship to the *Dasam Granth* being the second.
Akal Purakh	the One beyond time; the concept of the timeless Creator; a name for God
Akali	worshipper of Akal; a warrior Sikh, clad in blue, a high turban, and steel weapons. The term was copied from this traditional order and used by political parties such as the Akali Dal. The term is synonymous with the word 'Nihang'.
Akali Nihang	the traditional Singh warrior-guardians of orthodox Sikhism. Under the British, this order suffered heavily. A high-ranking Nihang Singh has a plume on top of a high canonical turban.
Akāl Ustati	the second composition within the *DG*. It expresses the spiritual world view of the Guru and explains how humanity has different shades that originate from the same source. See *Tva Prasādi Svaiye*.

akhaṅd pāṭh — unbroken reading; uninterrupted recitation of the entire *AG* or *DG*, by a relay of readers, normally comprising five Sikhs only

amrit — immortal; also the 'nectar of immortality' used in the initiation ceremony of the Sikhs and Khalsa. Various forms have existed from *Charan–Amrit*, *Kirpan–Amrit* to *khaṅḍe kī pāhul*, which predominates today. This term is also a name for God.

amrit saṅskār — see *khaṅḍe kī pāhul*

Aṅand Sāhib — a forty-verse *shabad*, composed in the Rāmakalī Rāg by Guru Amar Das. The first five verses and the concluding verse are usually recited on the completion of Sikh ceremonies, for example, *Rahirās Sāhib*.

ardās — a prayer or invocation at the conclusion of every Sikh ceremony. This is from the first stanza of the *DG* composition, the *Chaṇḍī dī Vār*.

āratī — literally, adoration; Guru Nanak's hymn in Dhanāsarī Rāg which is a part of the late evening prayer, the *Kirtān Sohilā*

Āsā — to hope, or desire. A *rāg* of the *AG* which expresses hope and high spirits (*Āsā kī Var*). It is a musical section of the *AG*. This *rāg* is also in *DG* and *Sarabaloh Graṅth*.

avatār — an incarnation of a deity. They are narrated and referred to many times in *AG*, *DG*, *Sarabaloh Graṅth*, Bhai Gurdas *Vārs*, and *Kabitts*.

baba — a term used for an elderly father or grandfather. It is a term of affection and respect used for holy figures and saints, for example, Baba Dip Singh.

Bachitra Nāṭak — the cosmic drama; the autobiography of the Tenth Guru which is historical in nature and also narrates his lineage in view of the previous *avatārs*

bānā — the external identity of a Sikh, which usually consists of the five *Ks*. A full traditional dress is still worn by some Sikhs such as the Akalis.

bāṇī — a word or utterance; the works of the gurus and the *bhagats* recorded in the *AG*, *DG*, and

	Sarabaloh Granth. The term can also mean Bhai Gurdas *Vārs* and *Kabitts*, as well as other compositions that are sung during kirtan.
Benatī Chaupaī	see *Chaupaī Sāhib*
bhagat	a devotee of God; a saintly person who practises *bhakti*
bhagat bāṇī	the *bāṇī* of the saints of the Bhakti Movement, which has *sant* and Sufi origins. Their *bāṇī* was recorded and compiled into the *AG* by Guru Arjan Dev.
bhai	an address, to mean brother or friend; also given for piety and learning, for example, Bhai Mani Singh
bhakti	adoration of a personal God
bhog	a ceremony which finalizes the complete reading of the *AG*, *DG*, and *Sarabaloh Granth*. There are *bhog* marks found at the end of the scripture in many old handwritten *granths*. This takes the form of the words *Ik Oankār* or a *swastika*-type symbol.
Brahmin	the members of Indian high caste. They are normally priests. In Sikhism, a Brahmin is irrespective of caste but a person who knows Brahm. This is in line with ancient Indian texts like the Bhagvat Gītā.
Braj Bhāshā	a central Indian language close to the Hindi language. The *DG* was written in this language. Braj Bhāshā literature was heavily employed in Sikh texts until the late twentieth century.
Buddha Dal	the moving *takht* of the Akali Nihangs, which derives its name from Baba Buddha, the martial instructor of Guru Hargobind. Various Akali Nihang Dals are subordinate to the Buddha Dal. The leader of the Buddha Dal was traditionally seen as the head of the entire Sikh nation and commander of the Sikh army, in addition to being the *jathedar* of Sri Akal Takht.
chanan	light or illumination
Chaṇḍī Charitra	composition within the *DG*, again extolling the virtues of the Goddess Chaṇḍi

Chaṇḍī dī Vār a composition within the *DG*, verses of which form the *ardās* of the Sikhs. It is one of the three compositions within the *DG*, which details the exploits of the goddess Chandi.

charaṅ the feet, usually symbolizing humility and devotion to God

charitra a tale or story; see *Srī Charitropakhyān*

Chaupaī Sāhib a prayer of protection that forms part of the evening, *Rahirās Sāhib*. This is also the concluding section from the *Srī Charitropakhyān* of the *DG*.

chhakkā a portion of the *DG* composition *Ugradantī*

Damdami Taksal literally, the mint of Damdama; a teaching school who claim their origins from Baba Dip Singh, a legendary Sikh martyr. They teach Gurmukhi and exegeses of Sikh scriptures as well as other texts. Sant Jarnail Singh Bhinderawale was a famous leader from this school.

dan wealth

darshan the vision, experience of being in the presence of God; to have an audience of an eminent person; to have an audience of the Guru (*AG*)

das a servant or slave; term used in devotion

Dasam Graṅth the scripture written by the Tenth Guru; a text of various themes, mostly focusing on fighting righteous war. It is respected by the non-martial Sikh orders—Udasis, Nirmalas, and Seva Panthis. It is worshipped as equal to *AG* by the Akali Nihangs and the school of learning, the Damdami Taksal. It is enthroned at two of the *takhts* of Sikh polity and was also enthroned at Sri Akal Takht.

Dasam Pādshāh kā Graṅth/ Dasveṅ Pātshāh kā Graṅth the original name of the *Graṅth of Guru Gobind Singh*

daskhat literally, signature. It refers to the signatures of the gurus on manuscripts and *hukamnāmās*; handwriting.

degh the cauldron of *langar* as well as sukha; see *sukha degh–tegh–fateh* a popular slogan used by the Khalsa in the eighteenth century. Its component parts are widely used in the *DG* and was employed on Sikh coins and *hukamnāmā*s.

ḍhaḍhī a bard or minstrel. Today this term is used for singers of *vīr ras*, who recite stories of the heroic deeds of the gurus and *shahīds*.

dharam universal Divine law; the civilized codes for life or duty; the righteous path; today construed to mean religious and *panth*ic duty

dharamsala the name for the place of worship for the early Sikh *panth*. Later this changed to gurdwara.

dharam yudh a righteous war, based on the principles of ensuring that war is propagated to reddress the balance between good and evil. This theme is narrated by the Tenth Guru in his *Bachitra Nāṭak* and throughout the *Granth of Guru Gobind Singh*.

faṛlā a loose plume or piece of turban cloth adorning the top of the *dastār* worn by Akali Nihangs. The cloth is always dark blue in colour.

gatkā a decorative art practised by Sikhs mainly as exhibitionist display. Also see *Shastravidiā*.

giani the wise or the knowledgeable; a learned person

gur, Guru the Divine Master, Enlightener, or Teacher

gurbāṇī Divine-inspired poetry of the gurus

gurbāṇī kirtan devotional singing of the gurus' poetry

gurbilās literally, praise of the Guru; hagiographic life narratives with focus on the Sixth Guru and the Tenth Guru as warriors

gurdwara literally, Guru's door; a Sikh place of worship in which the Sikh scriptures are venerated

gurmat the view of the Guru; the Sikh doctrine

gurmattā literally, Guru's intention; a resolution agreed on by the Sarbat Khalsa in the presence of the Sikh scriptures. This was undertaken by the Khalsa in the eighteenth century to resolve internal differences.

gurmukh true or facing the Guru; follower of the Guru

Gurmukhi	literally, from the Guru's mouth; the script in which the poetry of the gurus is written. It has become the script in which Panjabi is written by Sikhs.
Guru Granth Sahib	the *AG*, the primal Sikh scripture, the living embodiment of the Sikh gurus
Guru Khalsa	the Khalsa in its function as Guru; created by the Tenth Guru
Guru Panth	the *panth* in the role of Guru; the path laid down by the gurus. The final term is thus Guru Khalsa Panth.
guṭkā	a religious book; a small liturgical scripture
hari	name of God
Harimandir	the temple of God; the Golden Temple in Amritsar, the most sacred Sikh shrine
hartal	deletion; yellow orpiment paste used for deletion in the manuscripts of the *AG*, *DG*, and *Sarabaloh Granth*
hukam	command, will, Divine order; a passage from the *Guru Granth Sahib* chosen at random
Ik Oaṅkār	One Creative Being; the first and most fundamental sacred formula from the *AG*, also found throughout the *DG*
jap	name repetition; meditation
Jāp jī Sāhib	the first composition within the *AG*, written by Guru Nanak. It forms part of the daily *nitnem*.
Jāp Sāhib	the first composition within the *DG*, which forms a part of the daily *nitnem*. The composition is martial in nature and as a result it is recited by *Shastravidiā* practitioners.
jathedar	the leader or commander of a *takht*, or the leader of a military army
jhaṭkā	to kill with one blow; traditional method employed by the Akali Nihang Singh Khalsa to kill enemies and also used to kill animals for food. Killing is done using a variety of weapons, from guns to swords.
ju	the Bihari equivalent term of respect for the Panjabi or Hindi 'jī'.

kabitt	a certain type of poetic metre
kal	death; time
kathā	exegesis of the Sikh scriptures by a *giani*; the rendering of verses of the *AG*, *DG*, and *Sarabaloh Granth*, followed by the explanation and meaning of the verses
kaur	literally princess, a name used by female initiates of the Khalsa, as an equal to Singh (lion) for men
Khalsa	a religious/chivalrous order established by Guru Gobind Singh in 1699; literally, the pure, the ones from one source; the sovereign
khaṅḍā	a double-edged sword. It was used by the Tenth Guru at the first baptismal ceremony, and is therefore significant to the Sikh faith.
khaṅḍe kī pāhul	mystical 'knighthood' and 'baptism' of the double-edged sword. The initiation ceremony where five *bāṇīs* are read (from the *AG* and *DG*) and stirred with a sword. It is undertaken by new spiritual aspirants/warriors to enter the Khalsa Panth.
khatri	a merchant caste of Panjab. The gurus were Khatris.
kirpān	the sword of the Sikhs. This is one of the five *K*s or prescribed symbols worn by a Sikh initiated into the Khalsa.
kirtān	singing praises; spiritual music; one who performs *kirtān*
koftgari	a type of gold/silver decorative inlaying on metal objects
Krishnā Avatār	one of the largest compositions, it describes the characteristics of the Hindu god Krishna. However, the Tenth Guru reinterprets the story and brings it in line with his present struggles with the Mughals and Hill Rajas. The future Khalsa warrior, Kharag Singh, is described in this composition.
langar	the gurdwara kitchen from which sacred food is served to all, regardless of caste or creed; the sacred food from such a kitchen

mahalla	identifies which Guru is the author, Guru Nanak is designated 'Mahalla 1'; the second Guru, Angad, is designated as 'Mahalla 2'.
mahant	a head of a religious institution in the Udasi sect
mājh	a *rāg* associated with the Majha region of Panjab; one of the musical sections of the *AG*
malech	filthy; referring to foreign tyrannical powers
mantra	a sacred word to invoke Divine grace
masand	an administrative person acting for the Guru. The title was created by Guru Ram Das but later became corrupt, and as a result were chastised and disestablished by Guru Gobind Singh.
maya	worldly entanglements; illusionary and transient
mīrī–pīrī	the doctrine of unity of the temporal and spiritual. The Guru possesses temporal as well as spiritual authority.
Mughal	the Muslim rulers of India in time of Sikh gurus
nām	the Divine name; a term expressing the total being of Akal Purakh; the consciousness or presence of God
nāmāskar	salutation; to bow in humility
Namdhari	a reference to the branch of Sikhs emanating from the nineteenth century. They revere the *DG* in a way similar to other *samprādayās* of the Sikhs, that is, Akali Nihangs and Damdami Taksal.
nam japu	repeating the Divine name devoutly
nam simran	the practice of meditating on the Divine name
nirmalā	the pure one; the scholarly order of Sikhs who had influence and strength in the nineteenth century
nitnem	the liturgy of Sikh prayers that is recited daily
panch	five, select
Pañj Piāre	the five beloved; a reference to the five Sikhs who were willing to give their head to the Guru
panth	the keyword refers to the Sikh community; path, way, or system of religious beliefs
pauṛī	stanza of a *vār* or ode
Phula Singh	the Sixth leader of Budha Dal (Akali Nihangs) and Akal Takht
prasad	grace; kindness; mercy

Purakh	person; being; God
purātan	old, ancient, historical; one of the extant *Janamsākhī*
rāg	a musical mode or measure; a series of notes on which a melody is solely based
Ragamālā	literally, garland of musical modes, detailing the organization of the eighty-four *rāgas* of north India; the last composition of the *AG*
ragi	a Sikh *kirtan* singer, normally knowing *rāgas*
rahirās	literally, supplication; the evening prayer
rahit	the Khalsa code of chivalry or conduct
rahitnāmā	a Gurmukhi record of the *rahit*. There were several *rahitnāmās* written by the Guru's followers, that is, Chaupa Singh, Bhai Daya Singh, and so on. These early codes of conduct were used to form the modern-day Sikh Rahit Maryādā.
Rām	God; all-pervading Spirit. Hero of the Hindu epic Ramayana (Rama); also a designation for the all-pervasive God
Rāmakalī	a *rāga*; a section of the *AG*. It was particularly enjoyed by Yogis, due to the depth in the tone.
ras	delicious taste; enjoyment; spiritual rapture
rumala	a cloth for covering the *AG*
SGPC	Shiromani Gurdwara Parbandhak Committee. The Sikh organization which controls the main gurdwaras in Panjab. It was formed in the early twentieth century during the British Raj.
sabha	society or association
sach	true; eternal
sach khand	the realm of truth; Sach Khand—abode of Nirankar
sadh	saintly person
sahaj	the state of equilibrium resulting from spiritual practices
sahib	master, lord; a term of respect
samprādayā	traditional doctrine or a system of belief; order or a school of thought; a collection of individuals with a purpose to propagate *dharam*. All the different *samprādayās* of the Sikhs have belief in the *Granth of Guru Gobind Singh*.

sangat	congregation; group of devotees
sansar	transmigration
sant	saintly person in tune with God, often used for Guru
santhiā	traditional exegesis, consisting of grammatical, orthographic, and theological teachings
sant sipāhī	literally, a saint soldier; a reference to the Khalsa which is amalgamation of the saintly and the soldierly aspects
Sarbat Khalsa	the entire Khalsa, usually called together to make an important decision
Sarabloh	all iron; weapons of war; martial designation for the highest God, Nirankar
Sarabaloh Granth	the second of the Sikh martial texts. Though it is respected by the Sikh *samprādayā*—Udasis, Nirmalās, and Seva Panthis as scripture, it is only worshipped as equal to the *AG* alongside the *DG* by the Akali Nihangs. It also refers to the writing of the *avatār* of *Sarabaloh*.
sarguna	with qualities; having all forms
sewa	selfless service in a gurdwara
shabad	word; mystical poetry of the *AG*
shabad kirtan	hymn singing in Sikh tradition
Shastravidiā	the knowledge of weapons, seen as a martial art of the Sikhs. It is seldom practised by Sikhs in the modern age, but some Akali Nihangs still preserve this old tradition.
Shastra Nām Mālā Purāṇ	composition within the *DG*; literally, the rosary of weapons from the Purāṇas. The composition by the Tenth Guru weaves the names of weapons in a clever way.
Sikhi	the knowledge and experience of the Sikh dharma. Western scholars would call this Sikhism. It is composed of *gian*, which is the real experience of the scripture, and *dhian*, known as Zen in Buddhism.
Singh Sabha	a reform movement initiated in 1873. The Singh Sabha became an open area for a debate between the conservative Sanatan Sikhs and the radical Tat Khalsa.

So Dar — five hymns from the *AG* sung during the early evening as a part of the evening prayer called *rahirās*

So Purakh — four hymns from the *AG* recited as part of the evening prayer called *rahirās*

soraṭhi — a peaceful *rāga*; a section of the *AG*

Sri Akal Takht — literally, the timeless throne; seat of temporal authority of the Guru (*miri*). It is also known as the Akal Bunga, meaning the tower or palace of Akal. It is located in the complex of the Harimandir Sahib (*piri*) or Golden Temple at Amritsar. It is the highest seat of Sikh temporal authority; this was declared by Guru Hargobind Sahib in 1609. Traditionally, only the Buddha Dal Jathedar was the historical leader of Sri Akal Takht, for example, Akali Phula Singh.

Srī Charitropakhyān — the composition within the *DG*, which is composed of 405 *Charitras*. This composition was written by the Tenth Guru to show the seamier side of life. However, it also shows the strategies that are employed by humans to take advantage of the gullible individuals. As a result, it informs the reader of the perils they face by engaging in false ways.

Sri Hazur Sahib — situated at Nanded (Maharastra, India), where the Guru Gobind Singh ascended to heaven. It was here that the *AG* was declared to be the Guru of the Sikhs.

Sri Keshgarh Sahib — situated at Anandpur Sahib, Panjab, where the Tenth Guru gave birth to the brotherhood of the Khalsa

Sri Patna Sahib — situated in Patna (Bihar, India); the birthplace of Guru Gobind Singh

sukha — a cannabis drink made from almonds, black pepper, cardamom, and cloves

svaiye — stanza

takht — throne; one of the five centres of temporal power within the *panth*. The five *takht*s are situated at Amritsar, Anandpur Sahib, Damdama Sahib (Bhatinda district), Paths Sahib (Bihar), and Hazur

Sahib, Nanded (Maharashtra). Traditionally, there are four physical *takhts*. They are Sri Akal Takht Sahib, Sri Patna Sahib, Sri Keshgarh Sahib, and Sri Hazur Sahib; the Buddha Dal (Khalsa) is traditionally seen as the fifth.

Tarna Dal — in 1734, Akali Nihang Kapur Singh split the Akali Nihang Khalsa into the Buddha Dal (superior and comprising older, wiser, and battle-hardened warriors) and the Tarna Dal (comprising younger warriors). The Tarna Dal was further split into five groups.

Tat Khalsa — the original name of the Akali Nihangs of the eighteenth century before they split into Buddha and Tarna Dals. A name later adopted by the British Raj Victorian institutions that educated Sikhs.

tīsārā panth — the third way or path; a reference used in *DG* compositions like *Ugradantī* referring to the third path separate from the Hindus and the Turks, that is, the Khalsa

Turk — Mughal; hostile Muslim rulers or invaders. Note the distinction between a 'Musalman' and a 'Turk'—the latter is seen as oppressive.

Tva Prasādi Svaiye — ten stanzas which form a part of the *DG* composition *Akāl Ustati*

Udasi — member of the Udasi Panth, an order of ascetics who claim Sri Chand as their founder (Guru Nanak's eldest son); one of the oldest order of Sikhs and traditionally seen as the 'missionaries'

Vahiguru — wondrous praise to the Guru/God; an expression of the awe-inspiring God. There are various English spellings such as: 'Waheguru', 'Vahiguroo', 'Vahiguru', 'Vaheguru', 'Vaheguroo', 'Vahguru'—what most Sikhs use as a name for God.

vār — ballad. These are in the poetic form of an ode. Among the most famous compositions are the *vārs* attributed to Bhai Gurdas, who was the scribe and confidant of Guru Arjan Dev. In the

	AG, these are poetical compositions consisting of stanzas (*pauṛīs*) with preceding *saloks*. Vār is used in the *AG* and *DG*.
vīr ras	the warrior essence enshrined in *DG* and *Sarabaloh Granth*; the style of *chhands* employed in the Sikh scripture to bring out an energetic response in the reader
Zafarnāmah	forms part of the *DG* and traditionally appended with the *Hikāitāṅ*. This is not a composition as such but a letter written by the Tenth Guru to Emperor Aurangzeb, admonishing him for his actions.

Bibliography

Manuscripts

Anthology *AG/DG*, London, School of Oriental and African Studies (SOAS), MS. 44469, AD 1736.
Anthology, Bhai Maharaj Singh, *AG/DG*, British Library, London, Mss Panj, A4.
Anthology, Guru Nanak Dev University, Amritsar, MS. 771.
Baba Dip Singh, *Guṭkā*, Damdama Sahib, n.d.
Bhai Mani Singh *AG–DG* recension, New Delhi, AD 1713.
Das Granthī, lithograph, private collection.
DG, Amritsar, Guru Nanak Dev University, MS. 740, AD 1688.
DG Anandpurī, Darbara Singh, MS, AD 1695–6.
DG, Aurangabad, Bhai Daya Singh Gurdwara, Circa late 17th/early 18th century.
DG, Chandigarh, Punjab University, MS. 1190, AD 1698.
Singh, Mahan. *Dasam Granth dī Hazūrī Bīṛ dī Riporṭ* (*kujh bhag* 1752 *dā likhat*), Dehradun, Dr. Balbir Singh Sahitya Kendra, MS. 269, 25 January 1957.
DG, London, British Library, MS Panj. B39.
DG, London, British Library, MS Panj. D6. 'Devnagrī', AD 1847.
DG, London, Royal Asiatic Library, Tod MS. 121, AD 1827.
DG, Manchester, John Rylands University, MS 10, circa 18th century.
DG, Mata Sahib Deva Gurdwara, Hazur Sahib, n.d.
DG, National Museum, Delhi, n.d.
DG Patna recension, Patna, Takht Harimandir Sahib, AD 1698.
DG Patna *Misal* recension, Patna, Takht Harimandir Sahib, AD 1765.
DG, Takht Hazur Sahib, Nander, n.d.
Kavi Kankan, *Das Gur Kathā*, Amritsar, Khalsa College, ms. 1797A.
MS Chandra Shum Shere, Govinda Simha Vrttanta, Oxford, Bodleian Indian Institute Library, 1098.
MS Chandra Shum Shere, Govinda Sinha, Oxford, Bodleian Indian Institute Library, 1101.

Gobiṅd Gītā, extant manuscript, private collection.
Gobiṅd Gītā, Patiala, Language Department Library, 1891. From a copy dated AD 1744.
Rahitnāmā, manuscript, private collection.
Rahitnāmā, pamphlet, private collection.
Sarabaloh Graṅth, 1698. Available at http://www.gurmatveechar.com/books/Puratan.Sarbloh.Granth.Saroop.(GurmatVeechar.com).pdf (accessed September 2013).
Sau Sākhī, Amritsar, Khalsa College, S.H.R: 1455, AD 1714.
Srī Charitropakhyān, Chandigarh, Punjab University, AD 1723.
Ugradantī, manuscript, private collection.

Published Works

Adi Srī Gurū Graṅth Sāhib jī Saṭīk (*Faridkot vālā ṭīkā*). 4th ed. 4 vols. Patiala: Bhasha Vibhag, 1992.
Ahluwalia, M.M. *Kukas: The Freedom Fighters of the Panjab*. Bombay: Allied Publishers, 1965.
Ashok, Shamsher Singh, ed. *Prāchīn Vār te Jaṅgnāme*. 3rd ed. Amritsar: Shiromani Gurdwara Prabandhak Committee, 1983.
———. *Sādā Hath—Likhit Paṅjābī Sāhit*. Amritsar: Shiromani Gurdwara Prabandhak Committee, 1968.
———. *Punjabi Hath Likhatāṅ dī Sūchī*. 2 vols. Patiala: Punjab Language Department, 1961–3.
Ashta, D.P. *The Poetry of the Dasam Granth*. Delhi: Arun Prakashan, 1959.
Asiatic Society of Bengal. *Asiatick Researches: Or, Transactions of the Society Instituted in Bengal*, vol. 11. Calcutta, 1805.
Baden-Powell, B.H. 'Notes on the Origin of the "Lunar" and "Solar" Aryan Tribes and on the "Rajput" clans'. *Journal of the Royal Asiatic Society of Great Britain and Ireland* 31 (1899): 295–519.
The Badminton Magazine of Sports and Pastimes, vol. 23, 330. London: Longmans, Green, and Company, 1906.
Bali, A.N. *Glimpses of Punjab History*. New Delhi: printed by the author, 1969.
Ball, V., ed. *Tavernier's Travels in India by Jean B. Tavernier*. Vol. I. London: MacMillan & Co., 1889.
Banerjee, Indubhushan. '*Bachitra Natak*.' In *Evolution of the Khalsa*. Vol. 2. Calcutta: A Mukherjee, 1972.
Batra, Ravi. *Leadership in Its Finest Mould—Guru Gobind Singh*. Amritsar: SGPC, 1997.

Bayly, C.A. *Empire and Information: Intelligence Gathering and Social Communication in India, 1780–1870*. Cambridge Studies in Indian History and Society, no. 1. Cambridge: Cambridge University Press, 1996.

Bedi, Trilochan Singh, ed. *Sikhāṅ dī Bhagatmālā*. Patiala: Punjabi University, 1994.

Bevan, H. *Thirty Years in India: Or, a Soldier's Reminiscences of Native and European Life in the Presidencies,* from 1808–1838. Vol. 2. London: Pelham Richardson, 1839.

Bhalla, Hirday Ram. *Hanūman Nāṭak*. Amritsar: Chattar Singh Jivan Singh, 2001.

Bhalla, Sarup Das. *Mahimā Prakāsh*. Edited by Gobind Singh Lamba and Khazan Singh. 2 vols. Patiala: Bhasha Vibhag, 1971.

Bhangu, Rattan Singh. *Srī Gurū Paṅth Prakāsh*. Edited by Balwant Singh Dhillon. Amritsar: Singh Bros, (1841) 2004.

———. *Srī Gurū Paṅth Prakāsh*. Vol. 1. Translated by Akali Baba Santa Singh Nihang (Buddha Dal). Amritsar: Singh Bros, (1841) 2004.

Bhasauria, Teja Singh. *Khālsā Rahit Prakāsh*. Bhasaur: Panch Khalsa Diwan, 1917.

Bhatia, Narinder Kaur. 'Swayyas of Guru Gobind'. *Journal of Sikh Studies* 24, no. 1 (2000): 103–14.

Bhinderawale, Gurbachan Singh (Sant). *Gurbāṇī Pāṭh Darpaṇ*. Amritsar: Print Well, (1973) 1996.

Bindra, Pritpal, trans. *Chitro Pakhyaan: Tales of Male–Female Tricky Deceptions from Sri Dasam Granth*. Amritsar: B. Chatter Singh Jiwan Singh, 2002.

———. *Guru Kian Saakhian—Tales of the Sikh Gurus*. Amritsar: Singh Brothers, 2005.

———. *Tales in Persian (Hikayaat) from Dasam Granth*. Ontario: Sikh Social and Educational Society, 2002.

Bly, R. and J. Hirshfield. *Mirabai: Ecstatic Poems*. Boston: Beacon Press, 2004.

Brooks, H.F. *The Victories of the Sutlej*. London: Arthur B. Keen, Dublin, and Longman & Co., 1848.

Brown, K., ed. *Sikh Art and Literature*. London: Routledge, 1999.

Campbell, C. *The Maharajas Box—An Imperial Story of Conspiracy, Love and a Guru's Prophecy*. London: Harper Collins, 2001.

Chaudhry, B.B. *Gur Govind ki Darbarī Kavī*. Delhi: Svasitak Satiya Sadan, 1979.

Chopra, G.L. *The Punjab as a Sovereign State (1799–1839)*. Lahore: Uttar Chand Kapur & Sons, 1928.

Colburn's United Service Magazine and Naval and Military Journal. Vol. 3. London: Hurst and Blackett Publishers, 1857.

Cowper, H.S. *The Art of Attack: Being a Study in the Development of Weapons and Appliances of Offence, From the Earliest Times to the Age of Gunpowder.* Ulverston, Lancashire: W. Holmes, Ltd, 1906.

Craik, H. *Impressions of India.* London: Macmillan, 1908.

Crooke, W. *North Indian Notes and Queries.* Allahabad: Pioneer Press, 1894.

Cunningham, J.D. *History of the Sikhs.* Delhi: Low Price Publications, (1849) 1990.

Daljeet. *The Sikh Heritage—A Search for Totality.* London: Mercury Books, 2005.

Datta, A. *Encyclopaedia of Indian Literature.* Vol. 1. India: Sahitya Akademi, 1987.

Deol, J. 'Eighteenth Century Khalsa Identity: Discourse, Praxis and Narrative'. In *Sikh Religion, Culture and Ethnicity.* Edited by Christopher Shackle, Gurharpal Singh, and Arvindpal Singh Mandair, 25–46. Richmond: Curzon Press, 2001.

———. 'Illustration and Illumination in Sikh scriptural Manuscripts'. In *New Insights into Sikh Art.* Edited by Kavita Singh, 50–67. Mumbai: Marg Publications, 2003.

———. 'Text and Lineage in Early Sikh History: Issues in the Study of the Adi Granth'. *Bulletin of the School of Oriental and African Studies* 64, no. 1 (2001): 34–58.

Dhavan, P. 'The Warriors' Way: The Making of the Eighteenth—Century Khalsa Panth'. PhD thesis, University of Virginia, 2003.

Dilgeer, Harjinder Singh. *Akal Takht.* Jullunder: Punjabi Book Company, 1980.

Doré, Gustave. 'Indian Arms'. In *The Eclectic Magazine of Foreign Literature, Science, and Art,* 166–77. New York: E.R. Pelton, 1886.

Dorn, A. Walter and Stephen Gucciardi. 'The Sword and the Turban: Armed Force in Sikh Thought'. *Journal of Military Ethics* 10, no. 1 (2011): 52–70.

Dowson, J. *A Classical Dictionary of Hindu Mythology and Religion.* New Delhi: AES reprint, 2004.

Duggal, Devinder Singh, trans. *Fatehnamah and Zafarnama.* Jullundur: Institute of Sikh Studies, 1980.

The Eclectic Magazine of Foreign Literature, Science, and Art. 'Indian Arms'. *The Eclectic Magazine of Foreign Literature, Science, and Art.* Vol. 44. New York: Leavitt, Trow, & Co., August 1886.

Edinburgh Review, or Critical Journal. 'The Punjab'. *Edinburgh Review, or Critical Journal* (London: Longmans, Green & Co.) 89 (1849): 218–19.

Egerton, W. *An Illustrated Handbook of Indian Arms*. London: William H. Allen & Co., 1880.

———. *Indian Oriental Arms and Armour*. London: Arms and Armour Press, (1880) 1968.

Erndl, K.M. *Victory to the Mother: The Hindu Goddess of Northwest India in Myth, Ritual and Symbol*. New York: Oxford University Press, 1993.

Farquhar, J.N. 'The Fighting Ascetics of India'. *Bulletin of the John Rylands Library* 9, no. 2 (1925): 431–52.

Fenech, L. *Darbar of the Sikh Gurus: The Court of God in the World of Men*. New Delhi: Oxford University Press, 2008.

———. 'The Performative Nature of the Dasam Granth'. Paper Presented at the American Academy of Religion's Annual Meeting in November 2007 in San Diego, California.

———. *The Sikh Zafarnamah of Guru Gobind Singh: A Discursive Blade in the Heart of the Mughal Empire*. New York: Oxford University Press, 2013.

Figiel, L.S. *On Damascus Steel*. Florida: Atlantis Arts Press, 1991.

Fischer, D.H. *Historians' Fallacies: Towards a Logic of Historical Thought*. San Francisco: Harper & Row, 1970.

Friedlander, P. *A Descriptive Catalogue of the Panjabi Manuscripts in the Library of the Wellcome Institute for the History of Medicine*. London: The Wellcome Institute for the History of Medicine, unpublished.

Gandhi, Surjit Singh. *History of the Sikh Gurus (A Comprehensive Study)*. Delhi: Gurdas Kapur and Sons, 1978.

Garg, G.R. *An Encyclopedia of Indian Literature*. Delhi: Mittal Publishers, 1982.

Geikie, C. 'Samson and Eli'. *Hours with the Bible, or, the Scriptures in the Light of Modern Knowledge*. New York: J. Pott & Co, 1882.

Giani, Gian Singh. *Navīn Paṅth Prakāsh*. Reprint. Patiala: Bhasha Vibhag, (1888) 1987.

———. *Tvārīkh Gurū Khālsā*. Reprint ed. 2 vols. Patiala: Bhasha Vibhag, 1993.

———. *Tvārīkh Srī Amritsar*. Reprint ed. Amritsar: Kendri Singh Sabha Committee, 1977.

Giani, Pandit Narain Singh Ji. *Sri Dasam Granth Sahib ji Saṭīk*. 8 vols. Amritsar: Jawahar Singh and Kripal Singh and Co., (1932) 1992.

Gill, Amanpreet Singh. '1708—Remembering the Last Journey of Dasam Guru'. In *The Nishaan*. New Delhi: Nagaara Trust, Issue III/2008.

Gill, D.S. 'Relics of Guru Gobind Singh ji'. *Sikh Review* 548, no. 47 (1999): 49–53.

Gill, Mohinder Kaur. *Dasam Gurū Bāṇī de Rūp Modle*. Delhi: Manpreet Prakashan, 1999.

Gonsalves, Kiran and Michael S. Ojeda. *Deadliest Warrior: Season 2 Episode 6: Indian Rajput versus Roman Centurion*. Spike TV, Wednesday, 25 May 2010.

Grewal, J.S. *History, Literature, and Identity: Four Centuries of Sikh Tradition*. New Delhi: Oxford University Press, 2011.

Grewal , J.S. and Irfan Habib, eds. *Sikh History from Persian Sources—Translation of Major Texts*. New Delhi: Tulika, 2001.

Grewal. J.S. and S.S. Bal. *Guru Gobind Singh: A Biographical Study*. Chandigarh: Panjab University, 1967.

———. 'The Guru Granth and the Dasam Granth'. *Recent Debates in Sikh Studies—An Assessment*. New Delhi: Manohar, 2011.

Grierson, G.A. *The Modern Vernacular Literature of Hindustan*. Calcutta: Asiatic Society, 1889.

Griffin, L.H. Sir. *Ranjit Singh and the Sikh Barrier between Our Growing Empire and Central Asia*. Oxford: Clarendon Press, 1905.

Gupta, B.S. 'Guru Gobind Singh's Concept of God in *Jaap Sahib*'. *Spokesman Weekly* 29, nos 3–4 (1979): 25–6.

Gupta, H.R. *History of the Sikhs*. Vols 1–6. New Delhi: Munshiram Manohar Lal, 1984.

Gurdas, Bhai. *Kabitt Svaiye*. Amritsar: Singh Brothers, 2001.

———. *Vāra Bhāī Gurdās Saṭīk*. Edited by Bhai Vir Singh. 10th ed. Amritsar: Khalsa Samachar, 1984.

———. *Vāra Bhāi Gurdās (sampadan ate pāṭh nirdhārat)*. Patiala: Punjabi University, 1987.

Heath, I. *The Sikh Army 1799–1849*. Oxford: Osprey Publishers, 2005.

Henry F.B. *The Victories of the Sutlej*. London: Arthur B. Keen, Dublin, and Longman & Co., 1848.

Hookway, J.D. *M & R: A Regimental History of the Sikh Light Infantry 1941–1947*. Beckington, Bath, England: published by author, 1999.

Hughes, T.P. *A Dictionary of Islam*. London: W.H. Allen & Co., 1885.

Jaggi, R.S. *Dasam Granth dā Kartritav*. New Delhi: Panjābi Sāhitt Sabhā, 1966.

———. *Dasam Granth kī Paurāṇik Priṣṭhabhūmī*. Delhi: Bhārati Sāhitya Mandir, 1965.

Jaggi, R.S. *Dasam Granth dā Paurāṇik Adhiain*. Jalandhar: New Book Company, 1965.

Jaggi, R.S. and G.K. Jaggi. *Srī Dasam Granth Sāhib Pāṭh—Sampādan ate Viākhiā*. 5 vols. New Delhi: Govind Sadan, 2000.

———. *Bhāī Manī Siṅgh: Jīvanī ate Rachhnā*. Patiala: Punjabi University, 1983.

Johar, Surinder Singh. *Sikh Warrior Hari Singh Nalwa*. Delhi: National Book Shop, 2007.

Jones, R. *The Leisure Hour*. London: Religions Tract Society, 1894.

Kanwal, Harjinder Singh. *Dasmesh Bani Darpan: Translation of the Unique Banis of Sri Guru Gobind Singh ji Maharaj in Punjabi and English*. Delhi: Wellwish Publishers, 2002.

Kapoor, S.S. *Dasam Granth: An Introductory Study*. New Delhi: Hemkunt Press, 2003.

Kaur, Amritpal. *Dasam Gurū Bāṇī: Sañchār*. Patiala: Punjabi University, 1999.

Kaur, Beant. *The Namdhari Sikhs*. London: Sikhs Historical Museum, 1999.

Kaur, Madanjit. *The Golden Temple Past & Present*. Amritsar: Guru Nanak Dev University, 1983.

Kaur Singh, Akali Nihang. *Hazūrī Sāthī*. Lahore: Akali Patrika Press, 1934.

Kaushish, Svarup Singh. *Gurū Kiāṅ Sākhīā Krit Bhāi Svarūp Siṅgh Kaushish*. Edited by Piara Singh Padam. 2nd ed. Amritsar: Singh Brothers, (1797) 1991.

Khalsa, Nanak Dev Singh. *Gatka as Taught by Nanak Dev Singh, Book One—Dance of the Sword*. Phoenix, Arizona: GT International, 1987.

Khurana, Satnam Singh. 'Guru Gobind Singh: Scholar, Saint and Soldier'. *The Sikh Review*, 7, no. 1 (Jan 1959): 21–4.

Knowles, M. *Tap Roots: The Early History of Tap*. North Carolina: McFarland & Co. Inc., 2002.

Kohli, S.S. *Dictionary of Guru Granth Sahib*. Amritsar: Singh Brothers, 1996.

———, trans. *Sri Dasam Granth Sahib*. 3 vols. Birmingham: Sikh National Heritage Trust Publishing, 2003.

Lal, Bedi Singh. *Chānakā Rājnītī*. Amritsar: Chattar Singh Jivan Singh, 2003.

Lal, Bhai Nand. *Bhāi Nand Lāl Granthāvalī*. Edited by Ganda Singh. Patiala: Punjabi University, 1989.

Latif, Syad Muhammad. *History of the Punjab from the Remotest Antiquity to the Present Time*. Lahore: Sang-e-Meel Publications, 1997.

Lewin, T. *A Fly on the Wheel*. London: Constable & Company Ltd., 1885.

Loehlin, C.H. *The Granth of Guru Gobind Singh and Khalsa Brotherhood*. Lucknow: Lucknow Publishing House, 1971.

Lorenzen, D. 'Warrior Ascetics in Indian History'. *Journal of the American Oriental Society* 98, (1978): 617–75.

Luis, Francisco José. *Discourse, Praxis and Identity in Pre-Reformist Sikhism: A Study of the Nirmala Order*. School of Oriental and African Studies, 2013.

———. *Nirmalā Samprādāvā*. Unpublished PhD thesis, School of Oriental and African Studies.

———. 'Sex in Sikhi: The Erotic in the Sikh Tradition and the Politics of De-Eroticisation'. Unpublished paper.

Macauliffe, M.A. *The Sikh Religion: Its Gurus, Sacred Writings and Authors*. 6 vols. Oxford: Clarendon Press, 1909.

Mackenzie, C. *Life in the Mission, the Camp, and the Zenáná, or, Six Years in India*. Vol 1. London: Richard Bentley, 1853.

Mackinnon, Capt. D.H. *Military Service and Adventures in the Far East—Including Sketches of the Campaigns against the Afghans in 1839, and the Sikhs in 1845–6*. London: John Olliver, 1849.

Maclagan, E.D. *Census of India, Volume XIX: The Punjab and Its Feudatories. Part I: The Report on the Census*. Calcutta: Office of the Superintendent of Government Printing, 1892.

MacMunn, G.F. *The Martial Races of India*. London: Sampson Low & Co, 1933.

Madra, Amandeep. 'Guru's Relic under the Hammer'. http://news.ukpha.org/2008/03/gurus-relic-under-the-hammer/ (accessed 25 March 2008).

Malcolm, Lt. Col. J. *The Sketch of the Sikhs: A Singular Nation Who Inhabit the Provinces of the Punjab Situated between the Rivers Jamna and Indus*. London: John Murray, 1812.

Malhotra, Karamjit K. 'The Earliest Manual on the Sikh Way of Life'. In *Five Centuries of Sikh Tradition: Ideology, Society, Politics and Culture (Essays for Indu Banga)*. Edited by Reeta Grewal and Sheena Pall. New Delhi: Manohar, 2005.

Mandair, Arvind-Pal Singh. 'The Emergence of Sikh Theology: Reassessing the Passage of Ideas from Trumpp to Bhai Vir Singh'. *Bulletin of SOAS*, 68 no. 2 (2005).

———. 'Thinking Differently about Religion and History: Issues for Sikh Studies'. In *Sikh Religion, Culture and Ethnicity*. Edited by Christopher Shackle, Gurharpal Singh, and Arvindpal Singh Mandair. Richmond: Curzon Press, 2001.

Mandair, Navdeep. '(EN)Gendered Sikhism: The Iconolatry of Manliness in the Making of Sikh Identity'. *Sikh Formations: Religion, Culture, Theory* 1, no. 1 (2005): 39–55.

Mann, Gurinder Singh. 'Dasam Granth—There Is No Debate. The Magazine Approach to Guru Gobind Singh's Writings Dissected'. *Sant Sipāhī* (January 2008).

———. 'Descriptions of the Dasam Granth from the "Sketch of the Sikhs" in View of Sikh History'. *Sant Sipāhī* (April 2008).

———. 'Historical Sources on Sri Guru Granth Sahib and Sri Dasam Granth'. *Sant Sipāhī* (March 2010).

———. 'Sources for the Study of Guru Gobind Singh's Life and Times'. *Journal of Punjab Studies* 15, nos 1–2 (2008): 229–84.

———. 'Sri Dasam Granth—A Martial Sikh Scripture: Reflections from *Sikhan Di Bhagatmala*'. *Sant Sipāhī* (September 2010).

———. *The Making of Sikh Scripture*. New York: Oxford University Press, 2001.

———. 'The Relationship between Sri Dasam Granth and Bachitra Natak Granth'. *Sant Sipāhī* (June 2010).

———. 'The Role of the Dasam Granth in Khalsa'. Unpublished thesis. De Montfort University, Leicester, 2001.

Mann, Gurinder Singh and Kamalroop Singh. *Sri Dasam Granth Sahib: Questions and Answers*. London: Archimedes Press, 2011.

———. *Akali Phula Singh and His Turban*. Archimedes Press, forthcoming.

Mansukhani, Gobind Singh. 'Bachitra Natak: A Unique Autobiography'. *Spokesman Weekly* 28, no. 52 (1979): 19–20.

———. *Guru Ram Das, His life, Work and Philosophy*. New Delhi: Oxford & IBH Publishing Company, 1979.

———. *Hymns from Bhai Gurdas's Compositions*. Southall: The Sikh Missionary Society, 1988.

———. *Hymns from the Dasam Granth*. New Delhi: Hemkunt Press, 1997.

———. 'Some Manuscript Copies of the Dasam Granth Saheb'. *Sikh Review* 25, no. 4 (1987): 40–2.

Mar, W.D. *India of To-day*. London: Adam and Charles Black, 1905.

Marco, Manor Singh. *Sri Anańdpurī Bīṛh*. Delhi: Delhi Gurdwara Parbandhak Committee, 1975.

McLeod, W.H. *Early Sikh Tradition: A Study of the Janam-sakhis*. Oxford: Oxford University Press, 1980.

———. *Essays in Sikh History, Tradition, and Society*. New Delhi: Oxford University Press, 2007.

McLeod, W.H. *Prem Sumarag—The Testimony of a Sanatan Sikh*. New Delhi: Oxford University Press, 2006.

———. 'Reflections on Prem Sumarag'. *Journal of Punjab Studies* 14, no. 1 (2007): 123–32.

———. *Sikhism*. London: Penguin Books, 1997.

———. *Sikhs of the Khalsa: A History of the Khalsa Rahit*. New Delhi: Oxford University Press, 2003.

———. *Textual Sources for the Study of Sikhism*. Manchester: Manchester University Press, 1984.

———. *The Chaupa Singh Rahit-nama*. Dunedin: University of Otago Press, 1987.

———. *The Evolution of the Sikh Community: Five Essays*. Oxford: Clarendon Press, 1976.

———. 'The Problem of the Panjabi Rahitnāmās'. In *India, History and thought: Essays in honour of A.L. Basham*. Edited by S.N. Mukherjee. Calcutta: Subarnarekha, 1982.

———. *The Sikhs: History, Religion and Society*. New York: Columbia University Press, 1989.

Melikian-Chirvani, A.S. 'The Shah-Name Echoes in Sikh Poetry and the Origins of the Nihangs Name'. *Bulletin of the Asia Institute* (USA: Wayne State University Press) 16 (2006).

Mitra, R. *Indo Aryans Indo-Aryans: Contributions towards the Elucidation of Their Ancient and Medieval History*. London: Edward Stanford, 1881.

Morton, J. *The Poetical Remains of the Late Dr. John Leyden: With Memoirs of His Life, John Leyden*. London: Longman, Hurst, Rees, Orme, and Brown, 1819.

Muir, William. *Records of the Intelligence Department of the Government of the North-West Provinces of India during the Mutiny of 1857*. Vol. II. Edinburgh: T & T Clark, 1902.

Murphy, A. *The Materiality of the Past: History and Representation in Sikh Tradition*. New York: Oxford University Press, 2012.

Murray-Aynsley, J.C. *Our Visit to Hindostan, Kashmir, and Ladakh*. London: W.H. Allen, 1879.

Nabha, Kanh Singh. *Anekāth Kosh*. Amritsar: Sudarshan Press, 1928.

———. *Gurumat Mārtaṇḍ*. Amritsar: SGPC, (1962) 1978.

———. *Hum Hindū Nahiṅ*. Amritsar: Singh Brothers, 2000.

———. *Mahān Kosh*. Patiala: Bhasha Vibhag, (1930) 1999.

Nara, Ishar Singh. *Safarnama and Zafarnama: Being an Account of the Travels of Guru Gobind Singh and the Epistle of Moral Victory Written by Him to Emperor Aurangzeb*. New Delhi: Nara Publications, 1985.

Narotam, Tara Singh. *Srī Gurmat Niraṇe Sāgar*. Stone print, 1877.

———. *Srī Guru Tirath Sangrah*. Kankhal: Nirmal Akhara, 1883.

Narula, Surindar Singh. *Panjābi Sahitt dā Itihās*. 3rd ed. Jalandhar: New Book Company, 1969.

Nijhawan, M. *Dhadi Darbar: Religion, Violence, and the Performance of Sikh History*. New Delhi: Oxford University Press, 2006.

Oberoi, Harjot. *The Construction of Religious Boundaries: Culture, Identity and Diversity in the Sikh Tradition*. New Delhi: Oxford University Press, 1994.

Oman, J.C. *Cults, Customs and Superstitions of India*. London: T. Fisher Unwin, 1908.

Oppert, Gustav. *On the Weapons, Army Organisation, and Political Maxims of the Ancient Hindus, with Special Reference to Gunpowder and Firearms*. Madras: Messrs. Higginbotham & Co., 1880.

Orlich, L.V. *Travels in India: Including Sinde and the Punjab*. Translated by Hannibal Evans Lloyd. London: Longman, Brown, Green, and Longmans, 1845.

Orr, W.G. 'Armed Religious Ascetics in North India'. *Bulletin of the John Rylands Library* 24, no. 1 (1940): 81–100.

Osbourne, W.G. *The Court and Camp of Runjeet Singh*. London: Henry Colburn Publishers, 1840.

Padam, Piara Singh, ed. *Bhāī Kesar Singh Chhibbar krit Baṅsāvalīnāmā Dasi Pātashāhī kā*. Amritsar: Singh Brothers, (1769) 1997.

———. *Dasam Graṅth Darshan*. 2nd ed. Patiala: printed by author, (1968) 1982.

———, ed. *Puṅjabī Vārāṅ*. Patiala: Kalam Mandir, 1980.

———. *Kalam de Chamatkār*. Patiala: printed by author, 1981.

———. *Gurū Gobiṅd Siṅgh jī de Darbārī Rattan*. Patiala: Kalam Mandir, 1994.

———, ed. *Rahitnāme*. Amritsar: Singh Brothers, 2000.

———. *Srī Gurū Gobiṅd Siṅgh jī de Darbārī Rattan*. Patiala: New Patiala Printers, 1976.

Parkash, V. *The Sikhs in Bihar*. New Delhi: Janaki Prakashan, 1981.

Ram, Geela. *Gobind Gita*. Multan: Bharatiya Bhander, n.d.

Ram, Pandit Sharda. *Sikhā kā Rāj kā Vitihyā*. Edited by Pritam Singh. Jalandar Hind Publishing, (1866) 1956.

Rana, Y. 'SGPC [Shiromani Gurdwara Parbandhak Committee] Slams Auction of Guru's Relic'. http://articles.timesofindia.indiatimes.com/2008-03-30/chandigarh/27766624_1_body-armour-avtar-singh-makkar-sotheby-s-arts (accessed 30 March 2008).

Rawson, P.S. *The Indian Sword*. Danish Arms and Armour Society, Copenhagen, 1967.

Rinehart, R. *Debating the Dasam Granth*. New York: Oxford University Press, 2011.

———. 'Strategies for Interpreting the Dasam Granth'. In *Sikhism and History*. Edited by Pashaura Singh and N. Gerald Barrier, 135–50. New Delhi: Oxford University Press, 2004.

———.'The Guru, the Goddess: The Dasam Granth and Its Implications for Constructions of Gender in Sikhism'. In *Sikhism and Women*. Edited by Doris R. Jakobsh, 40–60. New Delhi: Oxford University Press, 2010.

Robinson, H.R. *The Arms and Armour Series: Oriental Armour*. New York: Walker and Co., 1967.

Ross, D. *The Land of the Five Rivers and Sindh*. London: Chapman and Hall, Limited, 1883.

Sagar, Sabinderjit Singh. *Hukamnamas of Guru Tegh Bahadur*. Amritsar: Guru Nanak Dev University, 2002.

Sandhra, Sharanjit Kaur. 'The Nihangs within the Great Sikh Court of 19th Century India'. Unpublished thesis. The University of the Fraser Valley, 2005.

Sandhu, P.S. *Selections from Sri Dasam Granth Sahib*. 2 vols. Amritsar: Singh Brothers, 2004.

Scott, George Batley. *Religion and Short History of the Sikhs—1469 to 1930*. London: The Mitre Press, 1930.

Sehgal, P. *Gur Govind Singh unkā Kaviyā*. Lucknow: Hindi Sahit Mandir, 1965.

Shackle, C. *Catalogue of the Panjabi and Sindhi Manuscripts in the India Office Library*. London: India Office Library and Records, 1977.

———. *An Introduction to the Sacred Language of the Sikhs*. London: SOAS, University of London, 1983.

Shah, Ami. 'Ugradanti and the Rise of the Tisar Panth'. *Journal of Punjab Studies* 15, nos 1 and 2 (2008): 181–97.

Shiromani Gurudwara Parbandhak Committee (SGPC). *Rehat Maryada—A Guide to the Sikh Way of Life*. Amritsar: SGPC, 1985.

Siddons, Capt. 'Translation of the Vichitra Natak.' *Journal of the Asiatic Society of Bengal* (Calcutta) xix, no. 1; xx, no. 2 (1851–2).

Simpson, William. 'Seated Holy Man with Figures'. Amritsar, Punjab, 1864.

Singh, Akali Baba Santa. 'Mukh Shabad'. In *Srī Dasam Grañth Darpaṇ*. Edited by Harbans Singh. Patiala: Gurbani Seva Parkasan, 2002.

Singh, Anurag. 'Sardar Jassa Singh Ramgharia—Servitor of Guru Panth'. In *Smriti Granth*. Mahahraja Jassa Singh Ramgharia Janam Samagam Committee, 2010.

Singh, Attar. *Sakhee Book or the Description of Gooroo Gobind Singh's Religion and Doctrines*. Allahabad: The Indian Public Opinion Press, 1876.

———, trans. *The Travels of Guru Tegh Bahadar and Guru Gobind Singh*. Lahore: Indian Public Press, 1876.

Singh, Avatar. *Khālsā Dharam Shāstar*. Amritsar: Gurmat Press, 1919.

Singh, Bawa Sumar. *Gurpad Prem Prakāsh*. Patiala: Punjabi University, 2000.

———. *Srī Gurū Pad Prem Prakāsh*. Lahore: Aftab-i Panjab, 1882.

Singh, Bhagat. *Missī Jāt dī Kartūt*. Amritsar: Sri Chandra Press, 1923.

Singh, Bhagwant. *Dasam Granth Tuk Tatakarā (Index)*. Patiala: Punjabi University, 2001.

———. *Dasam Granth dā Bāṇī Biorā*. Edited by R.S. Jaggi. Patiala: Punjabi University, 2001.

Singh, Bhai Narayan. *Illustrious Hero of the Akali Movement: Jathedar Bhai Kartar Singh Jhabbar—The Life and Times*. Translated by Karnail Singh. Amritsar: SGPC, 2001.

Singh, Bhai Santokh. *Kavī Chūṛāmaṇi Bhāī Santokh Singh jī Krit Shrī Gur Pratāp Sūraj Granth*. Edited by Bhai Vir Singh. 4th ed. 14 vols. Amritsar: Khalsa Samachar, 1964–5.

Singh, Daljeet and Kharak Singh, eds. *Sikhism: Its Philosophy and History*. Chandigarh: Institute of Sikh Studies (IOSS), 1997.

Singh, Darshan. *Akal Ustat: Praise of the Immortal Recitation by Guru Gobind Singh, 10th Guru of the Sikhs*. New Delhi: Gyan Sagar Publications, 1999.

———. *Poetics of Dasam Granth*. Amritsar: Gurprasad Publications, 2011.

———, ed. *Western Image of the Sikh Religion—A Sourcebook*. New Delhi: National Book Organisation (NBO), 1999.

———. *Zafarnama: Epistle of Victory Written in Persian by the Tenth Guru to Mughal Emperor Aurangzeb*. New Delhi: ABC Publishing House, 2000.

Singh, Diwan. *Glimpses of Chandi Chritra*. Mohali: Diwan Singh, 1996.

———. *How Vachitar Is Vchitra Natak?* Mohali: Diwan Singh, 1995.

Singh, Fauja. *Atlas Travels of Guru Gobind Singh*. Patiala: Punjabi University Publication Bureau, 2002.

Singh, Ganda. *A Select Bibliography of the Sikhs and Sikhism*. Amritsar: SGPC, 1965.

Singh, Ganda. *Bhai Naṅd Lāl Graṅthāvalī*. Patiala: Punjabi University Publication Bureau, 2000.

———, ed. *Early European Accounts of the Sikhs*. Reprint. Calcutta: Indian studies, past and present, 1962.

———. *Hukamnāme: Gurū Sāhibān, Mātā Sāhibān, Bandā Siṅgh ate Khālsā jī de*. 2nd ed. Patiala: Punjabi University Publication Bureau, 1985.

———. *Kavī Saināpati Srī Gur-Sobhā*. Patiala: Punjabi University Publication Bureau, 1987.

———. *Life of Banda Bahadur Based on Contemporary and Original Records*. Amritsar: Sikh History Research Department: Khalsa College, 1935.

Singh, G.B. *Srī Gurū Graṅth Sāhib diā Prāchīn bīṛ*. Lahore: Modern Publications, 1944.

Singh, Giani Avatar. *Nitnem Saṭīk*. Amritsar: Dam Dami Taksal, 1998.

Singh, Giani Hardeep. *Das Graṅthī*. Hazur Sahib, 2009.

Singh, Giani Isher. *Dasam Gurū Graṅth Sāhib jī de Khaṅḍaṇ dā Khaṅḍaṇ*. Ropar: Ramgarhia Furniture House, 1990.

Singh, Gurbachan Talib. *The Impact of Guru Gobind Singh on Indian Society*. Ludhiana: Lahore Book Shop, 1984.

Singh, Gurbaksh. *Gur Rattan Mal Sau Sākhī*. Edited by Gurbachan Singh Nayar. Patiala: Punjabi University, 1985.

Singh, Gurmukh. *Bhai Jaita Ji: Jiwan te Rachna*. Amritsar: Literature House, 2003.

———. *Historical Sikh Shrines*. Amritsar: Singh Brothers, 1995.

Singh, Gurtej. 'Two Views on Dasam Granth: An Appreciation of Ashta's and Jaggi's Approach'. In *Fundamental Issues in Sikh Studies*. Edited by Kharak Singh, Gobind Singh Mansukhani, Jasbir Singh Mann, 170–86. Chandigarh: Institute of Sikh Studies, 1992.

Singh, Harbans. 'The Bakapur Diwan and Baba Teja Singh of Bhasaur'. *The Panjab Past and Present*. Patiala: Punjabi University, Publication Bureau, October 1973.

———, ed. *The Encyclopaedia of Sikhism*. 4 vols. Patiala: Punjabi University, 1992.

Singh, Harkishan, trans. 'Ugradanti: Guru Gobind Singh's Adoration of Divine Mother', with an introduction by Kapur Singh. *Sikh Review* 8, no. 8 (1960): 8–13.

Singh, Jodhi and Dharam Singh. *Sri Dasam Granth Sahib, Text and Translation*. 2 vols. Patiala: Heritage Publications, 1999.

———. '*Bachitra Natak*. Some further exploration'. *Journal of Sikh Studies* 14, no. 2 (1987).

Singh, Jagjit. *Dasam Granth—The Real Issues*, Reprint, n.d.

———. 'Fictional Identity of Dasam Granth'. *Sikh Review* (August 1994): 21–4.

Singh, Jathedar Joginder. *Srī Hazurī Mriyādā Prabodh*. Nanderh: Takht Hazur Sahib, 1967.

Singh, Jathedar Kirpal. *Srī Akāl Takht Sāhib ate Jathedār Sāhibāṅ*. Amritsar: Chattar Singh Jivan Singh, 1999.

Singh, Joginder. *Srī Hazūrī Maryādā Prabodh*. Hazur Sahib: n.p., n.d.

Singh, Kamalroop. *Dasam Granth Re-examined: An Examination of the Textual History with Reference to Key Authors and Commentators*. Unpublished PhD thesis, University of Birmingham, 2013.

———. 'Gatka'. In *The Oxford Handbook of Sikh Studies*. Edited by Pashaura Singh and Louis E. Fenech, 459–71. New York: Oxford University Press, 2014.

Singh, Kapur. 'Qissa Rani Rup Kaur Da'. *Gurmat Prakash* (Amritsar: SGPC) (April 1959).

———. *Pārāśarapraśna*. Edited by Piar Singh and Madanjit Kaur. Amritsar: Guru Nanak Dev University, 1959.

Singh, Kharak and Gurtej Singh, eds. *Episodes from the Lives of the Gurus—Parchian Sewadas—English Translation*. Chandigarh: Institute of Sikh Studies, (1708) 1995.

Singh, Khushwant. *A History of the Sikhs*. 2 vols. New Delhi: Oxford University Press, 1977.

Singh, Kirpal. *A Catalogue of Punjabi and Urdu Manuscripts*. Amritsar: Sikh History Research Department, Khalsa College, 1963.

Singh, Kirpal and Prithipal Singh Kapur. *The Makers of Modern Punjab: What They Had to Say*. Amritsar: Singh Brothers, 2010.

Singh, Kuir. *Gurbilās Pātishāhī 10*. Patiala: Punjabi University, 2000.

Singh, Manjit. *Shastranāmā*. Amritsar: Chattar Singh Jivan Singh, 2005.

Singh, Manmohan. *Dasam Graṅth Vich Mith Rūpāṅtarṅ*. Amritsar: Lok Sahitya Prakashan, 1982.

Singh, Mohan. *A History of Panjabi Literature (1100–1932)*. 2nd ed. Amritsar: Kasturi Lal and Sons, 1956.

Singh, Mohinder. *Anandpur—The City of Bliss*. Birmingham: DTF Books, 2002.

Singh, Nahar and Kirpal Singh, eds. *Rebels against the British Rule (Guru Ram Singh and the Kuka Sikhs)*. New Delhi: Atlantic Publishers and Distributors, 1995.

———. *Two Swords of Guru Gobind Singh in England (1666–1708 AD)*. Delhi: Atlantic Publishers and Distributors, 1989.

Singh, Nanak. *Ik Miān Do Talvārā*. 2nd ed. Delhi: Navyug Publishers, 1962.

Singh, Nazer. *Guru Granth Sahib—Over to the West: Idea of Sikh Scriptures Translations: 1810–1909*. New Delhi: Commonwealth Publishers, 2005.

Singh, Nikky Guninder Kaur. 'Durga Recalled by the Tenth Guru'. *Journal of Religious Studies* 16, nos 1–2 (1988).

———. *The Feminine Principle in the Sikh Vision of the Transcendent*. Cambridge: Cambridge University Press, 1993.

———. *The Name of My Beloved: Verses of the Sikh Gurus*. San Francisco: Harper Collins, 1995.

Singh 'Nihang', Baba Ram. *Akāl Purakh kī Fauj*. Gurdaspur, n.d.

Singh 'Nihang', Gian, ed. *Srī Gurū Granth Sāhib jī*. Amritsar: Shiromani Gurdwara Prabandhak Committee, 1977.

Singh, Nihang Teja. *Adi Dasam Srī Gurū Granth Sāhib jī*. NK: Buddha Dal, 1980.

Singh, Pandit Narain. *Srī Dasam Granth Sāhib*. Lahore: Bhai Chattar Singh, 1940 (previously known as *Dasam Gurū Granth Sāhib Saṭīk*).

Singh, Parmjit and Amandeep Madra. *Sicques, Tigers or Thieves: Eyewitness Accounts of the Sikhs (1606–1809)*. New York: Palgrave Macmillan.

———. *Warrior Saints: Three Centuries of the Sikh Military Tradition*. London: I.B.Tauris, 1999.

Singh, Pashaura. *Life and Works of Guru Arjan*. New Delhi: Oxford University Press, 2006.

———. *The Guru Granth Sāhib: Canon, Meaning and Authority*. New Delhi: Oxford University Press, 2000.

Singh, Piar. *Gathā Srī Adi Granth*. Amritsar: Guru Nanak Dev University, 1992.

Singh, Rai Jasbir, ed. *Bhaī Kesar Chhibbar Krit Bansāvalināmā Dasān Pātshāhiān kā*. Amritsar: Guru Nanak Dev University, 2001.

Singh, Ran. *Dasam Granth Niraṅe*. Patiala: Panch Khalsa Diwan, 1919.

Singh, Randhir, ed. *Prem Sumārg*. Amritsar: Sikh History Society, 1965.

———. *Shabad Mūrat: Dasave Pātishāh ke Granth dā Itihās*. Amritsar: SGPC, 1962.

———, ed. *Shabadārth Dasam Granth Sāhib*. 3 vols. Patiala: Punjabi University, 1973–88.

Singh, Sahib. *Merī Jīvan Kahāṇī*. Amritsar: Singh Bros, 2001.

———. *Srī Gurū Granth Sāhib Darpaṇ*. Jallandhar: Raj Publishers, 1972.

Singh, Akali Nihang Sampuran. *Sūraj Vānisiyā Khālsā Panth. A Survey of Various Sectarian Movements among the Sikhs*. Amritsar: Svami Santoshanand, 1923.

Singh, Sardar Kapur. 'Qissā Raṇī Rūp Kaur dā'. In *Gurmat Prakāsh*. Amritsar: SGPC, 1959.

Singh, Sardul. *Rīpoṭ Sodhak Kommittī Dasam Patāshāhī Srī Gurū Granth Sāhib jī dī*. Amritsar: Vazirchand Printers, 1897.

Singh, Seva, ed. *Shahīd Bilās* (Bhai Mani Singh). Ludhiana: Panjabi Sahitt Academy, (1800) 1961.

Singh, Sewa, ed. *Dasam Granth dī Chonvīṅ Bāṇī*. India: National Book Trust, 1998.

Singh, Sher. *Dasmesh Darpaṇ*. Amritsar: Sikh Religious Tract Society, 1935.

Singh, Sikandar (Bhayee) and Roopinder Singh. *Sikh Heritage: Ethos & Relics*. New Delhi: Rupa & Co., 2012.

Singh, Sohan. *Gurbilās Pātishāhī Chhevīn*. Edited by Joginder Singh Vedanti and Amarjeet Singh. Amritsar: SGPC, 1999.

Singh, Surinder. *Sikh Coinage—Symbol of Sikh Sovereignty*. New Delhi: Manohar, 2004.

Singh, Taran. *Dasam Granth Rūp te Ras*. Chandigarh: Guru Gobind Singh Foundation, 1967.

———. *Dashmesh Darpaṇ*. Chandigarh: Guru Gobind Singh Foundation, 1967.

Singh, Teja. *Dasam Gurū Girāh Prakāsh*. Patiala: Panj Khalsa Diwan, n.d.

———. *The Gurdwara Reform Movement and the Sikh Awakening*. Jullunder: Desh Sewak Book Agency, 1922.

Singh, Teja and Ganda Singh. *A Short History of the Sikhs*—Vol. 1 (1469–1765). Patiala, 1989.

Singh, Trilochan. 'History and Compilation of Dasam Granth'. *Sikh Review* 3, no. 4 (1955): 51–60; 3, no. 5, 34–41; 3, no. 6, 44–52; 3, no. 7, 23–9.

———, trans. 'Selections from the Dasam Granth'. *Selections from the Sacred Writings of the Sikhs*. New Delhi: Orient, 2000.

———. *The Turban and the Sword of the Sikhs: Essence of Sikhism*. Amritsar: Chattar Singh Jivan Singh, 2001.

Singh, Trilochan and Anurag Singh. *A Brief Account of Life and Works of Guru Gobind Singh*. Amritsar: Chattar Singh Jivan Singh, 2002.

Sital, Jit Singh. 'Traditions and Customs of Nihangs'. *The Sikh Courier* (London: Sikh Cultural Society of Great Britain) 9, no. 12 (1977): 24–5.

Smith, R. Bosworth. *The Life of Lord Lawrence, 1849–1852*. London: Smith Elder & Co., 1883.

Smyth, G.C. *A History of the Reigning Family of Lahore: With Some Account of the Jummoo Rajahs, the Seik Soldiers and Their Sirdars*. Calcutta: W. Thacker and Co., 1847.

Snell, R. *The Hindi Classical Tradition: A Braj Bhāṣā Reader*. London: SOAS, 1991.

Srī Sarabaloh Granth Sāhib jī Saṭīk. Vol 2. Anandpur: Shiromani Panth Akali Buddha Dal, n.d.

Steinbach, H. *The Punjaub: Being a Brief Account of the Country of the Sikhs, Its Extent, History, Commerce, Productions, Government, Manufactures, Laws, Religion, etc.* London: Smith, Elder, & Co., 1846.

Steingass, F.A. *Comprehensive Persian—English Dictionary*. Reprint ed. Delhi: Oriental Books Reprint Corporation, 1981.

Stone, G.C. *A Glossary of the Construction, Decoration and Use of Arms and Armor: In All Countries and in All Times (Dover Military History, Weapons, Armor)*. New York: Jack Brussel, 1961.

Stronge, S., ed. *The Arts of the Sikh Kingdoms*. London: V&A Publications, 1999.

Syan, H.S. 'An Analysis of the Chritropakhyan as Sikh Didactic Literature'. Unpublished MPhil thesis, School of Oriental and African Studies, 2007.

Takkar, Amrit Lal. *Descriptive Catalogue of Panjabi Manuscripts in the Vrindaban Research Institute*. Vrindaban: Vrindaban Research Institute, 1996.

The Asiatic Annual Register, vol. XI—for the Year 1809. London: printed for T. Cadell and W Davies, etc., 1811.

Trueheart, Benjamin Adams. *Weapons Masters Episode 5—The Deadly Chakram*. Halfyard Productions for Discovery Channel, 13 September 2008.

Trumpp, E. *The Adi Granth or The Holy Scriptures of the Sikhs*. London: W.H. Allen and Company, 1877.

Usahan, D.S. *Prem Anbodh*. Patiala: Punjabi University, 1989.

Vahiria, Avatar Singh. *Khalsā Dharam Shāstar*. Lahore: Arorabans Press, 1894.

Walia, Varinder. 'Jathedar Dispels Doubts about Dasam Granth'. *Tribune India* (Online edition), 4 November 2008. http://www.tribuneindia.com/2008/20081104/punjab1.htm (accessed 10 April 2011).

Wilkins, C. 'The Sicks and Their College at Patna: 1st March 1781'. *Transactions of the Asiatick Society*. Vol. 1. Calcutta: Asiatick Society, 1788.

Williams, M. *Religious Thought and Life in India. An Account of the Religions of the Indian Peoples, Based on a Life's Study of Their Literature and on Personal Investigations in Their Own Country.* London: John Murray, 1883.

Wilson, H.H. 'Art. XI—Lecture on the present State of the Cultivation of Oriental Literature'. *The Journal of the Royal Asiatic Society of Great Britain and Ireland* 13 (1852): 191–215.

Wilson, J. *Final Report on the Revision of the Settlement of the Sirsa District in the Punjab*. Calcutta: Central Press Company 1884.

Wood, G. *The Uncivilised Races of Men in All Countries of the World.* London: G. Routledge and Sons, 1883.

Websites (last accessed in October 2014)

www.dasam.info
www.dasamgranth.org
www.globalsikhstudies.net
www.gobindsadan.org/dgranth.shtml
www.nanakshahi.com
www.patshahi10.org
www.punjabheritage.com
www.santsipahi.org
www.sarbloh.com
www.sarbloh.info
www.sarblohgranth.com
www.searchgurbani.com
www.sikhnet.com
www.sikhnugget.com
www.sikhreview.org
www.sikhs.org
www.sikhstudies.org/
www.sridasam.org
www.sridasam.org/dasam?c=t
www.sridasamgranth.com
www.tribuneindia.com

Index

About the Authors

Gurinder Singh Mann and Kamalroop Singh recently published a well-received book titled *Sri Dasam Granth Sahib: Questions and Answers* (2011), which is an introductory guide and contains the authors' responses to fifty questions about the scripture. It was the top-selling book on Sikhism on Amazon for a number of months.

Kamalroop Singh

Kamalroop Singh completed his PhD on textual history of the *Dasam Grańth* (*DG*) while writing this book, titled 'Dasam Granth Re-examined' (http://etheses.bham.ac.uk/4285/; accessed 28 July 2015). His PhD research involved the in situ examination of numerous manuscripts, both known and previously unknown, as well as historical sources to evaluate how the *DG* was created and compiled. He has undertaken fieldwork locating some of the earliest recensions of the *DG*. He also has an MPhil in Sikh studies from the University of Birmingham, during which he studied the *rahitnāme* or Sikh codes of practice and formation of the Sikh scriptural canon. Kamalroop Singh has given many lectures and seminars throughout the UK and internationally. Some of his lectures related to the *DG* in the UK include a talk on 'The Liturgy and Praxis of the Dasam Granth' at the Oxford University and 'A Discussion of the Scriptures of Guru Gobind Singh in Relation to Sikh History and Praxis' at the Punjab Research Group in 2008. Most recently, his paper, 'The Textual History of the Dasam Granth Sahib' was included in the conference on 'Dialogues With(in) Sikh Studies: Texts, Practices, and Performances' at the University of California, Riverside, in 2013. The lectures form the material for the present book. He has also worked closely with museum curators in the area of Sikh manuscripts. The author is working on various projects including the publication of his PhD thesis on the textual history of the *DG*, and a critical examination of the *Sarabaloh Grańth*, as well as the translation of the *Das Gur Kathā*. He also has a number of essays that are published, including one on the Sikh martial art, *Gatkā*, in the *The Oxford Handbook of Sikh Studies* (2014).

Gurinder Singh Mann

Gurinder Singh Mann is an independent researcher in the area of Sikh studies. He started his research in the late 1990s that was formulated in his dissertation, 'The Role of the Dasam Granth in Khalsa'. This was part of his MA in South Asian religions in 2001 at De Montfort University, Leicester. This is one of the first Western works on the Sikh scripture since Loehlin (1971). He has participated and given presentations at two international conferences on the *DG* which include '300 Years of the Dasam Granth' at the International Seminar on the Sri Dasam Granth, Sacramento, California, in 2008. Here he outlined the history of the *DG* through historical sources and early manuscripts. He also considered Sikh relics and British sources of the *DG*: 'The Granth of Guru Gobind Singh—A Historical Journey through Rare Manuscripts and Relics of the Khalsa' at the conference on 'The Legacy of the Khalsa—The Eternal Scriptures (Khalsa Di Virsa)' at San Jose, California, in 2013. He also presented his paper titled 'Understanding the Dasam Granth Debate in the UK: Responses by Sikh Youth from the Internet to the Gurdwara' at the conference on 'Young Sikhs in a Global World', Lund University, Sweden, in 2013. With regard to new literary sources on the *DG*, he gave the presentation, 'Dasam Granth: A Historical Perspective of the Khalsa from Eighteenth Century Texts' at the Sikh Studies Conference at Imperial College, London, 2014.

The author has also contributed several articles to the Sikh magazine *Sant Sipāhī* between 2008 and 2010. He also discovered a rare English translation of the *Prem Sumārag Grańth* by John Leyden in 2006. This was presented in a project titled the 'Anglo-Panjabi Literature and Publishing Initiative' which showcased the translations in 2011. He is currently working on a series of books looking at the relationship between the British and the Sikhs, as well as working with Kamalroop Singh on the *marayādā* of Takht Hazur Sahib and the history of the Akali Nihangs.